PHRASES *that* SELL

Ultimate Phrase Finder to Help You Promote Your Products, Services, and Ideas

Edward Werz and Sally Germain

CB

CONTEMPORARY BOOKS

Library of Congress Cataloging-in-Publication Data

Werz, Edward W.
    Phrases that sell : the ultimate phrase finder to help you promote
your products, services, and ideas / Edward Werz and Sally Germain.
       p.   cm.
    Includes index.
    ISBN 0-8092-2977-3
    1. Advertising—Language—Handbooks, manuals, etc.   2. Slogans—
Handbooks, manuals, etc.   3. English language—Terms and phrases.
4. Creative writing—Handbooks, manuals, etc.   I. Germain, Sally.
II. Title.
HF5827.W47   1998
659.13'2—dc21
                                          97-43790
                                             CIP

Interior design and production by Susan H. Hartman

Published by Contemporary Books
A division of NTC/Contemporary Publishing Group, Inc.
4255 West Touhy Avenue, Lincolnwood (Chicago), Illinois 60646-1975 U.S.A.
Copyright © 1998 by Edward Werz and Sally Germain
Printed in the United States of America
International Standard Book Number: 0-8092-2977-3

18   17   16   15   14   13   12   11   10   9   8   7   6   5   4   3   2   1

Contents

Acknowledgments

WE would like to acknowledge our many friends and colleagues who enthusiastically shared with us their favorite copywriting ideas and "phrases that sell." Very special thanks to our creative partners Janice and Allan, who make it all fun, and thanks to Kay Sherman for her invaluable suggestions and advice.

Introduction

ANYONE who writes advertising, sales, or promotional copy has those moments—hopefully few and far between—where he or she draws a blank, hits the wall, or is just plain stumped. Don't let anyone tell you otherwise!

And just like any other craftsperson, the copywriter needs a box of tools he or she can rely on, to rummage through in hopes of finding just the right thing to help solve the problem at hand. For the writer, this box of tools includes a dictionary, a thesaurus, and, from now on, the powerful idea stimulator, *Phrases That Sell*.

Phrases That Sell is the result of over 50 years of combined creative work selling countless products, services, and ideas to consumers and businesspeople across the United States and beyond. We've tried to pack into this handbook the basics of writing effective advertising copy and more than 5,000 sample phrases that might be used or adapted to sell just about anything and everything. By browsing through the pages of this unique resource, the writer will be bombarded with phrases and concepts that will provide ideas, stimulate creativity, and give new direction to the work in progress.

We hope that you will enjoy using *Phrases That Sell* and that it becomes an indispensable resource that you will call on time and time again.

How to Write Copy That Sells

WRITING persuasive copy is both a science and an art. True, the competent word-smith must follow the basic rules of copywriting to create a written promotion that will sell his or her product, service, or idea. These rules will be outlined in the following section. They are the results of trial and error. Thousands of advertising writers have tested them over time and have incorporated the ones that work into their everyday writing techniques. But beyond these rules, it is the writer's creative and artistic talent that takes over to make the copy unique and memorable.

The novice may begin by adhering to the rules alone in an effort to "get it right." This often results in cookie-cutter copy that lacks energy and persuasive power. Some of us believe that rules are made to be broken—but that is only after they've been learned and absorbed. It is only when the novice is so comfortable with the basic rules of copywriting that these become second nature, that he or she can move past them into a new, more fulfilling, effective, and rewarding dimension of writing. This brief introduction to writing good copy is aimed at helping the copywriter arrive quickly at that special place.

The 10 Basic Rules of Copywriting

The following rules are not set in stone. And highly skilled copywriters may use all, few, or even none of them to create copy that sells. If you examine copy that is really able to connect with the reader, however, more often than not it will follow at least a few of these tried-and-true principles:

1. Know your audience.
2. Understand your product or service.
3. Find your principal selling position (PSP).
4. Write benefit-oriented copy.
5. Choose active versus passive words.
6. Short sentences and short words can add up to big ideas.
7. Use formats that promote.
8. Use offers that sell.
9. Tell your reader what to do.
10. Tout your name.

Know Your Audience

Before you pick up your pen or turn on your word processor, understand your audience—the men, women, children, businesspeople, hobbyists, or the multitude of others who you hope will respond to your copy. It's these people who will see and read your ad that determine the language you choose to tell your story.

Often, the prospects for a product are a fairly homogeneous group—graduating seniors, new parents, recent home buyers. But this is not always the case. To pinpoint your ad's readers, you'll want to review exactly who your target prospect is and the advertising medium in which your ad will appear.

To discover the profile of the ideal prospect, copywriters delve into the buying history of the company. Included in this discovery process are the following:

1. Surveys or questionnaires of buyers
2. Demographic studies
3. Buyer focus groups
4. Analysis of mailing-list results
5. Review of advertising-media results
6. Interviews with marketing personnel
7. Survey of company literature
8. Review of the competition's marketing

The conclusions about the perfect prospect that come from using this process become the basis of how you approach writing your ad. If your product is a new allergy medication and your target audience consists of doctors who will be prescribing the medication, your ad will be very different than if you are trying to build consumer awareness for the same product.

For example:

- Doctors want to learn about a medication's efficacy and contraindications, while consumers want to learn how the product will relieve their symptoms.

- Doctors are comfortable with medical terminology and technology, while consumers are familiar with simple, direct language.

- The cost of the medication may not be a consideration of the medical professional, while it may be critical to a consumer.

The alert copywriter will study the company's customer profile and delve into the ad medium's demographics well before the first word is written.

Understand Your Product or Service

Before you can write compelling copy about a product or service, you need to fully understand the product and its features, and how a potential customer will benefit if he or she decides to buy your product. If, for instance, you are promoting a service that brings freshly cut flowers to the customer's office twice a week, you will want to know more about the service. Questions you would want answered might include:

- What type of flowers are provided?
- Why are the flowers provided special?
- What exactly does freshly cut mean?
- Where are the flowers grown?
- How are the flowers arranged?
- In what type of container are the flowers displayed?
- How long will the flowers stay fresh?
- Are the flowers fragrant?
- When and how are the flowers delivered?
- What is the cost of the flowers?
- And so on.

When you have all the pertinent facts about the product's features, you can then begin to construct the corresponding benefits. If the flowers are hard-to-find, exotic, tropical varieties, your benefit might be the prestige and beauty of displaying rare flowers from around the world. If they are delivered before the workday starts, twice a week, the benefit might be hassle-free delivery without any disruption of the business day. As you can see, before benefits can be created, you need to have as much information as possible about the product. You can gather this information from brochures, spec sheets, advertisements, news releases, interviews, etc. The more you know, the more benefits you can offer, and the more powerful your sales message will be.

Find Your Principal Selling Position (PSP)

The principal selling position (PSP) is your product's or service's most attractive benefit, viewed from the buyer's perspective. The PSP becomes the focus of your copy, around which other, less important, benefits are presented. Once a list of product features and benefits is created, your marketing team will decide on the PSP. All the benefits are weighed regarding their potential effect on your prospect. When agreement is reached on which benefit you believe will present your product most powerfully to its target audience, the PSP has been selected.

For instance, if your product's design provides extraordinary ease of use and that benefit is what makes it stand out from the competition, the focus of your copy should be targeted toward that selling advantage. The ad's headline and body copy would emphasize how the product's design makes it amazingly user-friendly. This feature eliminates cumbersome operations, therefore saving the buyer time and effort.

Famous PSPs include:

Maytag appliances—Service, Trouble-Free

Hertz Rent-A-Car—Fast Check-In

Crest toothpaste—With Fluoride to Decrease Cavities

Volvo automobiles—Safety

Prudential insurance—All Dependability

Disney—Family Values

United Airlines—Friendly Service

Wheaties cereal—Nutrition for Athletic Performance

Visa credit card services—Convenience

Energizer Batteries—Durable and Long-Lasting

Write Benefit-Oriented Copy

The bottom line of many consumer-vendor relationships is often "What can you do for me now?" This is never truer than when applied to writing advertising copy. Compelling promotional copy creates an emotional bond with the reader. It may identify and appeal to a basic need in the reader such as the need to feel loved, secure, recognized, attractive, healthy, sexy, and so on. Effective copy is interactive or action-provoking. This means that if the copy is successful, it will create a gut-level connection that ultimately motivates the reader to act. The reader's action is just what the copywriter is hoping for: a visit to a store, the return of a coupon expressing interest, or the purchase of a product or service. For words to have that effect on a prospect, they must strike a powerful chord. The reader must instantly understand "what you [the vendor] will do for him or her [the consumer] now."

Here are two descriptions of the same product. Read each and decide which one would have the greatest effect on the target prospect—an average American teenager.

> *Sunblast Suntan Lotion contains all-natural ingredients: sesame oil, sea buckthorn oil, watermelon extract, and aloe-vera gel, all designed to protect your skin from the harsh rays of the sun and produce a deep tan.*

> *Make heads turn all summer long with Sunblast Suntan Lotion. Its all-natural formula and soothing moisturizers combine to offer ultimate sun protection and the kind of deep, alluring tan guaranteed to attract the opposite sex.*

The first description focuses on the product itself and its ingredients. It provides important facts. This is a purely intellectual connection with the prospect. No emotional impact is made. The relationship between the advertisement's facts and the reader's needs is not clear. The reader must stretch to make the connection.

The second description zeroes in right away on the benefits of using the product. The copy tells the reader that, sure, the product protects the user, but it also helps produce the kind of tan the user has fantasized about—one that is appealing to the opposite sex. The connection here is one the reader feels. When the prospect's emotions are touched and the fulfillment of his or her basic needs are promised, the prospect is likely to be roused into action.

It is clear that a typical teenager deciding on which suntan lotion to purchase would most likely be motivated by the second approach over the first.

For a further example, here is a list of product features along with a possible benefit that might be highlighted for each one.

Product Feature	Benefit
Informative magazine.........................	Makes the reader more interesting.
All-wheel-drive automobile	Gives the driver confidence and control in all weather conditions.
Fewer calories in cereal	Helps the reader look good in form-fitting attire.
Prudent investment services............	Allows the reader to retire comfortably.
Reliable, on-time service....................	Reader avoids hassles and frustrations.

Choose Active Versus Passive Words

I'm sure you remember some of those English classes from your school days. Certainly, one of the subjects covered was parts of speech—specifically, verbs. The verb is the element of the sentence that describes the action taken and is expressed either in the active voice or the passive voice. The active voice is generally more direct and has more energy and momentum than the passive voice. For instance, if the verb is "to buy," a sentence using the active voice might be: "Shoppers buy the new cherry-filled chocolates by the handful."

In comparison, using the passive voice, that same sentence might sound like this: "The cherry-filled chocolates were bought by shoppers by the handful."

As you can see from this example, writing copy in an active voice gives your words an intensity, energy, and passion that draws the reader in and produces the results the copywriter wants. Passive copy, on the other hand, has no emotional power and may leave the reader flat and uninterested.

The active voice refers to a sentence's subject in relation to its verb. In a sentence using the active voice, the subject acts—"the waitress serves dinner," "the buffing machine shines the floor," and "flowers brighten the room." Conversely, in sentences using the passive voice, the subject receives the action or is acted on—"dinner is served by the waitress," "the floor is shined by the buffing machine," and "the room is brightened by the flowers."

Here's another example:

Drivers love the safety of driver- and passenger-side air bags. (Active)

The driver- and passenger-side air bags are loved by drivers. (Passive)

In the first sentence, the focus is on "drivers," the subject. In the second sentence, however, the emphasis is on "air bags," the object. As a skilled writer, you will want to design your copy to connect with the product's potential buyer, and that's certainly the driver, not the air bags. The first sentence is stronger and will have a more powerful effect on the reader.

Whenever possible, use the active voice when writing advertising copy. Not only are active-voice sentences more forceful, they are less complicated and easier to understand. They are crisp, clear, to-the-point, and effective.

Short Sentences and Short Words Can Add Up to Big Ideas

"No-frills" advertising copy is brief, direct, and delivers a knockout punch every time. When you're about to say something in ten words, see if you can say it in eight, or six, or four. Because, when it comes to copy, being concise is a virtue. Eliminate irrelevant or redundant words or phrases, cut out puffery and pompous language. Big words only confuse as well as get in the way of your message. Say what you mean just the way you would when talking with a friend. Substitute big words with the smaller words you'd use in conversation. Simply stated, say what you have to say and move on to the next benefit. By reducing language to the essentials, your message will be lean, on target, and energy-packed. Short, powerful words create an urgency and rhythm that drives home your sales message so it has the best chance of getting noticed.

Don't say, "You'll be cognizant of the exhilaration of movement." Instead, say, "You'll love the speed."

Don't say, "It exhibits a user-friendly interface." Instead, say, "It's easy to use."

Don't say, "As of this date, all orders will be processed in 48 hours." Instead, say, "Orders received today are shipped tomorrow."

Always think of yourself when writing copy. You be the judge. Would you stop and read a long paragraph filled with multisyllable words? Of course not! Write for the lazy reader. We have met our enemy and the enemy is us.

Use Formats That Promote

Just like an architect uses a blueprint or an engineer uses a schematic drawing to give his or her project direction, the copywriter has access to proven format formulas that will provide his or her copy with a structure that captures readership, inquiries, and sales. Some proven format formulas include strong headlines, benefit-oriented body copy, and bulleted selling points. A discussion of these techniques follows.

The number-one challenge to any copywriter is to get the attention of the prospect and hold that attention—so the ad is read and motivates the reader to act. Grabbing the reader's attention is a creative challenge. As we flip through the pages of a magazine or click from one television station to another, the writer's window of opportunity to interest us—the reader/viewer—lasts just a few seconds. How can the copywriter compete with all the other ads, articles, programs, and more fighting for the consumer's attention?

The answer is to open up the copywriter's bag of tricks and pull out a technique that helps grab and keep attention. Here are a few that are sure to work.

Strong Headlines

I'm sure you've seen ads in magazines with a full page of small-print copy. How can an ad like that work? Who would stop to read it? The answer is that the headline is what pulls in the reader and keeps the reader interested long enough to read the entire ad.

Invariably, the headline is in bold type and teases the reader with an intriguing question or statement. In fact, the headline may very well have taken more time to write than the entire ad. It's that important! The famous headline that sold more piano lessons than any effort before or since read, "When I sat down at the piano, my friends all began to laugh. But when I began to play. . . ." This headline tells a story. It whets the appetite and forces the reader to want to learn how the story ends. A headline is like a drillmaster's command. It immediately captures the audience's attention and puts everyone on alert. Once this has been accomplished, instructions, facts, and benefits are heard and acted on.

Headlines that work are short, crisp, and easy to read. They may take the form of:

Intriguing questions: "Are you ready to retire today?"
Provocative statements: "Turn $1 into $10,000 in two weeks."
Promises of value: "Get 35 miles per gallon."
How-tos: "How to brew beer right at home."
Inside information: "Seven secrets to finding the perfect mate."
Testimonials: "Bill Gates swears by it."

Some effective headline examples include the following:

Would you spend $1 to save $1,000?
Eighty-seven miles per gallon!
How I lost 25 pounds in 10 days without dieting
Learn what 99 out of 100 people don't know that causes them to fail
The razor blade that went to the moon and why
What your stockbroker will never tell you
Three times the life of ordinary tires
Engineered to put engineers out of work

Body Copy

Support for your headline comes from the body copy of your ad. The body copy must hold the interest that the headline created and inform the reader of the product's or service's benefits. Copy should be focused, short, and benefit-oriented. It elaborates on the interest raised by the headline, creates a need for the product, resolves objections, and, step-by-step, leads the prospect to a buying action.

Usually, an ad will promote a single selling proposition. Every product or service has multiple features and benefits. However, the writer must isolate the predominant one as the focus of the copy. Jumping from selling point to selling point confuses the reader, does not allow the writer to develop any selling point fully, and makes the ad lose focus. By elaborating on the single selling proposition in the body copy, the ad's central theme is consistent, direct, and powerful.

Let's look at golf equipment as an example of focused body copy. For a golf club, that single selling proposition might be performance. The headline brings the prospect to the table by grabbing his or her attention. The body copy serves up the headline's selling proposition with focused copy.

Headline: Add 25 Yards to Your Drive with the New ProGolf Titanium Driver

How many strokes would you cut off your score if you could add 25 yards every time you used your driver? A typical golfer could lower his or her handicap by five or more strokes. Now, with the ProGolf Titanium Driver, you can add distance and accuracy to your game. You'll amaze your foursome and maybe, finally, win that club championship you've been after for years.

The secret is in the oversize, titanium club head. It provides you with a sweet spot 30 percent larger than ordinary drivers, giving you cleaner, truer ball strikes. This means more fairways hit and lower scores. Plus, the power generated by the scientifically designed titanium shaft and head will produce greater head speed than you ever imagined. You'll be hitting your second shots from so far up the fairway, you'll feel like a pro.

Notice how this advertising copy cites features and, then, immediately focuses on how those features benefit the buyer. An oversize club head helps the buyer achieve his or her goal—a lower golf score.

Bulleted Selling Points

One of the most effective ways to drive home the benefits of a product or service is to list them above the body copy of an ad. This is accomplished with the use of bullets (•). Each bullet provides or lists a different feature or benefit. Bullets reinforce the headline and body copy and can be thought of as a selling shorthand. The prospect's attention is naturally drawn to the short list of points within the copy. The message is delivered quickly, effectively, and painlessly. Ideally, bulleted copy should flow from most significant benefit to least (but all should be important). Keep the bullets to a manageable handful. Too many spoils their effectiveness. Here's an example of bulleted copy selling the book *Phrases That Sell*:

- More than 5,000 ready-to-use advertising phrases
- Organized so you can find the perfect phrase in just seconds
- Eliminates writer's block
- Stimulates your creative juices
- Includes a primer on writing copy that sells

The smart copywriter uses format principles such as intriguing headlines; short, focused, benefit-filled body copy; and bulleted selling points to deliver a knockout blow to the prospect. While not every one will hit the canvas, you'll make many TKOs resulting in significant interest and sales in your product or service.

Use Offers That Sell

Like fine wines, offers that sell are cultivated with care and brought to the table at just the right moment. The offer is the natural conclusion to an ad. It presents the product or service in a manner that's hard to turn down. It changes "like" into "love" and makes the couch potato get up, reach for the telephone, and call that toll-free number you provided in big, bold type.

Well-conceived offers generally follow these six guidelines. The offer is:

1. an exceptionally good deal. Either the price has been significantly cut or free merchandise or service is available.
2. easy to understand. It can be stated in just a few words.
3. limited as far as availability and/or date-sensitive. One must act quickly or the offer will expire. This creates a feeling of urgency for the prospective buyer.
4. a high perceived value. The perceived value is often higher than the actual value of the offer.

5. risk-free for the buyer. This is frequently achieved with a money-back guarantee.

6. credible. If any offer sounds too good to be true, it will arouse suspicion in the prospect, which negatively affects sales.

Some examples of proven-effective offers include:

Free 30-Day Trial

Buy One . . . Get One Free

Pay only $1 and receive five ____s valued at $49

Free, No-Risk Subscription. Receive the first three issues.
    Pay only when satisfied.

End-of-year 50 percent off sale

Buy Two . . . Get One Free

Tell Your Reader What to Do

Smart copywriters never leave the prospects' reactions to their ads to chance. Rather, they tell the readers exactly what is expected of them in specific terms. Their instructions are concise, concrete, and direct.

Too often you see advertising that makes you scratch your head and say "so what?" The writer has left the potential buyer at a loss. What is the reader expected to do? Without clear instructions, all the work that went into developing the ad is wasted.

Here are a few examples of the kinds of instructions copywriters give to prospects that leave no question about what the reader should do next:

- Write, call, or fax for your free prospectus.
- Come right down to see us today. We're keeping the store open until 10 P.M. for preferred customers only.
- Visit our new interactive display in the Standard Building lobby on Tuesday, November 11th. Hours: 9 A.M. to 5 P.M.
- Mail the coupon for your free sample.
- Call the toll-free number now to reserve your complimentary issue.

- To find out your discount rate, call 1-800-555-5555.
- To take advantage of this limited offer, call today.
- Reserve your ____ today while quantities last.
- For a confidential review, please call me today.

Tout Your Name

Every time you create an advertisement or promotion, you have the opportunity to build recognition for your company and product by plugging your corporate or brand name. If your company has a good reputation, you certainly will want to take advantage of it by emphasizing name recognition. If you are a start-up company, you won't want to miss the chance to begin to build goodwill by touting your name.

These are a number of practical and effective ways to promote your name in your copy:

1. Tell the reader who you are in the headline. An example is, "The Fast and Easy Way to Manage Your Finances . . . Brought to You by XYZ Company." A second example is, "Before You Buy Your Next Computer . . . Ask the Experts at MicroTechnologies."

2. Use your logo. Place it in a prominent location in the ad for instant visual recognition.

3. Use your slogan. Often your audience best knows you from a popular company slogan or tag line.

4. Always place your company name, address, and telephone number at the bottom of the ad. These days, companies also often add their fax number and e-mail number.

5. When it's appropriate, include your name in the ad's copy, testimonials, etc.

When a company consistently employs some or all of these methods to place its name in front of its potential customers, it is building a foundation of recognition that will bring immediate and future sales.

We'd like to add a short note about testimonials, awards, and reviews. The strength of these credibility enhancers cannot be overemphasized. People want to learn what others think. And if the objective third party who is quoted is an expert, or someone with like interests, or an individual in their field, it couldn't be better. Studies have shown that when consumers read ads, they often jump right to the testimonial. Therefore, whenever possible, reinforce your message with the element of trustworthiness found in these effective devices.

Seven Steps to Writing Winning Slogans

THE following seven steps designed to help you write winning slogans have been culled from interviews with top copywriters. The list was created from a consensus of the ideas that these experts use in their everyday work as creative writers. No single copywriter offered the list exactly as presented. Yet, on average, these steps or ones similar appeared in most of the lists we received. We're happy to share them with you.

You may find that you can create successful slogans by following only a few of these steps and ignoring others—and that is fine. Creativity is a very personal process and your approach may be a unique one. But if you are drawing a blank or need a jump start to spark your creative juices, this list may be just what you need. Try some of the ideas or customize them to fit your own style. The results will speak for themselves.

STEP 1—
Decide on Your Objective

Writing slogans can be easy, but coming up with the perfect slogan that hones in on the specific message you wish to convey about your company, product, or service takes time, planning, and thought. Some typical objectives a company might set for a slogan include:

- Building company name recognition
- Establishing a positive feeling about the company or its products
- Communicating an idea/concept and linking it to your company
- Creating customer loyalty
- Offering a new marketing strategy
- Positioning a product or service
- Reinforcing the historical image of the company
- Establishing credibility

A well-conceived slogan can meet any of these objectives or a combination of two or more. However, the more concepts one wishes to convey through a slogan, the more diluted the slogan may become and the less effective it may be. Conversely, the more specific a slogan is, the more limiting it may be.

Take the example of a company that sells lightbulbs. The slogan, "We're not light on bulbs," tells a great deal about the company and its products. But in the future, if the company wanted to sell lamps or other electrical fixtures, the slogan might need to be changed. Therefore, a vision of the company's future and the direction its growth might take should be considered when creating your slogan.

Slogan development usually comes from one of two sources. First, with newly formed organizations, top executives often establish a slogan or tag line at the time the company name, letterhead, and logo are formulated. Second, an in-house marketing department or outside advertising or public-relations company may recommend a slogan to complement a sales or marketing campaign. Whoever makes the decision, the objective must be clearly stated before the creative process begins.

Naturally, clearly understanding your market is essential. For instance, if you are selling a product or service to children (and they will be making the buying decision), the nature of the slogan will be very different from one that appeals to bankers. Additionally, developing a slogan for a child's toy will be very different from creating one for a carpet-cleaning service. Keep your audience in mind at all times!

STEP 2—
Develop a List of Key Words or Phrases

With your objective established, your next step will be to form a list of words or phrases that describes the product or service and targets the specific quality you have isolated as most important to the buyers who you are targeting. For example, the objective of a company that markets a mutual fund might be to reinforce the fund's name with a slogan that touts its performance history. The key-word list might look like this:

- Reputation
- History
- Prudent
- Conservative
- Growth
- Sound investing
- Proven performance
- Stable management
- Outstanding research
- 25 years of success
- Reliability
- Year after year

The list of key words can be developed by brainstorming, reviewing company literature, checking out the competitor's literature, surveying key customers, searching through trade publications (articles and ads), and using a dictionary and thesaurus. Once you are satisfied that your list of key words fairly represents the qualities you wish to promote, it is time to move on to the next step.

STEP 3—
Use Creative Association

Creative association helps you develop new and insightful marketing ideas. It consists of two processes, focus and comparison. First, you must focus on your objective and the key-word list you've developed. By focus, we mean to keep these ideas foremost in your mind. Much like meditation, during which one repeats a mantra, you must continually think about the slogan and your objective. Second, with the slogan's focus in your mind's eye, stimulate your creative imagination. The stimulation can come from anywhere and everywhere. It is accomplished by comparing and contrasting key words and phrases with words, objects, and thoughts.

Let's take a closer look at this using our previous example. We want to develop a slogan to enhance our mutual fund's image and we've developed a list of key words. With this in mind, we look to stimulate our imagination. The stimulation could come from browsing in a bookstore, or walking through a department store or down a busy street. We could watch a television program or leaf through a magazine. As images and words appear, new ideas relating to your product or service are generated. Thinking about the key words "proven performance," you might see a car ad saying "It's a keeper." This spurs the thought that "Our customers stay with us for the long term." From this point ideas flow—"We're with you for life," "Invest for life," "The company that invests in your life," "The investment for life that makes more than cents," etc.

STEP 4—
Use Creative Mapping

This powerful tool can be thought of as "brainstorming on paper." One simply writes down key words or phrases, then draws lines connecting ideas that are related in some way to one another. It is very important not to censor or inhibit this process by judging if the idea is worthwhile or not. Every idea should be written down no matter how abstract or far-fetched. As phrases begin to come closer to a usable concept, words can be circled or underlined. Creative mapping is often executed on a large piece of paper or written on a blackboard or whiteboard. Quickly, the map takes on a life of its own as it grows and spreads across the paper/board with multiple ideas. Thoughts that seem more on target are elaborated on while less-attractive concepts reach dead ends.

Here's an example of creative mapping. Notice how the concept evolved from key words to fuller ideas to a final slogan concept.

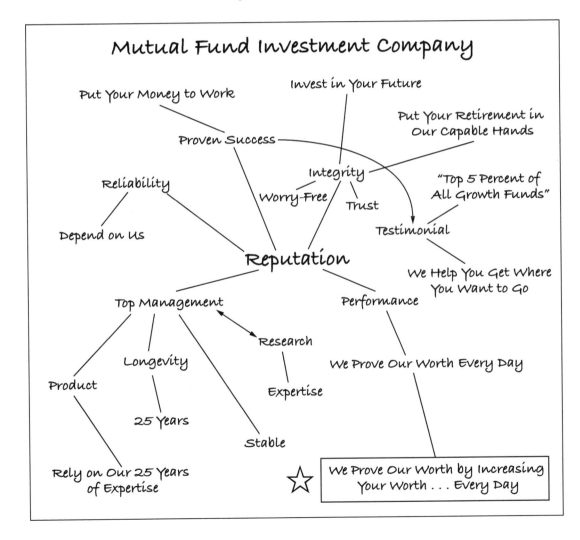

STEP 5—
Narrow Down Your Choices

The processes of creative association and creative mapping will produce many good ideas. Of course, it is important to eliminate some so that only the best are left for further scrutiny. Narrowing down your choices is the task of the "slogan committee." The slogan committee is usually made up of marketing, advertising, and public-relations personnel. Once it is decided how many choices you think you will need, each member of the committee creates a hierarchy of slogans by numbering each remaining choice from the best to the worst. As soon as this is completed, the committee can meet to select a master list of choices.

STEP 6—
Begin Reality Testing

Your list of slogans has now been narrowed down to a select few, and it is time to test each slogan's effectiveness. To do this, create a new list of the possible situations in which you might use your new slogan. For example, this list might look like the following:

1. Company letterhead
2. Capability brochure
3. Annual report
4. Musical jingle
5. Sales sheets
6. Business cards
7. Television advertising
8. Product packaging
9. Trade-show signage
10. Imprinted giveaways

It is surprising how often a slogan will work well only on certain materials and not others. As you try the slogan out, you may see that it's too long, awkwardly phrased, or doesn't really satisfy the most important criteria for a slogan that you established early on in the process.

In some instances, a slogan is developed for a single purpose. If this is the case and the slogan works, your reality testing is complete. However, in circumstances where the slogan will be used in a multitude of communication media, testing it against a list similar to the previous one has great value.

STEP 7—
Consider the Legal Implications

Before you choose a slogan for your business, it is important to make sure that it is protectable under the law. A slogan that is protected has more value to your company than one that can be copied by competitors, thus losing its uniqueness.

Keep in mind that a slogan is a trademark. Therefore, you need to follow a series of steps to make sure your slogan isn't too similar to someone else's slogan or trademark. If you get sued for trademark infringement or unfair competition, the penalties could be severe—you could end up paying the plaintiff all the profits you earned from using that slogan, incur attorneys' fees and, perhaps most inconvenient, be required to change all your stationery and marketing materials.

Here are four steps you may want to follow:

1. Ideally, you should consult an attorney experienced in trademark law to give you an opinion about whether or not your slogan will infringe on a third party's rights. There are a number of good ways to locate a trademark or intellectual-property attorney.

   - Your local bar association may have a referral service. Bar associations are generally organized by city or county, and the telephone number will be listed in the white pages; if you cannot find the name or telephone number of the local bar association, try calling the nearest courthouse and asking for this information.

- If you have an attorney you use for general business advice, he or she may be able to provide a recommendation.
- The International Trademark Association, known as INTA, is the professional organization for practitioners in trademark and related areas of the law. You can call INTA in New York City at 212-768-9887 and ask for the name of a member in your geographic area. While membership in the INTA is not a guarantee of legal ability or client satisfaction, it does indicate that the lawyer was sufficiently interested in trademark law to join the organization.
- The *Martindale-Hubbell Law Directory* is a listing of lawyers by state of practice. The listings often provide the educational and professional background of the lawyer. Often lawyers who are specialists in trademark or intellectual-property law describe themselves as such in this directory. Some libraries carry this directory (law school libraries almost certainly will) and the information is also available via the Internet at www.martindale.com. Again, a listing in the directory is not an endorsement of the lawyer.

2. The lawyer will most likely recommend a search of existing trademarks to determine if any third parties are using a similar trademark or slogan. A complete search should include records of the U.S. Trademark Office, the various state trademark offices and directories, and databases relevant to your industry. (There are circumstances when a less-comprehensive search would be appropriate.) The lawyer may use an outside firm to perform the search. These search firms typically charge from $350 to $400 for a comprehensive search with results in five business days; faster services can be obtained for a higher fee. It may be tempting to order a search yourself. However, a nonspecialist

may not know which third-party trademarks are problems. For example, your proposed slogan may not be identical to an existing registration but still could be a problem. On the other hand, if the exact slogan you proposed is already in use but in a completely different industry, there may not be a problem. What you are paying your lawyer for is his or her expertise in evaluating the search, knowing the legal standards, and providing practical advice.

3. Here are a few hints in developing your slogan:
   - The more descriptive or common the slogan, the harder it will be to prevent someone else, even a competitor, from using it. For example, "the best service in the industry" may accurately describe your business, but unless you have been using that slogan for a few years and established significant name recognition, a court will probably not help you stop a third party's use of virtually the identical slogan.
   - Keep away from a slogan that sounds like your competition—that's just asking for trouble.
   - Once you have cleared your slogan, take the right steps to protect it from third parties and to make it more visible to your customers.
   - Consider filing for a federal trademark registration for your slogan. Consult your trademark lawyer for the benefits and costs involved.
   - Use the slogan in a font or typeface or logo that makes it stand out from the rest of your copy or stationery.
   - If the slogan does not have a federal trademark registration, use one of the following symbols: ™ for a slogan used in connection with goods or products—i.e., "Head for the mountains of Busch™," for beer—and ˢᴹ for a slogan used with services—"Fly the friendly skies ˢᴹ" for airline services. While these symbols do not have any legal significance, they can increase customer awareness of your slogan. Note: You can only use the ® symbol for a federally registered trademark.

- Take prompt action if a competitor uses a confusingly similar trademark or slogan. If you allow similar slogans to proliferate, not only will customers become confused, but your slogan will lose its distinctiveness and its value for you will diminish.

Popular Slogans

Here are examples of slogans that have proved themselves successful over the years and are familiar to most Americans. In fact, a large percentage of adults can name the product just by hearing the slogan:

We Make Money the Old-Fashioned Way: *E. F. Hutton*

Don't Leave Home Without It: *American Express*

I Love What You Do for Me: *Toyota*

Just Do It: *Nike*

It's the Real Thing: *Coca-Cola*

It's Everywhere You Want to Be: *Visa*

Plop, Plop, Fizz, Fizz, Oh What a Relief It Is: *Alka-Seltzer*

Gentlemen Prefer Hanes: *Hanes hosiery*

Delta Is Ready When You Are: *Delta Airlines*

The Night Belongs to Michelob: *Michelob*

Fly Me: *National Airlines*

Take Pictures. Further: *Kodak*

Exactly: *Hertz*

Passion for the Road: *Mazda*

Perfect from Beginning to End: *Sassoon Hair*

Reach Out and Touch Someone: *AT&T*

Where's the Beef?: *Wendy's restaurants*

The Computer Inside: *Intel*

The Dependable People: *Maytag*

Where Discover Is a Real Adventure: *Busch Gardens*

Mmm Mmm Good: *Campbell's soups*

We Bring Good Things to Life: *General Electric*

Better Sound Through Research: *BOSE*

We Work Hard So You Don't Have to: *Dow*

It All Makes Sense: *Sprint*

Designed for Living: *Corelle*

Something Special in the Air: *American Airlines*

Bullish on America: *Merrill Lynch*

We Try Harder: *Avis*

Breakfast of Champions: *Wheaties*

This Bud's for You: *Anheuser-Busch beer*

Don't Risk It. Wisk It: *Wisk*

Johnson's. Where the Best Ideas for Babies Are Born: *Johnson & Johnson*

Be All That You Can Be: *U.S. Army*

When It Rains, It Pours: *Morton Salt*

How Do You Spell Relief?: *Rolaids*

No One Knows Pancakes Like Aunt Jemima: *Aunt Jemima*

Sometimes You Feel Like a Nut: *Almond Joy*

Just Slightly Ahead of Our Time: *Panasonic*

What a Luxury Car Should Be: *Lincoln*

When It Absolutely, Positively Has to Be There in the Morning: *Federal Express*

The Quicker Picker-Upper: *Bounty Towels*

Please Don't Squeeze the Charmin: *Charmin bathroom tissue*

Get a Piece of the Rock: *Prudential insurance*

Have You Driven a Ford Lately?: *Ford*

The Softer Side of Sears: *Sears*

You're in Good Hands: *Allstate insurance*

See What Develops: *Polaroid*

Does She Or Doesn't She?: *Clairol*

Never Had It, Never Will: *Seven-Up*

When You Care Enough to Send the Very Best: *Hallmark*

Just a Better Fever Medicine: *Children's Advil*

Genuine Chevrolet: *Chevrolet*

Better Care Makes Better Kittens: *Kitten Chow*

Like a Good Neighbor: *State Farm insurance*

Takes a Licking, Keeps on Ticking: *Timex*

Bet You Can't Eat Just One: *Wise Snacks*

It's Not Nice to Fool Mother Nature: *Chiffon margarine*

Pepsi Generation: *Pepsi-Cola*

It Takes a Tough Man to Make a Tender Chicken: *Perdue poultry*

Wouldn't You Really Rather Have a Buick?: *Buick*

If It's Got to Be Clean: *Tide*

The Quiet Company: *Northwest Mutual Life*

Descriptive Qualities/ Products and Services

Age Before Beauty

A centuries-old technique

A modern heirloom

A tradition since _____

An age-old tradition

Antiaging breakthrough

Born of centuries of experience

Delight young and old alike

Feel and look young again

Feeling the effects of aging? Then,
_____

For the young at heart

Founded on old-world traditions

Keeps you young at heart

Look younger, feel younger

Looks new, year after year

Looks years younger

No matter what your age

Passed on for generations

Recover your youth

Resists the signs of aging

Stay mentally and physically fit
with _____, no matter what
your age

Takes years off

The world's oldest

Turn-of-the-century

We'll make you feel young again

Where ancient meets modern

Where past meets present

You'll look years younger

Young and fresh

Younger looking in just 10 days

Younger than springtime

You're never too old

You're never too young

Beauty at Every Turn

A beautiful sight wherever you put it

A beauty of a _____

A delicate and intricate design

A harmonious blend

A natural beauty

Accents the beauty of _____

Add beauty to _____

Adds a touch of beauty to your day

Adds atmosphere

An airy, delicate design

An aura of gentle beauty

An eye-pleaser

Artistically inspired

As beautiful as it is practical

As good as they can look

As lovely as can be

Attractive, welcoming, and useful

Beautiful all on its own

Beautiful anywhere!

Beautiful basics

Beautiful from any angle

Beautiful in its simplicity

Beautifully crafted

Beauty and craftsmanship that will never go out of style

Beauty based on simplicity and utility

Beauty beyond measure

Beauty comes from the inside

Beauty that stands the test of time

Blends beautifully with many styles

Breathtaking enough to make double takes the response you'll come to expect

Brighten your day with _____

Delightful to look at and hold

Engineered for a lifetime of beauty and service

Enhance your beauty

Enjoy the tranquil beauty of _____

Ethereal beauty

Exceptional beauty

Exquisitely subtle

Graceful beauty

Indulge in the beauty of _____

It can only be described as breathtaking

Its beauty alone merits admiration

Lasting beauty

Lithe, luxurious, lovely

Looks so good outside, it will make you feel good inside

Make a beautiful impression

Natural opulence and serene beauty

Never looked so good

Not only a joy to look at but _____

Oh, so pretty!

On top of its good looks, _____

Others pale in comparison
Pleasing patterns
Pleasing to the eye
Poised for beauty
Practicality and beauty
Provides a dramatic accent
Restore its original beauty with _____
Simply stunning
Singularly dramatic beauty
So beautiful. Nature's own pale in comparison.
So exquisite no one will guess
So terrific, you'll surely be noticed
Spectacular beauty
Standout status
Step up to the beauty of _____
Stunning beauty
Sure to draw admiring looks

The beauty of contrasts
The belle of the ball
The effect is enchantment
The magic and the beauty of _____
The prettiest under the sun
The rare and exciting beauty of _____
The sensuous feel and beauty of _____
There's no mistaking its beauty
Tranquil beauty
Transcendent beauty
Turn heads with the beauty of _____
Unsurpassed beauty
Will snare its share of attention
Years of beauty
You can't lose when you look this good
You'll display yours with pride

The **Choice** Is Yours

A clear choice when only the best will do

A dazzling array of styles

A fit for every taste

A great alternative to _____

A popular choice. And for a good reason.

A practical choice

A refreshing alternative

A variety unmatched anywhere else

A wonderful merger of old and new

All the brands you want

An enormous assortment

An extensive selection

An ideal choice

An unrivaled selection

At home or on the road

Available in English or French

Available in several finishes

Best for selection

Carefully selected

Choices. Choices. Choices.

Choose from many distinctive styles

Choose one!

Choose one that fits your individual need

Comes in a variety of shapes and sizes

Compare your choices

Extensive, on-the-shelf inventory

For a broad range of _____

For any taste or budget

For contemporary and traditional settings

For home or travel

For the best selection

From budget to deluxe

Has multiple talents

Huge selection

If you had to choose just one, this would be it

If you need it, we have it

Imagine the possibilities

It's your choice

Just-right options for _____

Large or small

Largest collection available

Lots of choices

Make up your own mind

New merchandise arriving daily

No quantity too large or too small

Nobody offers more variety or more choices

Now in stock

Order now for best selection

Perfectly suited for day and evening

Reflecting your many moods

Since variety is the spice of life

Stretch your options

Such possibilities!

Suitable for entertaining and everyday use

The best choice for _____

The better choice

The choice for all your _____ needs

The largest selection

The luxury of choice

The one you've been waiting for

The options are endless

The selection you deserve

The size you need at a price that's right

The smaller, friendlier, more personal choice

The smartest choice you'll ever make

The superior choice

There's only one

Thousands to choose from

Today's discriminating choice

Unmatched selection

Value, choice, and selection

We have more of what you want

We have the right one to suit your needs

We stock a large inventory

What better choice!

Wide selection of custom-finished styles available

You can get it all at _____

You have choices in life

You'll find everything you're looking for

Your one-stop shop

Your only choice

The Classics

A classic design

A classic for today

A classic, homespun, country look

A classic of the period

A classic presence in any room

A classic version

A country classic

A favored classic

A modern classic

A new American classic

A proven classic

A summertime classic

A timeless classic

A true classic from generation to generation

Add classic style to your _____

An all-time classic

An enduring classic

An instant classic

An old classic with a new twist

An updated classic

Blends the classic and contemporary

Classic and refined

Classic compositions in shimmering hues

Classic designs for every type of _____

Classic details at affordable prices

Classic fit

Classic good looks

Classic value

Classic yet revolutionary

Classically designed

Classically elegant

Classically handsome

Clean and classic

Comfortable classics

Considered the standard

Cool and classy

Distinctive. Classic. Lasting.

How do you make a classic new?

In classic style

Like all true classics, it transcends the boundaries of time and style

The classic beauty of _____

Timeless and classic

Truly an American classic

What makes it a standard?

Color Beyond Compare

A bold turn of shapes and colors
A bright spot in your day
A brilliant splash of color
A burst of color
A coaxing collaboration of colors
A colorful mosaic
A dense abundance of color
A fabulous mix of color and texture
A fantastic flash of color
A profusion of colors
A rage of color
A rhythm of color
A rich range of colors
A riotous display of colors
A sea of color
A vibrant slice of color
A warm glow
A whirl of colors
A wild fusion of color
Adds a little sunshine
All in a soothing desert palette
An artist's palette of colors
An exuberant expression of color and
    design
An impressionistic palette of colors
Awash in supercharged color

Bold strokes of bright color
Born of the sun
Bright and bold
Brightly colored
Brilliant, lasting color
Candy colors
Casts a lovely glow
Charged with incandescent color
Cheerful, bold colors
Citrus colors
Cleaner white
Color à la mode
Color excitement
Color for all seasons
Color is the key
Color your world with _____
Color-coordinated
Colors you'll look great in
Complementary colors
Cool, luscious colors
Creates a beautiful, subtle palette
Deep, intense, impassioned color
Deeply radiant color
Drama in black and white
Drenched in color
Earth-inspired colors
Earth-toned shades
Explosive colors
Eye-popping colors

Fresh and colorful

Fresh, crisp, and colorful

Fresh spring colors

Funky colors

Get a jump on the newest fashion colors

Gives a welcoming glow

Glowing colors

Goes beyond the pale

Great color, great texture, great prices

High-visibility color

Hot colors! Cool sophistication!

Hot, shocking colors

In brilliant color

In full color

In glorious color

In matching colors

In natural colors

In vivid colorations

Infused with unexpected color

Inspiring color

Makes a contemporary statement on the use of color

Mellow colors

Mouthwatering shades

Multipastel

Opulent colors

Painted in bold brush strokes

Pepped-up colors

Punch-bowl colors

Pure colors

Rainbow of colors

Reminiscent of an Impressionist's palette

Rich colorations

Rich, deep hues

Rich in texture, detail, and coloring

Show your true colors

Simple texture and exhilarating color

Soft colors

Softly sun-washed colors

Sorbet colors

Sparked by brilliant jewel tones

Spectacular parade of color

Spirited colors

Spring colors

Subtle hues

Sun-drenched

Sun-softened colors

Sun-spun colors

Sun-washed palette

The importance of color

The power of color

The prettiest colors under the sun

The soft touch of celestial hues

Tone-on-tone

True-to-life colors

Very tempting colors

Vibrant color combinations

Vibrant, desert colors

Vibrant tones

Warm colors and exuberant designs

Warm, spicy hues

Watercolor shades

Welcoming, warming tones

When spring is in the air, your thoughts turn to color

Whispers of color

Will give you a color boost

With a burst of color

Wonderful, country colors

Your most flattering color

Comfort Starts Here

A breakthrough in comfort

A casual favorite

A cozy way to _____

A home away from home

Advanced comfort technology

All the amenities of home

All-day comfort

As cozy as can be

Beauty, comfort, durability, and
    ease of care

Blends comfort and good looks

Blissfully comfortable

Broken in

Built for comfort

Casual and contemporary

Casual feel and comfort

Combines convenience and comfort

Comfort and luxury combined

Comfort never looked so good

Comfort you instantly feel at
    home in

Comfortable contours

Constant comfort control

Cool and comfortable

Couldn't be more comfortable

Country casual

Cozy and welcoming

Creature comforts you'll appreciate

Curl up with _____

Defines comfort

Designed for comfort

Do it in comfort

Easy comfort

Efficiency, personality, and comfort

Enjoy the comforts of home

Ergonomically designed

Feel right at home

Feel the cares of the day fade away

For a higher level of comfort

For all-season comfort

For easy comfort

For luxurious comfort

For optimum comfort

For total relaxation

Go-anywhere comfort

Help you stay comfortable

Incomparable comfort

Just right for after a long day

Just the right amount of comfort

Leisurely comfort

_____ made comfortable

Made for life's relaxing moments

Made to (keep you cool, take the
    heat, etc.)

Make yourself at home with _____

Moves freely

Need a little pampering?

Nonstop comfort

Old-world charm. New-world comfort.

Optimally comfortable

Our recipe for relaxation

Plenty of room

Plush, cozy softness

Premium comfort

Provides hours of relaxation

Pure comfort that's never out of style

Pure, relaxing comfort

Raise your comfort level

Relax in total comfort

Relax with the luxury of _____

Relaxed fit

Roomy and durable

Sensuous lines and unsurpassed comfort

Serene solitude

Snuggle into _____

So comfortable you'll forget you have them on

So soft it feels like floating on a cloud

Soothing comfort

Stylishly comfortable

The epitome of comfort and style

The most-comfortable _____ ever created

The most comfortable you've been in a long time

The perfect fit

True comfort

We take the pain out of _____

Will help you _____ more comfortably

With an emphasis on comfort

You can relax now

You'll experience an overwhelming sense of relaxation

Your headquarters for extra comfort

You've never been more comfortable

A-1 Craftsmanship

A flawless finish

A masterful creation

A master's touch

A work of art

Aesthetics, precision, ultimate craftsmanship

Beautifully crafted

Beautifully rendered

Beautifully tailored

Brilliantly executed design and construction

Combines yesterday's craftsmanship with today's fit and function

Crafted by pure genius

Craftsmanship and care

Created by master artisans

Created for you . . . by hand . . . one at a time

Earns superior marks for construction, comfort, and durability

Enhanced with rich and harmonious materials

Excels in endurance and eye appeal

Exceptional craftsmanship

Exclusively handcrafted

Exquisitely crafted

Fine workmanship

Finest made anywhere

Finished by hand

Flawlessly carved

From the finest master craftsmen

Gives your _____ a look of importance

Handmade by dedicated artisans

Has the texture and appearance of a fine heirloom

Impeccably crafted

Individually hand-sculpted

Made from the finest materials available

Masterfully crafted

Mechanical ingenuity

Meticulous commitment to craftsmanship

Meticulous workmanship

Old-world attention to detail

One-of-a-kind workmanship

Painstakingly hand-fashioned

Powerfully built

Precision engineering

Quality and handmade craftsmanship

Quality construction throughout

Quality craftsmanship in every detail

Quality workmanship

Rare workmanship

Richly textured

Smooth, flawless finish

State-of-the-art engineering

Substantially built

The pleasures of beautiful workmanship

The secret's in the way it's made

Unexpected artistry

Unsurpassed craftsmanship

Using the fine techniques employed by early craftsmen

We make it right!

Weighty, solid, and built for long service

Well constructed

With detail and care

World-class design and construction

You'll be proud to present

Credibility

A bold claim—but we know that it's true

A proven leader

A recognized world leader

A _____ your mother would approve of

American-made

America's favorite

America's largest retailer of _____

America's most-prestigious _____

America's most-trusted resource for

_____

And we can prove it!

Approved by _____

As one satisfied customer told us,

_____

As seen on TV

Centuries of experience went into this

Come see what all the fuss is about

Critically acclaimed

Don't be confused by cheap imitations

Editor's Choice

Endorsed by _____

Experience counts

Experience it!

Extensively researched

Find out why our customers return again and again

Four out of five users prefer _____

From popular designers whose names we cannot divulge

From the same company who brought you _____

Glowing recommendations

Has been in our family for more than 50 years

Here's what others say about us:

Highly recommended

Highly regarded

In test after test, ours is proven the best

Includes a Certificate of Authenticity

Internationally renowned

It's true!

Kids love _____

Laboratory-tested

Made right on the premises

Made under expert supervision

More than 100,000 people have successfully used this product

Most critics agree that ours is the best

My doctor recommends _____

Newly patented

No wonder it's #1

#1 doctor-recommended

#1 on everyone's list

100 years of experience go into every one

One of the year's 10 best

Order one and see for yourself

Our _____ speak with authority

Patent-pending

President's Choice

Proudly made in the U.S.A.

Rated "Best" by an independent panel

Rated #1

Researchers have proven the benefits of _____

Respected worldwide

Scientific tests have proved it!

Spanning five decades

Take advantage of our expertise

The acknowledged pacesetter

The brand doctors recommend most

The choice of champions

The choice of competitors around the world

The choice of professionals

The critics' choice

The first authorized _____

The industry's pacesetter

The leader in _____

The market leader

The most-trusted name in _____

The official _____

The one used by champions

The only product ever proven to _____

The original

The proven name in _____

The recognized leader in _____

The _____ Seal of Approval

The source for professionals

The ultimate authority on _____

This is the genuine article

This is what everyone is raving about

Thoroughly researched

Top-rated

Trust our experience

We bring expert advice right to you

With the experts

World's foremost _____

Years of knowledge and experience

Your home-care experts

We **Deliver**

Always in stock

Always ready for delivery

Ask for our rush delivery

Call toll-free

Count on us to get it there when you
need it

Delivered to your door every month

Delivering the service you deserve

Delivery, morning, afternoon, or night

Delivery when you want it

Express shipping available

Fast delivery

Fast, dependable delivery

Faster order turnaround

Fax us your orders

Free delivery

Free next-day delivery

Free overnight-shipping upgrade

How fast do you need it?

Immediate shipping

In stock for immediate delivery

International shipments

Just tell us when you need it

Most orders shipped in 24 hours

On-time delivery

Order today. Delivery tomorrow.

Overnight delivery

Prompt delivery

Ready to ship anywhere

Rush service available

Same-day shipping

Satisfaction always delivered

Ships next day

Want it right away?

We deliver anywhere

We deliver conveniently to your home

We pay for your shipping

We ship straight from our extensive
stock

We ship worldwide

We'll get it there faster

When you need it in a hurry

White-glove delivery

The **Durability** Advantage

Adds strength and substance
All-terrain
Always looks like new
Assured of long life
Best-built
Built for commercial use
Built for rugged use
Built to last a lifetime
Built to last . . . made to perform
Built to take your toughest abuse
Built with added strength
and durability
Can take a beating
Crafted for years of use
Delicate-looking yet so strong
Designed for years of heavy-duty use
Designed to weather any challenge
Don't be tempted by a quick fix
For maximum durability
Heavy-duty
Here today. Here tomorrow.
How long will it last?
Industrial-strength
Ironclad
It's tough!
It's very sturdy!

Keeps like new
Lightweight, yet rugged for heavy-duty
use
Long-term durability
Looks as fresh and appealing today as
when it was first created
Made to last
Maintains that like-new look and feel
Nearly indestructible
Reassuringly sturdy
Reinforced for added strength
Remarkably rugged
Resists damage like no other
Rugged construction
Rugged enough to withstand constant
use
Rugged industrial quality
Rugged, no-nonsense
Scratch-resistant
Shrugs off the hard knocks of _____
So durable it frequently outlasts its
owners
So strong you can _____ without
damage
Soft yet substantial
Specially reinforced
Stands up to the elements
Stays new longer
Strength meets style
Strong enough for him

Strong yet flexible

Stronger, more powerful

Sturdy and functional

Sturdy features

Sturdy yet lightweight

Superior construction

Superstrong

Tarnish-resistant

The best way for more than 50 years

The last _____ you'll ever need

Tough as nails

Valued for their strength and versatility

Virtually indestructible

Virtually unbreakable

We don't sacrifice strength for convenience

Wears like iron

Will last a lifetime

Will last for generations

Will maintain its _____ after years of use

Will never wear out

Will provide many seasons of service

Withstands everyday wear and tear

Withstands heavy-duty usage

Withstands the roughest abuse imaginable

Years of use

Your best friend in extreme conditions

Easy as One, Two, Three

A breeze to use

A real convenience

A simple pleasure

A snap to apply

A speedy and simplified approach

A true pleasure to use

A truly portable _____

All under one roof

Always ready when you are

Anywhere, anytime, anyplace

As easy as taking a walk

Assembles in minutes

At a glance

At the touch of your fingertips

Available at fine stores everywhere

Because of our superior process

Brings _____ right to you

Call free anytime

Call now and shop at leisure in your home

Call 24 hours a day

Can be conveniently stored

Carrying convenience

Comes already assembled and ready-to-go

Comes with complete instructions

Compatible with your easy outlook

Control at the touch of a single button

Convenience. Service. Savings.

Conveniently located

Deceptively simple

Detailed instructions

Do-it-yourself

Easier than you think

Easily within reach

Easy access

Easy-access _____

Easy and ready to use

Easy assembly

Easy care

Easy does it

Easy portability

Easy to care for

Easy to carry

Easy to do

Easy to get to

Easy to live with

Easy to make. Hard to resist.

Easy to understand

Easy to use

Easy to wear. Hard to wear out.

Effortless action

Everything you need in one easy-to-use package

Extra storage space

Fast, easy set up

Flawless reputation

Folds up for easy storage

For easy access

For information on our catalog or a showroom near you

For your convenience

Goes anywhere

Hands off

Has never been easier

Hassle-free shopping

Headache-free

In one motion

In the comfort and safety of your own home

Installs in seconds

It simplifies your life

It's as simple as _____

It's doggone easy

It's in the bag!

It's our job to make your job easier

It's pure convenience

It's that simple!

Just one step away

Just turn the key

Kiss your hassles good-bye

Leave the bother behind

Less effort, less fatigue

Lets you keep both hands free

Loose and relaxed

Maintenance is a breeze

Make _____ work for you

Makes _____ a snap

Makes _____ disappear

Makes it easy

Makes the job a breeze

Makes your life easier

Minimum attention gets you maximum results

No experience necessary

No more hassles

No muss. No fuss.

No problem!

No searching. No bending.

No tools required

Now in a store near you

_____ on the go

One-hand carrying convenience

One-stop shopping

One-touch control

Only _____ miles from the center of town (from the business district, etc.)

Open until _____ o'clock every evening, for your convenience

Optimal convenience

Perfect for beginners

Perfect for home or office

Quick access

Quick assembly, comes apart just as
   easily

Quick, easy set up

Ready to _____

Ready to eat

Ready to hang

Requires minimal care

Right in your own backyard (kitchen,
   home, etc.)

Right on your doorstep

Right there

Safe, quick, and easy

Seems spontaneous and effortless

Simple enough for a child to use

Simple pleasures

Simple. Relaxing. Safe.

Simplify your life

Simply touch a button

Smooth sailing

So easy even a child can do it

So easy even an adult can do it

So easy to use

Space-saving

Step-by-step

Step-saving

Storage is simple

Take the drudgery out of _____

Takes the guesswork out of _____

The easy way

The epitome of ease

The handiest one you'll ever own

The living is easy when _____

The simpler, the better

The world's most effortless _____

The _____ you've always wanted is
   just a telephone call away

There's no easier way

To make your work easier

To meet all your needs

Too good to be this easy

Turn it on and it's ready to go

Under one roof

Usable anywhere

User-friendly

Very easy to use

_____ without leaving home

We have a store near you

We never close. Twenty-four-hour
   service.

We'll make every time as easy as the
   first

We'll take it from there

We've made it easy

Whenever you need it

Why strain yourself?

With a flick of your wrist

With a flip of the switch

With a minimum of effort
With a push of the button
With a touch of your finger
With a turn of the handle
With one easy touch
With seductive ease
Within arm's reach
Within easy reach

Without moving a muscle
Without the problems
Work-saving
You can even take it with you
You can use it wherever you please
You won't believe the simplicity
You'll wear it with ease
Your one-stop source for _____

Effective, Efficient, and Professional

A business assistant you can count on

A formula so advanced that _____

A formula that really works

A valuable resource

Against all odds

All your professional needs met

An executive privilege

Ask the pros

Become an expert

Brings efficiency to your home or office

Builds sales

Designed to meet today's demands

Designed with efficiency in mind

_____ does it right, and does it fast

Efficiency, beautifully styled

Everything you need for that professional look

Expand your business potential

Experience, expertise, and service combine for unparalleled results

Feel relief in a matter of minutes

Feel the excitement

For five-star results

For people on the go

For professional-looking _____

For professional results

For results that are out of this world

For your business needs

Get the facts

Gets the message out

Give our experts a call

Give your work an air of professionalism

Gives you the same edge as the pros

Handles tough jobs

Has the know-how you need to do the job you want

Held to the highest standards

Helps maximize efficiency and productivity

Helps you turn wasted hours into productive ones

Highly effective

Identify business trends

If your business is ready to cash in on _____, learn how with _____

If you've been wondering how to get your business moving

Impressive results

Increase work flow

Increases efficiency

Instant organization

It pays to know

Knowledge and know-how

Looks good and works hard

Makes an instant impact

Measured by professional standards

Optimum efficiency and productivity

Our leading-edge professionals will provide you with _____

Our _____ means business

Perfect for any type of business

Perfect to promote your business

Practical, efficient, and economical

Preferred by professionals

Professional _____ right in your own home

Professionally installed

Proven effective

Put to work for you

Puts an end to clutter

Save space, increase efficiency

Save time, frustration, and money

Sends a message of professionalism

Strictly business

Suits every business need

Superbly efficient

Take a tip from the professionals

The best way to make your point

The ideal business partner

The information you need to succeed

The kind of professionalism that is expected from top performers

The most complete information available

The perfect business companion

The _____ professionals depend on

The way to reach all your goals

Unleash your potential

Use it tonight, see the progress tomorrow

We can help your business succeed. Call us today!

We did it!

We know what we're doing

We make things happen

We make your dream a reality

We mean business

We produce results

We want your business

We're famous for our super service

We're the experts

We're the professionals

What could be more practical?

Whatever it takes

When it comes to _____, we're all you need

When you need professional help

Will command your respect

Work with a team of experienced professionals

You name it, we've done it!

You'll be amazed at how we get things done!

You'll have total control

A Tradition of **Elegance**

A hint of elegance

A reflection of your uncompromising good taste

A regal touch

A relaxed elegance

Adds instant distinction

An elegance worthy of family heirlooms

Beautifully tailored, subtly detailed

Capture the splendor of _____

Celebrate our tradition of elegance

Cool elegance

Dressed-down elegance

Easy yet elegant

Elegance for easy living

Elegance richly defined

Elegant and inviting

Elegant. Luxurious. Fun.

Elegant simplicity

Elegant solutions

Elegant. Understated. Unsurpassed.

Elegant, yet sporty

Elegant, yet still affordable

Elegantly rustic

Eloquence distilled to its essence

Enchanted elegance

Enter a world of gracious living

Entertaining elegance

Evokes the feel of rich elegance

Evoking the grace and style of ancient Greece

Exceptional elegance, exceptionally well priced

Exceptional. Elegant. Extraordinary.

Experience the elegance

Formal elegance

Functionally elegant

Grace, comfort, and refinement

Graceful and elegant

Hand-engraved for a personal touch

Hand-tailored elegance

Here's an elegant way to _____

Let yourself be pampered by elegance

Make room for grandeur

Makes an elegant statement

Modern, easy, and elegant

Museum-quality brilliance

Natural opulence

Opulent textures

Perfect for the woman of elegance and mystery

Quietly sophisticated

Refined elegance

Relaxed, contemporary elegance

Rich elegance

Self-assured elegance

Sheer elegance

Simple, elegant, and sure to become a classic

Stately and simple

Subtle elegance

The art of hand-tailored elegance

The epitome of elegance

The grace and majesty of _____

The opulence of _____

The picture of elegance

Traditional elegance

Truly a work of art

Ultramodern elegance

Unabashedly elegant

Uncontrived elegance

Understated elegance

Well appointed

Yesteryear's elegance in a _____

Exclusively Ours

A charming collector's item

A once-in-a-lifetime experience

A perfect fit because it's custom-made for you

An exclusive assortment

At its rarest

Available only from _____

Be the only one in your neighborhood to own one

Best in its class

Collectors' edition

Commissioned exclusively for us

Created for connoisseurs

Creates a spectacular custom look

Custom-designed

Custom-fitted

Custom-made

Customized at no extra cost

Designed exclusively for _____

Designed with you in mind

Exclusively ours and irresistibly priced

Expresses your personal style

Extraordinary and rare

For a select few

For preferred customers only

For those who view the world differently

From our exclusive collection

Hard to find

In a class by itself

Individually numbered and signed

Invented just for you

Lets you customize

Limited edition, unlimited style

Limited space available

Made to order

Never before and never again

No ordinary product is quite like this

No other _____ even comes close

Of rare and distinctive character

Once experienced. Never forgotten.

One of the best-kept secrets

One time only

Only at _____

Our exclusive _____

Our exclusive tribute to _____

Our _____ gets immediate attention

Our own exclusive creation

Our signature look

Produced in a limited edition

Rare, exotic, and provocative

Registered, limited edition

Signature style

Simply unforgettable

Sought after by collectors

The best of its kind

The choice of those in-the-know

The favorite of experts

There's no feel in the world like

_____

To suit your tastes

To your specifications

Virtually any design can be created for you

We had you in mind when we designed _____

While supplies last

You'll catch every discriminating eye

Your one and only chance

Fashion! Style! Design!

A bold new look

A brilliant mix

A charming accent for any spot

A dazzling effect

A decorator's delight

A dramatic backdrop

A dreamy swish of _____

A fetching _____

A flare for _____

A French flair

A fresh look

A gem of a _____

A go-with-anything basic

A great way to create a splash

A handsome statement

A lavish display of _____

A little touch that means a lot

A lively look

A look beyond compare

A look that's uniquely different

A marriage of _____ and _____

A modern essential

A perfect balance

A perfect fit

A pretty pick-me-up

A racy collection

A real head-turner

A refreshingly clean look

A return to glamour

A ripple of texture

A selection of top names you'll recognize

A sensational new look

A simple statement of style

A sleek new level of style

A slimming silhouette

A smashing look

A spirited accent

A sportier look and feel

A sporty look

A striking yet simple accent

A study in simplicity

A stunning addition

A sure conversation piece

A sweep of great drama

A taste for the exotic

A touch of dazzle

A traditional favorite

A *très chic* version

A true attention-getter

A vivid accent

A wardrobe essential

A weathered look

Absolutely charming

Accent on simplicity

Accented with _____

Add character to _____

Add drama without added costs

Add pizzazz

Add sparkle to _____

Adds a world of atmosphere to _____

Adds flair

Adds that special touch

All the features you look for

Always fashionable

Always flattering

Always just right

An authentic reproduction

An impressive showpiece

Angular lines

Artfully presented

Artfully shaped

As spellbinding as _____

Authentically styled

Barely there

Because first impressions count

Beyond your imagination

Body-slimming silhouette

Boldly patterned

Both rugged and stylish

Bring springtime into your home any time of the year

Can do big things for your image

Captures the look of _____

Career-chic

Carefree and casual

Casual, contemporary, and romantic

Casual grace

Catch their eye

Charming and whimsical

Cheerful and charming

Chic and striking

City-smart

Cleverly coordinated

Combines texture and design

Commands attention

Complements just about any home's interior

Contemporary flair

Contemporary spirit

Country-style

Create your own contemporary look

Crisp, clean lines and fine detail

Current and cool

Curve-conscious

Dazzling detail, color, and clarity

Dazzling, unique, and contemporary

Decorative and a little bit different

Defining style

Delicate and magical

Delicate details

Delicate yet dignified

Demure and delicate

Designed to flatter

Distinctive accents

Distinctly designed

Does the job fashionably

Dress it up with _____

Easy to accessorize

Easy to wear, hard to resist

Effortless style and easy care

Embellished with _____

Endless enchantment

Exceptionally detailed

Exert your femininity

Expertly contoured

Express your own sense of style

Eye-catching appeal

Fashion-friendly

Fashionable and functional

Fashionably original

Fiercely feminine

Fits like it was made for you

Flattering shapes

Flatters a woman's body

Flawlessly fashioned

Flirtatious and feminine

Fluid style

For a high-tech look

For a lasting impression

For a look that's uniquely yours

For a more youthful, vibrant appearance

For a touch of drama

For the people you love

For the sophisticated gentleman

For the style-conscious

For the well-appointed home

For those who want to be noticed

Form-flattering

Frankly feminine

Fresh and flawless

Fresh as a breath of spring

From modern to traditional

From simplicity comes glamour

Fun fashions

Gentle curves

Get that winning look

Give it style and sophistication

Glamour beyond your imagination

Glamour is back!

Glistens in the night

Goes with everything

Graceful lines

Gracefully draped

Guaranteed conversation pieces

Guaranteed flattery

Has an all-American feel

Has everything you need

Has more inherent appeal than any you already own

Her time to shine!

High-styled

Hottest new styles

If you want to always look your best

Impeccably tailored

Impressive and attention-getting

In proper style

Incredibly sleek

It's a great look!

It's all in the fit

It's an attitude

It's one of the nicest we've seen

It's out of this world

It's pure delight

It's your turn to shine

Just gorgeous!

Just the perfect finishing touch

Just the right degree of _____

Keep warm in style

Lends charm and personality

Less is more

Light and cool

Look sharp

Look your very best

Looking pretty has never been simpler

Looks too good to be so practical

Made for each other

Make an indelible impression

Makes a powerful statement of style

Makes a statement of style and quality

Mixable and matchable

More style. More fashion.

Multiply your wardrobe options

Mystical and magical

Nothing boosts your image more

Nothing short of sensational

Offers unmatched luxury

Old West charm

Opulent curves

Oriental opulence

Our unmistakable style

Perfectly streamlined

Perks up any (meal, outfit, room, etc.)

Playfully designed

Pleases the eye

Probably what first caught your eye

Progressive designs

Provides the finishing touch

Pulls everything together

Pure design

Pure flattery

Pure simplicity

Pure, uncluttered lines

Put your best foot forward

Redefines glamour

Reflects your personal style

Refreshingly distinctive

Relaxed sophistication

Remarkable for its _____

Retro-styling

Rhythmic lines

Rich with detail

Richly embellished with _____

Riveting splendor

Rustic yet refined

Savvy dressing

Seductively simple

Sense of style

Sensual designs

Sets the stage for the magic to begin

Shaped to fit

Sheer style

Shimmer and shine

Show your good taste

Simple and uncluttered

Simple styling, perfectly accented

Simple yet elegant

Simplicity at its best

Simplicity, functionality, and great aesthetics

Simplicity with an elaborate twist

Simply eloquent

Sizzling-hot styles

Sleek and contemporary

Sleek, simple, and stylish

Slim and simple

Slim-line styling

Smartly designed

So very dapper

Soft and feminine

Soft and flowing

Soft and graceful

Soft, supple, durable

Spare yet substantial

Specializing in the exotic

Spectacular is the only word for _____

Springtime fresh

Striking in any combination

Style in an instant

Styled to make a lasting impression

Styled with a new twist

Styles that sizzle!

Stylish, easy, and perfect

Stylish simplicity

Suits you perfectly

Sweeping lines

Tailored, contemporary, and sporty

Tailored to perfection

Tasteful presentation

That special look you've always dreamed of

The art of detail

The best and the boldest

The best you can be

The designers' choice

The epitome of simple chic

The essence of all that is feminine and genteel

The essence of excitement

The exotic look and feel of _____

The feminine touch

The height of sophistication

The inviting curves of _____

The look of a champion

The master of simplicity

The new glamour

The quality of understatement

The sheerest whisper of _____

The style you've been looking for

The subtle new shape of _____

The ultimate conversation piece

Thoughtfully designed

Tip your hat to the spirit of the Old West

To attract those lingering looks

Traditional and trendsetting

Traditional European design

Trendsetting flair

Trendy and savvy

True-blue glamour

Unexpected details abound

Unprecedented charm

Unquestionably feminine

Utterly beguiling

Very chic

Visually seductive

Waist-smoothing

Warm, rustic, casual look

We add details the others leave out

We can hardly wait for you to admire it in your own home

We make a bold statement

Wear-it-with-everything beauty

We'll change the way you see yourself

We've perfected casual chic

What a great look!

What should you wear?

When appearance matters

Where space is a concern and style a priority

Will add interest to any room

Will dazzle any setting

Will instantly dress up your room (outfit, garden, etc.)

With a fresh, clean look

With a piece like this in your closet, you'll always have something to wear

With an accent on style

With couturier-inspired detail

With flair

With panache

Without the glitz

Wonderfully rustic and primevally appealing

Wonderfully wild!

Wondrous shapes

Works together brilliantly

Wow fashions!

You too can look like a _____

You'll like our style

You'll look pretty in _____

You'll love the look

You'll never want to take it off

Your fantasy of sophistication

A Few of Your **Favorite** Things

A medley of favorites

A sportsman's dream

A welcome addition

A _____ you'll treasure

An absolute essential

An asset for every home

An experience that will touch your soul

An experience you can't describe

An experience you'll never forget

An exquisite collection

An extraordinary environment

An indescribable experience

An uncommon experience

An unforgettable experience

_____ are a girl's best friends

_____ are a man's best friend

At last!

Because we care

Beyond all expectations

Brilliantly conceived

Completely satisfying

Deserves special treatment

Essential for men

Every home needs one

Experience all the benefits

Experience it for yourself

For a lasting first impression

For a more desirable you

For that special individual

Gives you that magic touch

Hats off to _____

Here's the best part

Here's what you'll gain

If you want to make a particularly good impression

If you were on a desert island, this is one item you'd want to have along

Irresistible for women

It has that special something

It's a must-see!

It's a showstopper

It's incredible!

It's magic!

Just right for _____

Just what you need

Let us work our magic!

Lucky you!

Meet the challenge

Must-have

Now you have no excuse

Paradise found

Quicken the pulse with _____

Savor the finer things in life

Simply wonderful

Something to write home about

Something you can be proud of

Stimulating and seductive

Take your best shot

The excitement is building

The lure of _____

The star of the season

The stuff dreams are made of

The way you like it

There's something special about

_____

Treat yourself royally

Treat yourself to something special

We bring it to you

We can tell you the advantages in just one line

We make a world of difference

We make your fantasies happen

We still care about the basics

We wouldn't think of using anything less

Welcome back!

We'll make your dreams a reality

We've done your homework for you

What a great idea!

What's in it for you?

What's least expected is often most wonderful

With that special *je ne sais quoi*

You can have it all

You can't have too much of a good thing

You can't imagine life without _____

You deserve nothing less than _____

You gotta have it!

You never knew it could be this good

You'll be glad you did

You'll be proud to have _____

You'll be wild about_____

You'll delight in our _____

You'll enjoy years of compliments

You'll love every minute of it

You'll love everything about them

You'll love it!

You'll want to capture the moment

You'll want to show it off

You'll wonder how you ever lived without it

You're in luck!

You're the secret of our success

You've earned it

Special **Features**

A friendly professional staff
Absolute confidentiality guaranteed
Abundantly illustrated
All inquiries welcome
Allergy-tested
And pays long-term dividends, too
Batteries included
Beautifully personalized
Childproof
Completely reusable
Corrosionproof
Crease-resistant
Dishwasher-safe
Dissolves instantly
Easy installation
Easy to close
Easy to grip
Easy to open
Extends reach
Extra lightweight
Fade-resistant
Folds flat
Fragrance-free
Free exam
Free monogramming
Free refills

Free transportation
Full of all the standard features
Fully adaptable
Fully assembled
Fully automatic
Fully lined
Fully portable
Fully reversible
Gift certificate available
Hand-cut
Hand-polished
Hardware included
Hard-wearing
Impact-resistant
Imported from _____
Includes full-function remote
Individual instruction offered
Infinitely expandable
Kid-friendly
Less shrinkage
Lifetime limited warranty
Long-wearing
Low maintenance
Machine-washable
Maintenance-free
Maximizes storage
Maximum strength
Meets any price
Meets OSHA standards

Microwave-safe
Monogrammed
Never fades
Never needs polishing
Never wilts
No annual fee
No assembly required
No maintenance necessary
No setup required
Nonallergenic
Nonskid backing
Odor-free
100 percent fragrance-free
Outstanding features
Oven-safe
Premeasured
Quiet operation
Ready to use
Reduces glare
Removes instantly
Rust-resistant
Scratch protection
Self-cleaning

Self-stick
Service contract included
Shatterproof
Shatter-resistant
Shuts off automatically
Slips on easily
Specially insulated
Stain-resistant
Stays cleaner longer
Stick-resistant
Stress-free
Suitable for framing
Ultraportable
Vandalproof
Wall-mountable
Waterproof
Water-repellent
Wide selection available
Wind- and water-resistant
Wrinkle-free
Your choice of fabrics
Your choice of finishes

High **Finance**

A small investment goes a long way

A small investment will pay you a big dividend

An amazing moneymaking opportunity

An investment in your future

Be financially free

Business mastery

Change your financial destiny now

Deferred payments

Double your income

Easy financing and free advice

Easy payment plans available

Effectively deal with financial difficulties

Financing available

For the financial freedom you want

For the shrewd investor

Go for the gold

Greatest return on your investment

High profit margins

Improve your bottom line

Invest in excellence

Minimal investment

Moneymaking

Now you can earn more than you ever dreamed of

Protect your family's income

Protect your financial future

Substantial earnings potential

To lock in these great rates

We deliver profits for your business

We'll save you a fortune

With an eye toward profitability

You'll watch your money grow!

Your tools for business success

Fun, Fun, Fun

A dream come true

A festive choice

A little on the wild side

A measure of pleasure

A moment to remember

A touch of whimsy

A tribute to quiet excitement and adventure

A triple delight

A wonderful way to share in family fun

Absolute heaven

Add a festive touch

Add some luxury to your fun

Add zip

Adds fun to your life

Adventure calls

All in good fun

All the elements of fun

An unexpected pleasure

Appeals to your sense of adventure

Are you game?

Burst loose

Celebrate good times shared

Celebrate life!

Challenging. Exciting. Invigorating.

Come join the fun

Discover the magic of _____

Doubles your fun

Easy, fun, and effortless, too

Enjoy *la dolce vita*

Enjoy more free time

Enjoy the best life has to offer

Enjoy the good life

Experience the thrill of _____

Experience the ultimate

Experience the zest of life

Extra pleasure

Fantasy takes flight with this _____

Flights of fancy

Flirty fun

For everyone to enjoy

For that rare combination of leisure and excitement

For the most joyous occasions

For your outdoor (summer, winter, nighttime) enjoyment

Fun and affordable

Fun and eye-catching

Fun and fanciful

Fun. Fanciful. Functional.

Fun for the whole family

Fun in the sun

Fun-loving lifestyle

Get more fun for your money

Get the most out of life

Give in to temptation

Gives your spirits a lift

Go ahead and indulge

Go ahead and really celebrate

Go a little wild

Good clean fun

Grab hold of the good life

Guaranteed to heighten your enjoyment

Guarantees you a lifetime of pleasure

Have fun with _____

Have more fun!

Have the time of your life

Having fun never goes out of style

Hot! Fun! Sexy!

Hours of pleasure

If we don't carry it, it can't be much fun

If you need instant gratification

Imagine the pleasure

Indulge! You deserve it.

Indulge yourself

Insist on the best

Invigorating. Involving. Thrilling.

Irresistibly playful

It adds up to pure pleasure

It's cool!

It's festive and fun

It's time to play

It's time to unwind

Join the party!

Just in time for the party season

Just plain fun

Laugh all the way to the _____

Learn to relax with _____

Less work, more play

Let the good times roll

Let us tempt you

Lift your spirits

Live like you never lived before

Live the good life

Live your dreams

Loads more fun

Looking for a big thrill?

Made for your enjoyment

Make every moment special

Makes _____ almost a pleasure

Makes your routine more fun

One of life's pleasures

Pamper yourself

Pleasure beyond expectation

Pleasure personified

Provides hours of fun for the whole family

Pure pleasure

Put some fun in your _____

Put your feet up and relax

Ready to enjoy

Remember fun?

Rev up the party

Savor the good life

Savor the moment

See how the best can get better

Sit back and enjoy life

Small pleasures

So easy to enjoy

Some temptations are too great to ignore

Spend more time enjoying yourself

Spur-of-the-moment fun

Step into a whole new world of fun

Summer fun!

The fun never ends at _____

The fun starts here

The life of the party

The practical made fun

The sheer pleasure of _____

The ultimate adventure

The wild one

To experience the thrill of _____

To feel like a free spirit

Treat yourself to unparalleled pleasure

Turns the simplest gathering into a gala occasion

Unwind with _____

We're full of surprises

We've got all the fun stuff you like

What's your idea of fun?

When was the last time you bought something that brought you this much pleasure?

When was the last time you had this much fun?

When you're feeling your oats

When you're ready to let loose

Where the fun never stops

Whimsical motifs

Why limit your enjoyment?

Wild nights

With enviable style

With pleasure

Wonderfully whimsical

Wow! What a blast!

You can enjoy it anywhere

You'll never be bored

Your whole family will enjoy _____

You're invited to a new world of pleasure

You've never had this much fun!

A **Gift**, Especially for You

A delicious gift

A delightful keepsake

A fresh and lively way to send your best wishes

A generous token of your esteem

A gift as individual as you are

A gift every woman would love

A gift of great taste

A gift she'll always remember

A gift that will be appreciated all year long

A gift that will endure through the years

A gift that's just plain fun

A gift which is a reflection of your good taste and consideration

A gift with distinction

A gift you'll be proud to give

A golden gift idea

A great gift for someone special

A great gift idea!

A lavish gift, for you and yours

A lovely gift for your hostess

A lovely way to convey your love

A loving gift

A loving gift for that special someone

A most memorable gift

A much-appreciated gift

A perfect gift for the gourmand

A perfect way to express your sincere thanks

A popular gift to commemorate that special occasion

A remembrance for those on the top of your list

A sensitive gift for yourself or a friend

A sweet way to remember that special someone

A symbol of _____

A thoughtful gift given with personal feeling

A timeless gift to make the moment

A treasured gift

A tried-and-true gift standout

A very special gift to receive, a pleasure to own

Always a welcome gift

Always appropriate

An exceptional gift of elegance

An inspired gift for _____

An inspiring gift of hope and love

An instantly pleasing gift

An unforgettable gift

An unforgettable way to show her how special she is

As a gift or to keep for yourself

Check out our Mother's Day specials

Connoisseurs will love this!

Don't forget Mother's Day!

Especially for Mom

Especially for the one you love

For a one-of-a-kind gift

For any occasion. For every occasion.

For life's memorable occasions

For someone you love

For that special occasion

For that special someone

Free engraving

Free gift with purchase

Gifts she'll love to wear

Give a gift that will become a family heirloom

Give as a symbol of thanks, friendship, or affection

Give her a few choices

Give the gift of a lifetime

Give them something truly special

Give your family a gift they'll cherish

Give yourself the precious gift of _____

If you're considering what to give that special someone

Inspires all-around good cheer

It doesn't need to be a special occasion

It will be treasured forever

It's shorthand for thank-you

Let her know you're thinking of her

Looking for a great baby gift?

Makes a great housewarming gift

Makes a memorable gift

Makes an exquisitely thoughtful gift

No gift will be more appreciated

One of the most unique gifts we've ever seen

Our products make memorable gifts

Perfect for those special moments

Remind that special someone of your love

Say thank-you in first-class style

Send a loving message

Send the best to that someone special

She'll treasure it forever

Show her with _____

Show that you choose your gift with care

Show your family or a special friend how much you care

The best way to say Happy Valentine's Day

The gift that works 365 days a year

The ideal way to express your devotion and thoughtfulness

The right gift choice for _____

The search is over!

The sweetest gift you can give

The ultimate gift of love and romance

There's no lovelier tribute
They make great gifts, too
To honor those you esteem
Treat someone you love to a _____
Truly a gift from the heart
Two gifts in one
What better way to say thank-you

When that very special occasion calls
  for something extraordinary
Who wouldn't enjoy receiving _____
_____ will appreciate your creativity
Will express the right sentiment for any
  occasion
Worthy of the occasion

Guaranteed!

A guarantee you can count on

A recipe for success

All our products are guaranteed to please

All purchases backed by a $_____ manufacturer's guarantee

All work guaranteed

Best guarantee in the business

Famous for our 100 percent money-back guarantee

Free replacement parts

Free service for the lifetime of the product

Guaranteed! A lifetime of precision results

Guaranteed for a lifetime

Guaranteed in writing

Guaranteed lowest prices

Guaranteed privacy

Guaranteed results for the life of the product

Guaranteed to please

Guaranteed to work for you, 60 minutes an hour, 24 hours a day

Guarantees the highest standard of excellence

I will personally guarantee it!

If you don't _____, we'll buy it back

If you're not fully satisfied _____

Ironclad guarantee

It's not just a guarantee, it's my promise to you

Lifetime guarantee

Lifetime Replacement Guarantee

Look for our assurance of quality and value

Made to last a lifetime

Manufacturer's lifetime warranty

Money-Back Guarantee

150 percent price protection

100 percent protection or your money back

One-year guarantee on all purchases

One-year warranty

Our guarantee is in writing

Our guarantee is one of the best in the business

Our promise

Risk-free—satisfaction assured

Risk-free with our guarantee

Satisfaction guaranteed

365-day guarantee

Unconditionally guaranteed

We stand behind our products 100 percent

We will not be undersold

Will never go out-of-date

You'll get results—guaranteed!

Your guarantee of quality

Healthy Living

A challenge for the body

A great pick-me-up

A healthful way to _____

A nutritional breakthrough

A soothing influence

A true measure of health

An amazing cure for _____

Antibacterial

Ask your doctor about _____

At-home relief with _____

At last! New relief for _____

Be healthy and fit

Boost your energy

Boosts vitality

Brings instant relief

Builds healthy bones

Calcium-enriched

Clinically tested

Controls anxiety

Deep relaxation is yours in minutes

Deep relief from stress

Discover all you can be

Discover alternative paths to good health

Dissolve tension

Doctor-approved

Fast, easy treatment

Feel better!

Feel revitalized all over

Feeling good has never been easier

Feeling your oats

For a beautiful body

For a speedy recovery

For complete relief

For that healthy glow

For your well-being

Gives you a superior workout

Good health is within your reach

Happiness. Prosperity. Good health.

Have energy to spare

Heal yourself with _____

Healing properties

Help your system stay in top condition

_____ helps bring relief

Helps your body fight off _____

Here's relief

High in fiber

High in nutritional value

If you treasure your health

If you want to take good care of yourself

If you're looking for the way to stay healthy

Increased endurance

Increases concentration

Instant energy

Instant relief

Just what the doctor ordered

Keep your kids healthy with _____

Lasting energy

Leaves you feeling refreshed, relaxed, and invigorated

Less fatigue, more fun

Lose the weight you want

Low-calorie

Low in fat

Low in sugar

Maximum strength

Melts pain away

Need more energy?

No side effects

Now you can look your best

Permanent weight loss

Prevent the pain of _____

Prevention is the best medicine

Protect yourself from fatigue

Proven to relieve pain

Provides the energy you need when you need it

Refresh yourself with _____

Rejuvenates your body and spirit

Relax. Renew. Rejuvenate.

Relieve the unpleasant effects of _____

Relieves symptoms

Relieves tension and stress

Restore physical vigor

Revitalize your life

Revitalizes your body

Safe and drug-free

Soothes pain

Spirited. Refreshing. Energizing.

Stop _____ before it starts

Stop pain now

Stop smoking forever

Strengthen your immune system

Supports your active lifestyle

The next best thing to a cure

The picture of health

The secret to healthier-looking skin

Too good to be this healthy for you

We'll help you be your best every day

Will make you feel good all over

Without drugs

Won't keep you awake

Won't put you to sleep

Works for children, too

You can recharge your health with _____

Your health-care experts

It's Your **Imagination**

A clever problem solver

And now for our next trick

Beyond your imagination

Beyond your wildest dreams

Captures your imagination

Conveys a sense of creativity and innovation

Create your own _____

Design your own _____

Don't let a good idea slip through your fingers

Even better than you thought possible

Explore creative solutions

Fresh perspectives

Give your creativity free rein

Imagine yourself _____

In-depth insights

Instant creativity

It's a neat idea!

Just the way you imagined it

Let your imagination run wild

Make your dreams come true

Make your work say "creativity"

No, it's not your imagination

Now imagine it with _____

One clever idea after another

Puts your imagination into overdrive

Ready for your personal stamp

See it and believe

Take control of your creative vision

Taps your true creativity

The possibilities are as endless as your imagination

Try for a moment to imagine

Unleash your hidden creative powers

Unlimited possibilities

Unlock your hidden creative potential

Walk on the wild side

We had an idea!

Your imagination is the only limit

Innovative and Original

A hint of the unexpected

A new experience

A pioneer in _____

A priceless treasure

A real conversation starter

A refreshingly new idea

A revolutionary new kind of _____

A step ahead of the pack

A striking new approach to _____

A sure conversation opener

A true innovation

A unique addition to any home or office

A unique, scientifically developed formula

Ahead of its time

Ahead of the pack

Announcing a major breakthrough

Anything but traditional

Are you ready for something different?

Be a pacesetter

Breakthrough device

Brings a whole new dimension to the world of _____

Captures the spirit of innovation

Don't look back

Even the best traditions need an update

Everything and anything except the ordinary

First time ever

For a new experience

Fresh and creative

Fresh ideas

Fresh, innovative styling

Get it straight from the source

Imaginative design

In a whole new way

Incomparable individuality, aesthetics, and quality

Inconceivable until now

Innovate with _____

Innovators, not imitators

Introduces the first _____

It's electrifying!

Just when you thought they had everything

Never before seen

New, revolutionary

Now there's a novel idea!

On the cutting edge

One-of-a-kind treasure

Opens up a new world

Our best discovery yet

Our _____ have changed to meet your needs

Our updated version

Rare and unusual

Seeing is believing

Set the trend

Surpasses all your expectations

Takes it one step further

The finest ever developed

The latest in medical technology

The most-advanced _____ available

Unlike any other

Way ahead of the competition

We can help make yours stand out

We may not have a crystal ball, but _____

With a new twist

Years ahead of the field

You won't believe your _____

You'll wonder why no one has thought of it before

You're always a step ahead with _____

You're guaranteed the unexpected

You've never settled for the ordinary

Nature's Best

A fusion of science and nature

A gift of nature

A natural alternative to _____

A natural wonder

All natural

All-natural fibers

All-natural formula

An excellent natural source for _____

Brings the beauty of nature indoors

Built for the great outdoors

Call it a natural attraction

Celebrates nature

Chemical-free

Deserves natural loving care

Earth-inspired artistry

Elements of nature

For all who yearn for a return to traditions

For nature lovers

For the old-fashioned natural look

Fresh . . . naturally

Gives you back what nature takes away

Improve on nature

Infused

Inspired by nature

It's a natural

It's nature's defense against _____

Let us show you how to improve on Mother Nature

Looks so real you'll have to look twice

Made of all-natural ingredients

Mother Earth's very best

Natural care

Natural ingredients

Natural relief

Natural support

Natural warmth

Naturally appealing

Naturally inspired

Nature-friendly

Nature's answer to _____

Newest naturals

No additives or preservatives

No preservatives added

Nothing artificial added

100 percent biodegradable

100 percent natural

Organic ingredients

Organically grown

Provides all the benefits of nature

Pure and natural

Straight from nature

The answer to nature's design

The essence of nature

The language of nature

The natural alternative

The natural art of _____

The natural choice

The natural essence of _____

The natural way to treat _____

To please your nature-loving sensibilities

Warm and natural

We make nature smarter

With natural ingredients

Without the use of harmful chemicals

Works quickly and naturally

Your love of nature

New and Improved

A brand-new you

A breath of fresh air

A familiar style updated with a new direction

A fresh approach

A look that's entirely new

A new benchmark in _____

A new dimension

A new, exciting approach to _____

A new _____ that will give you _____

A new twist

A revolutionary new breakthrough

A safe new way to _____

A step forward in good looks and comfort

A step in the right direction

A whole new approach

A whole new breed

A whole new look

Adds a new dimension to your _____

All merchandise is factory-fresh

An interesting update

An old favorite for a new generation

An update on tradition

An updated interpretation

Anticipate new opportunities

As fresh as if it had been created yesterday

As good as new, in just three steps

At last it's here!

Back by popular demand

Based on your suggestions

Before . . . After . . .

Better than ever

Better than new

Better than the old days

Break out of the mold

Change is good

Changes to meet your needs

Come see what's new

Don't settle for things as they are

Everything old is new again

Exciting news!

Experience it in a whole new way

Finally, a new _____

First in its field

For a great change of pace

For an instant change of effect

Fresh, new, and contemporary

Gain the upper hand

Gives you a fresh start

Grandma never had anything like these!

Groundbreaking design

Here comes _____

Here it is!

Hot off the _____
Important news!
Improves the quality of your life
Infused with fresh, new energy
Instant update
Introducing _____
Introducing the new breed of _____
Introducing the new you!
Introducing the newest member of our family
Introducing the next generation
_____ is here!
It's a brand new world
It's new!
Let us shatter any myths
Like never before
Loaded with new features
Look at us now
Made better by _____
Makes a world of difference
New, complete starter set
New, enriched
New, this month!
No more waiting!
Now all other brands are history
Now available
Now available for home use
Now the best is even better
Now there's a better way
Our latest and greatest

Ours isn't old hat
Ready for a change?
Reinvent yourself
Say good-bye to _____
Shows steady improvement, time after time after time
Starts right here
Take it one step further
Take your business to the next level
Takes a fresh look at _____
The latest and the greatest
The latest in _____
The latest sensation
The new best thing
The new generation of _____
The new way to _____
The newest crop of _____
The one the world has been waiting for
Time for a change
Tired of the same old _____?
Up-to-the-minute
Updated and improved
Updated and upgraded
We make things better
We proudly present _____
We reinvented the _____
We'll change your life
We'll fix all this
We'll give it a new look and new life

We're back and better than ever

We're bursting with new ideas

We're new

We're one of the new breed

We're pleased to announce _____

We're proud to introduce _____

We're putting out the welcome mat

Why follow tradition?

Why reinvent the _____?

You'll like what you see

You'll see the difference

You'll throw your old one away

Your days of waiting are over

You've never experienced anything like it before

Odds 'n' Ends

A helping hand to _____

A personal oasis

A source of inspiration

A special place to retreat from the world

An invitation to _____

And that's just the tip of the iceberg!

And that's not all!

Appearances can be deceiving

Beware of imitations

Bring it to life with _____

Building your business to compete takes _____

Call and ask about _____

Celebrate a personal victory

Compare these two

Competitive edge

Contrary to popular belief

Cool stuff!

Create a sense of community

Discover the mysteries of _____

Don't be shy

Don't even think about it until you read this

Don't hesitate

Don't hide

Enhance your career

Find that long-sought-after item

For added impact

For busy people

From the inside out

Genuinely down-to-earth

Get in gear

Give in to your primal urges

Gives you the freedom to be yourself

Has never made more sense

Heartwarming

Here's how we compare

Here's just a sampling

Here's the real payoff

If you value your _____, then read this!

In a word: _____

Isn't this what (summer, winter, Christmas, etc.) is all about?

It may seem impossible but _____

It will put you in the limelight

It's all about your image

It's good news!

It's just the beginning

Just like (magic, mother used to make, at the movies, etc.)

Just the right blend

Keeps it sparkling clean

Keeps you on track

Let go of worry

Let us surprise you

Live a more fulfilling life
Live the legend
Make a smart decision
Minimize the damage
Not just a pleasant distraction
Nothing's friendlier than _____
Poignant and captivating
Preserve the moment with _____
Put your best foot forward
Recipe for success
Reserve early!
Say good-bye to _____
See yourself as you never have before
Soft and calming
_____ speaks for itself
Stop dreaming. Wake up to _____
Take a peek at _____
Take your next step
That's one-upmanship
The best-kept secret
The collector's source
The friendliest one around
The top ten reasons to _____
The truth about _____

There's no reason for you to _____
Think about it
Three good reasons why you need a _____
Three steps to _____
Totally indetectable
Try us first!
Turn your worst nightmare into a pleasant dream
We specialize in _____
We've got big plans for you
What's stopping you?
When you experience _____, you experience _____
Why us?
Will cast its spell
Win glory in the marketplace
You are cordially invited to join
You'll be set for life
You'll get a royal welcome
Your complete _____
Your pot of gold at the end of the rainbow
Your ship has come in
You're invited

Special **Offers**

All items must be sold

An added bonus

An Early Bird Special

An incredible offer

An offer worth investigating

An offer you can't refuse

And a surprise free gift

Annual maintenance program

Ask about our special quantity discounts

At a fraction of the cost

At a price that may surprise you

Be our guest

Below-cost sale

Below dealer cost

Blowout sale. Everything must go!

Bulk pricing available

Buy now. Pay later.

Buy now. Pay nothing until January 1st.

Buy one, get one free

Call for your free product demonstration today

Call for your free sample

Call for your free trial

Call today for a free price quote

Come in and pick up your entry form today

Come in by _____ and save _____ percent

Come in for your free demonstration

Competitively priced

Complimentary membership

Courtesy transportation

Deferred payment

Don't miss out on our March Mania Sale

Early-sign-up discount

Enjoy additional savings when you _____

Enroll now

Experience the freedom of _____

Expert instruction available

Extra luxury, affordable cost

First month free service

Free catalog

Free consultation

Free gift with any first-time order

Free gift with any order of _____ or more

Free home estimates

Free illustrated price list and color brochure

Free No-Risk Demonstration

Free offer

Free one-month unlimited trial

Free _____ when you buy

Full refund available

Get an advance look
Get two for the price of one
Grand Opening Event
Half price
Has never been more affordable
Hurry, offer ends today
Information-packed
Kids are free
Ladies' day
Last chance to _____
Last five days. Hurry in!
Limited-time offer
Lowest prices of the season
Make no payment until _____
90-day in-house trial
No cost. No obligation. Nothing to buy.
No interest charges for 90 days
No minimum
No obligation to buy
No payment necessary until _____
On-site extended service agreement available
100 percent satisfaction 100 percent of the time
Only four easy payments
Order a free sample
Preferred customers shop one day early
Preseason sale

Price protection
Priced lower than our competitors
Priced to sell
Receive _____ with a purchase of more than _____
Refer a friend and receive a $ _____ gift certificate
Request your free bulletin
Sale held over
Save money on freight
Send for your free bonus today
Send no money now!
Senior citizens' discount
Significant savings
Special Anniversary Offer
Special introductory offer to new customers
Special off-season rates
Special rebate offer
Special sign-up bonus
Special trial offer
Superior value with professional results
Terrific values and special offer for the entire family
The best anywhere, at any price
The modern, affordable luxury
This check is yours if _____
To order, use our handy postage-paid envelope
Top-notch values

Uncompromising quality with
  conservative pricing

Unlimited access

Unlimited usage

Valuable money-saving coupons

Warehouse Sale

We accept all credit cards

We'll let you preview

We'll meet or beat any competitor's
  price

We're cutting prices

We're proud to make this extraordinary
  offer

Without the designer price tag

World-class at half the cost

You can't beat the price

You're under no obligation

Yours free

Yours free with any purchase

An **Old-Fashioned** Bit of Nostalgia

A blast from the past

A nostalgic look at _____

A perfect way to remember

A piece of nostalgia

A tradition that will last forever

An attractive, old-fashioned appearance

An old-fashioned favorite

Back to basics

Become a part of a beautiful tradition

Brings back memories

Captures the spirit of yesteryear

Celebrate a personal victory

Centuries-old design

Combines the elegance of the past with the energy of the future

Country-cottage charm

Create an aura of Victorian romance

Echoes a past era

Enjoy the best of yesterday, today

Evokes another era

From a bygone era

From a centuries-old source

Join us in a new tradition

Just like Grandma used to make

Old-fashioned and romantic

Old-world craftsmanship

Old-world grace

Preserve the tradition

Recalls a charming bygone era

Recalls _____ of years gone by

Recapture the thrill of _____

Re-create the magic of _____

Remember what it used to feel like?

Remember when _____

Reminiscent of 18th-century design

Reminiscent of the Victorian era

Reminiscent of times past

Small-town charm

Step back to the past

Takes you back to simpler times

That speaks of antiquity

The ageless charm of _____

The look and feel of the 1950s

The old-fashioned way

The timeless value of a treasure from the past

The tradition continues

Turn-of-the-century

Vintage-inspired

What an **Opportunity!**

A once-in-a-lifetime opportunity
A unique opportunity
An essential for _____
Available one time only
Be prepared
Don't be left behind
Don't make a move without it
Don't miss out!
Don't pass up this opportunity
Experience firsthand the future of _____
Free Opportunity
Get ready for praises galore
Gives you the competitive edge
Growth opportunity
Hard to resist
Have I got a _____ for you!
Helps people live their dreams
Here's your chance
How lucky can you get!
If you pass it up you'll be passé
_____ is finally within your reach
Is this all possible? Absolutely!
It begins by taking the first step
It's worth all the trouble
Last chance!

Learn how to help yourself
Like the promise of spring
Moneymaking Opportunity
No limits
Now it's your turn
Once-in-a-lifetime
Once you try it (see it, hear it, etc.), you'll want one of your own
Opportunities like this come only once in a lifetime
Opportunity knocks
Opportunity of a lifetime
Rare opportunity
Sign up now
Take advantage of a unique opportunity
Take the plunge
The adventure begins here
The chance of a lifetime
The place to be
The prize at the end of the rainbow
This year's hottest opportunity
Too good to pass up
Uncover a priceless treasure
Undreamed-of opportunities
Unequaled opportunity
We're offering you a once-in-a-lifetime opportunity
We've got the _____ of your dreams

When _____ just isn't enough

Where to go once you've reached the top

Will take your breath away

Your chance to _____

Your gateway to the good life

Your treasure chest of _____

Your treasure map to _____

Proven **Performance**

A brilliant performer

A new standard

A real price performer

A unique combination of styling, performance, and handling

Achieve peak performance

All-night relief

An impressive performance

Beats its competitors in every way

Become an overnight success

Bigger and better performance

Built to perform. Priced to compete.

Cleans and polishes

Creates order out of chaos

Critically acclaimed performance

_____ does it all

_____ does the trick

Don't miss the mark

Don't take our word for it. See it. Feel it. Decide for yourself.

Double performance

Everybody needs a little help sometime

Everything you need to succeed

Exceeding expectations

Expands with your needs

Experience the difference

For a strong performance, you've come to the right place

For optimum accuracy

For the kinds of results the pros get

For the performance of a lifetime, choose _____

For top performance

Gain the edge

Handles the whole job

Hardworking _____ for hardworking people

High-performance tools

Improve the performance

It does the job

It really works

Lets people know you mean business

Low profile, high performance

Make the move to _____

_____ means performance

Nothing works better

Our best performance

Our _____ works as hard as you do

Perfection personified

Performance. Convenience. Value.

Performance—every time!

Performance-inspired

Performance plus

Proves its worth time and time again

Really gets the job done

Rigorously tested for performance

Six reasons to buy from _____

Smoothly. Quickly. Efficiently.

Stands up to all your tough jobs

Stands up to rough use in the real world

Tackles the really tough jobs

The best part is that you can do it, too

The high-performance choice

The ultimate in performance

The unsung heroes of the day

Trouble-free performance

Unerring precision

Up to 10 years' performance

Visible results in 24 hours

Watch them work their magic

We are serious about performance

We can help you put it all together

We define performance

We did it, now you can, too!

We make ours work harder because you do

We set a new standard of performance

We'll improve the performance of your business

We'll show you how

We're good at _____

We're proud of our performance

When performance counts

When there's lots to do

Wins the gold

Works hard and looks great, too!

Works hard for you

Works wonders

Yes, you can!

You want more out of life and you'll get it with _____

You won't find another company that can top our work

Your satisfaction is very important

You're the reason for our success

Perennially **Popular**

A blue-ribbon _____

A crowd-pleaser

A family favorite for more than 100 years

A favorite of executives, leaders, and trendsetters

A hot property

A longtime favorite

A name you can trust

A natural winner

A perennial favorite

A summertime favorite

A testament to _____

A tried-and-true summertime pleaser

All-time favorites

Always a favorite

Always the center of attention

An old favorite

Back by popular demand

Begin your own tradition

Best bet

Best ever!

Best for long-term satisfaction

Best in sales! Best in quality!

Bestseller

Certain to satisfy anyone's taste

Check us out

Choose your favorite

Come see what people are talking about

Consider the source

Destined to become a favorite for years to come

Don't be fooled by pretenders

Don't just take our word for it

Don't settle for an imitation

Ever-popular

Everyday favorites

Everyone loves a _____, and you will too!

For the _____ lover

For the _____ maven

For the now generation

For the serious enthusiast

Has a devout following

Has all the features you love the most

Has long been a favorite

Hits the spot

I learned the three steps to _____ success, and you can too!

Incredible but true

_____ is wonderful!

It will be welcomed by all!

It's good to be back!

It's not your imagination

It's on everyone's lips

Join millions of satisfied users

Just stand back and watch

Just try it!

Listen to what people are saying about us:

Make a splash with _____

Makes it one of our most popular

Most-distinguished

Much sought after

No other _____ satisfies so many tastes

Nobody knows _____ better

Our bestseller

Our customers rave about this one

Our favorite

Our most popular

People are talking about us!

Preferred over all others

See for yourself

Serious _____ can't manage without it

Standard issue

Startling authenticity

Sure to be a crowd-pleaser

Sure to be a holiday favorite

Sure to delight your guests

The first choice of almost anyone who loves _____

The legendary _____

The most intelligent way to _____

The most preferred

The new leader

The _____ of your dreams

The one you can agree on

The perfect conversation piece

The strongest new name in _____

The tradition continues

This is what everyone is raving about

Universally appealing

Used by millions

Used for generations

Used worldwide

We knew we had a winner when _____

We know from experience that it's true!

We love _____!

We love skeptics!

Well-earned reputation

What could be more appealing than _____

What is everyone saying about us?

Will claim the hearts of all who see it

Will quickly become your favorite

Will take the world by storm

With universal appeal

World-renowned

You be the judge

You can't go wrong

You'll become a fan

You'll rave about our _____

You'll truly cherish this

You'll wow 'em with _____

Your kids will love them

You're in good company

Make a **Powerful** Statement

A powerful masterpiece
A showstopper
Celebrate the power of _____
Combines power and technology
Compact, yet powerful
Experience the power
Explode with power
Feel the power of _____
Gets you big results
Harness the power of _____
It's a powerful weapon against _____
It's a powerhouse!
Knocks you off your feet
Knocks your socks off
Lightweight yet powerful

More powerful than ever
Nothing compares to the power of a
_____
Packs a punch
Packs a wallop
Powerful _____ for powerful people
Proven powerful and effective
Puts Atlas to shame
The great American _____
The most potent tool
The power of _____
The power to change your life
The power you need
The power you want from a _____
The strong, silent type
Tiny but powerful
To present yourself powerfully
We deliver the power of _____
We'll help you unlock the power of
_____

The **Price** Is Right

A comfortable fit for any budget

A real find, at an excellent value and price

A superb value

A toast to extraordinary prices

Absolutely free

Act now. The savings won't last forever.

Added value

Affordable luxury

Affordable prices that are sure to fit into even the tightest budget

All the benefits for a fraction of the cost

All the fun for less than half the price

Amazing values

An economical choice

An exceptional value

And a whole lot more

And much, much more

And the price?

Another reason to buy _____

Ask about our quantity discounts

Astounding value

At a cool, cool price!

At a price you'll appreciate

At a very modest price

At great prices

At no extra charge

At prices you can live with

Best for price

Best prices always

Best prices, direct from the factory

Built to your specifications at an affordable price

Bulk pricing available on request

Buy a bargain

Buy direct

Buy more, save more

Call for our winter specials

Convenient payment plans

Cost-effective

Costs pennies a day to operate

Cut costs

Don't miss our money-saving _____

Each comes with something extra

Early-Bird Discounts

Easy payments

Economical alternatives

Elegant look, inexpensive price

Eminently affordable

_____ equals value

Everyday discount prices

Everything must go

Few other _____ offer so much

Fits your budget just right

For any budget

For less than you expected

Free for all _____

Get more for less

Get more for your money

Get more than your money's worth

Gives you so much for so little

Great buys

Great style, great price

Great value for the money

Here's a little incentive

Here's what you'll save

High perceived value

Honest savings

Hot buys

Hot values at cool prices

Huge discounts

Imagine buying _____ and still having enough money to buy _____

Incredible deals

Insist on excellence and affordability

Inventory clearance

Irresistibly priced

Isn't it time you stepped up to a new level of value?

It looks the same but costs much less

It pays to hire us

It's a Holiday Happening

It's worth every penny

Just right for the price-conscious buyer

Last-chance savings

Less than _____ per day (per year)

Looks like a million bucks

Low prices available until June 1st

Low prices every day

Lowest prices of the year

Make money

Make the most out of your _____ dollars

Many included extras

Money-saving

More for your money

More Savings. More Value.

Much more than a _____

Never pay retail again

Never undersold

New low price

Nice prices

No fees, no hassle

No investment required

No-nonsense prices

No start-up costs

Now it's simple to save

Now you can own a _____ at a fraction of the regular cost

Offer good while supplies last

Offers the best price and warranty

On a budget?

Once-in-a-lifetime savings

One of the best values we have to offer

One reduced rate for all

One-time-only prices
Order now and save
Order toll-free
Our best buy
Our prices are competitive
Our prices are unbeatable
Outdistance the competition in price and value
Packed with value
Pay-as-you-go options
Pay less at _____
Pennysaver products
Perfect _____ at a surprisingly perfect price
Potentially saves you hundreds of dollars
Price-perfect
Priced right for _____
Priced to buy
Priced to get your attention
Priced to please
Real luxury at everyday prices
Save money and boost response
Save on all your future orders
Save time and money
Saves you money
Saves you the big bucks!
Savings and convenience
Savings Galore
Savings that sizzle

So much for so little
Special savings for students
Start saving now. Call _____
Starting at less than _____
Storewide savings
Stretch your budget
Student-discount program
Summer steals
Super Values
Superfast and affordable
Tailored to your needs and budget
Take advantage of our Summer Vacation Savings Specials
The affordable alternative
The best deal in town
The choice for value
The deal of the year
The price is nice
The prices you want
The sales event you've been waiting for
The value leader
Too good to be this affordable
Turn in this cash voucher for your special discount
Unbeatable value
Unbeatably priced
Unbelievable _____ at believable prices
Value-added

Value-priced

Volume pricing available

We buy direct and pass the savings on to you

We discount price, not quality!

We give you a lot for a little

We will beat any advertised price

We will meet any advertised price

We'll match any competitor's price

Where price and quality meet

Why buy from our competitors when _____?

Why pay a lot more?

Why pay more and get less?

Why spend a fortune if you don't have to?

_____ without spending a whole lot of money

Wonderfully inexpensive

Worth its weight in gold

You can pay more or you can get more

You'll always get our best possible prices

You'll get big savings along the way

Quality Counts

A breakthrough in quality

A clear-cut winner

A commitment to quality

A cut above the rest

A first-class offer

A hallmark of quality

A honey of a _____

A little piece of heaven

A luxurious personal indulgence

A masterpiece of quality, design, and color

A modern masterpiece

A perfect ten

A standout in any room

A statement of quality

A step above the rest

A stroke of genius

A symbol of quality for 50 years

A symphony of purity

A testimony to our meticulous attention to details

A touch of brilliance

A trove of special treasures

A true collector's item

Absolutely brilliant

Adds a note of authenticity

All things aren't equal

Almost too nice to use

Always get the best

Always outstanding

Among the finest produced today

Among the world's best

An earthly treasure

An exquisite piece

An heirloom-quality _____

An unbeatable _____

An unforgettable piece

As good as it looks

As you'd expect from a product of this quality

At its best

Authentically detailed

Award-winning

Best for quality

Better from the inside out

Better than store-bought

Better than you ever dreamed

Bridges the gap between casual and elegant

Brings luxury to everyday living

Can't be improved

C'est magnifique!

Charming in every detail

Clearly the best

Come see our quality line of _____

Comes closer to perfection

Compare us to our imitators

Consider the merits

Consistent quality

Cream of the crop

Created with painstaking care

Dare to compare

_____ defines excellence

Deserving of high praise

Designed as the ultimate reward

Discover the difference

Discover the wonders of _____

Don't accept second best

Don't compromise

Don't sacrifice quality

Don't settle for less

Dreams are made of this

Enduring quality

Engineered for a lifetime of beauty and service

Even we were impressed by the looks and quality

Exceeds industry standards

Exceeds your highest expectations

Exceptional in every way

Experience the best

Experience the luxury

Experience the upper limits of _____

First class

First-class treatment

First quality

For the look of success

For those who appreciate quality

For those who respect inherent value

Fresh every time

Get on the path to greatness

Get serious

Get the real thing

Go first class, all the way

Great _____s aren't made overnight

Handmade details abound

Hand-painted

Hand-sewn

Has been pared to perfection

Has the look and feel of imported, made right here in America

Have you ever experienced heaven on earth?

Heads above the rest

Heirloom quality

Helps preserve the quality

Highest grade available

How does your _____ measure up?

If you appreciate exquisite detail, you'll love _____

If you want the best

Immerses you in luxury

Impeccable in every detail

Impeccable quality

In peak condition

Indulge in outright luxury

Investment-quality _____

It doesn't get any better than this

It goes anywhere

It keeps on getting better

It's a home run

It's that good

It's the ultimate

It's unbelievably good

It's what we do best

Jaw-dropping quality

Just as perfect as it should be

Just what you would expect from luxury

Leave the best for last

Legendary quality

Live the good life

Live your dream

Long recognized as the world's finest

Luxuriously fashioned

Luxury is yours

Made from selected, supreme quality _____

Made using American construction

Made with a style and substance rarely found nowadays

Makes an impressive statement

Meets the highest standards

Mint condition

Museum-quality brilliance

No attention to detail has been spared

No other measures up

Nothing could be finer!

Nothing is more precious

Now you can own something priceless

Obsessed with quality

Of the highest quality

Once you have ours, your others will gather dust

100 percent pure

One of the finest made anywhere

Only the best survive

Only the best will do

Others fall short

Others talk about quality, we deliver it

Our customers demand the finest

Our _____ made the difference

Our _____ say achievement, quality, and success

Passes every test with flying colors

Perfect from the beginning to the end

Perfect—the first time and every time

Practically perfect

Precious future heirlooms

Precision results

Premium quality

Presidential quality

Prime quality

Proven superiority

Pure. Complete. Perfect.

Pure indulgence

Pure star quality

Putting quality first

Quality and precision

Quality at a great price!

Quality counts

Quality is a full-time commitment

Quality is on everyone's mind

Quality is the key

Quality materials ensure a lifetime of use

Quality speaks for itself

Quality without compromise

Quite simply luxurious

Ranks among the finest

Richly styled

Satisfy your taste for the good life

Second to none

See how great it can be

Settle for nothing less than the best

Simply unbeatable

Some of the best in the world come from _____

Sometimes more is definitely more

Stand out from the crowd

Surpasses all others

Surpasses your highest dreams

Surround yourself with the finest

Synonymous with excellence

Synthetic with the look of handmade

Taken to new heights

Takes it to the max

The best. All in one place.

The best in the business

The best in town

The best of all worlds

The best of the best

The best one on the planet

The best possible _____

The best we've ever used

The clearest sign of quality

The difference between nearly right and exactly right

The difference is in the details

The enriching touch

The finest on earth

The finest on the market today

The genuine article

The highest quality you can expect

The industry benchmark

The intelligent choice

The leader when it comes to _____

The leading _____

The little things that make all the difference

The look of handmade

The material of choice

The new standard

The next best thing to _____

The next thing to perfection

The one and only one to consider

The perfect addition

The perfect touch

The quality alternative

The quality you've been looking for

The quintessential _____

The perfect blend of craftsmanship and art

The picture of perfection

The real thing

The right combination

The sign of a great _____

The standard by which all _____ are judged

The ultimate in _____

The ultimate luxury

The world's finest collection

There's no competition

There's no finer example

There's simply no comparison

This year's best

Tomorrow's heirloom

Top gun

Top-notch quality

Top quality

Treat yourself to something decadent

Treat yourself to the best

Uncompromising quality

Unique museum quality

Unsurpassed facilities

Very grand

We don't cut corners on quality

We improve on perfection

We make it great

We searched until we found the finest ones available

We set the standard

We took a classic and made it even better

We use nothing but the best

Well worth your attention

We're obsessed with quality

We're the first and the finest

What could possibly be more perfect?

What's the difference?

When it really matters, turn to _____

When quality is important

When quality is your absolute priority

When you demand excellence

When you're looking for a sign of excellence

Where excellence makes a difference

Why not use the best?

Will impress the most-discriminating connoisseur of detail

With an accent on quality

World's best _____. Period.

Worthy of center stage

You couldn't ask for a better _____

You haven't seen _____ until you've seen ours

You know a good product when you see one

You owe it to yourself to expect more

You'll be delighted with the quality you get for the money

You'll be spoiled for life

You'll never regret buying the best

You'll recognize the hallmarks of quality

You'll see the quality yourself

You'll think you've found perfection

Your every dream come true

You're in for a treat

You Can **Rely** on Us

A favorite old standby

A lifetime of _____

A name of stature

A sure bet

A _____ that really works

A _____ to last a lifetime

A _____ you can count on

An essential reference

And for years to come

Ask the man who owns one

Be prepared for anything

Built to last forever

Consider us friends you can rely on

Count on us

Crafted in our own plants

Crafted to last a lifetime

Creates an instant _____

_____ delivers!

Designed to handle your toughest assignments

Designed to meet any challenge

Each and every time

Effortless—Reliable—Affordable

Eliminates the worry and hassle

Enhanced stability

Exceptionally lasting

Finally, something that really works

For a lifetime of use

For generations to come

For now and forever

For over a century

For years, we've been helping businesses like yours

Forever may be too much to expect

Give us a call. What do you have to lose?

Goes the distance

Handed down over the years

Has staying power

Here's why millions of men and women rely on us

It will last your lifetime and your kids' lifetimes as well

It's a fact!

It's more than up to the task

It's what you get every time

Just refuses to wear out

Known for our stability, reliability, and integrity

Lasts for weeks, not days

Lasts forever

Lasts from season to season

Lasts longer than ever before

Leave it to us

Let us rescue you

Looks great through years of use

Made to last—and last—and last

Never fails!

No fading

No gimmicks!

No lemons!

No more hype

Not only looks the part, but delivers

Order risk-free

Order with confidence

Ours will never (fade, leak, wear out, etc.)

Peace of mind when you need it most

Perfect for every occasion

Preserve for generations to come

Preserved forever

Problem-free

Products you can depend on

Proven 100 percent fail-safe for over 25 years

Reduced wear and tear

Rely on the leader

Rely on us

Reuse year after year

Shop with confidence

_____ shouldn't be a gamble

Some _____ come and go, but these will last a lifetime

Some things never change

Sturdy and steady

Sturdy enough for everyday use

Take our advice

Take the guesswork out of _____

Ten times more accurate

Tested! Proven! It Works!

The company you can count on

The last _____ you'll ever buy

The legacy of the future

The _____ of the future

The one you can count on

The only ones you'll need

The only proven way to _____

The perfect alternative to _____

The _____ professionals rely on

The ultimate luxury . . . peace of mind

The word *quit* is not in our vocabulary

The world's leading authority on _____

There when you need us

There's no gamble for you

Today's _____ are tomorrow's _____

Tried-and-true

Try our products worry-free

Unique, trouble-free operation

Uses a precision-controlled process

Virtually indestructible

We deliver

We keep our promises

We promise total satisfaction

We stand behind our product

We test what we sell

We won't let you down
Wear for years to come
Wear-tested
We'll give you the edge you need
We're there to help
We've got everything covered from
    A to Z
We've got you covered
What you see is what you get
When dependability is a must
When you expect more
Will be remembered for years
    to come
Will be treasured for years to come
Withstands the elements
Withstands the test of time
Won't bend or break
Won't rub off
Works day and night
Works every time

Works under any conditions
Worry-free
Year after year after year
Year in and year out
Years of carefree use
Years of maintenance-free service
You can breathe easier with _____
You can rely on our experience,
    expertise, and commitment
You demand it, we deliver
You know you can relax with _____
You'll always have it when you need it
You'll be confident with _____
You'll go the distance
You'll never have to worry about
    _____
You'll risk nothing
You'll use it with pleasure for years to
    come
You're not alone

Romance Is in the Air

A favorite of brides

A little mystery is good for romance

A reflection of your heart

A romantic addition

A romantic flourish

A romantic setting

A sweet keepsake

A toast to romance with _____

A token of your love

A touch of magic

Add a romantic touch

All about love

An air of romance

An elegant, romantic atmosphere

Anything your heart desires

As an expression of love

Bestow a romantic touch to _____

Brings out the romantic in all of us

Brings the romance and warmth of times gone by

Captures the romance and adventure of _____

Conveys your heartfelt affection

Create an inviting mood

Created just for lovers

Creates an atmosphere of romantic sophistication

Dreamy and enchanting

Enjoy a romantic evening

Evokes the romance of a grand era

Fall in love with _____

Feel the magic

For a more romantic view of the world

For lovers of _____

For your love of special moments

For your true love

Get ready to fall in love all over again

Has a delicate Victorian appeal

Has held your heart ransom ever since

Instant romance!

_____ is for lovers

It's romance

Learn the secrets of _____

Leaves no doubt about the depth of your feelings

Light romance

Light up your evening with _____

Make love sparkle

Perfect for the one you love

Romance, fantasy, and fun

Romance is back!

Romance is our byword

Romantic glow

Rustic yet romantic

Secluded. Mystical. Enchanting.

Sensuous and luxurious

Share precious moments together

Show them you care with _____

Show your love with _____

Sophistication, romance, and simplicity

Speaks of love and romance

Sure to steal your heart

The mystique and romance of _____

The perfect blend of fun and romance

The picture of romance

Timeworn and romantic

To proclaim your affection

To romance the heart

You'll fall in love all over again

You'll fall in love with _____

We're romantically inclined

When romance is in the air

Where mysteries, romance, and
memories meet

Wildly romantic

Will capture your heart

Will melt your heart

With a hint of romance

Wrap her in love

You'll want to keep it close to your
heart

Safety Features

A pioneer in establishing safety standards

A potential lifesaver

A safe and gentle way

A safer way to _____

Accident-proof

Accidents can be avoided

Acts as a deterrent

Adds extra security

Affordable safety

Cushions and protects

Designed for safety

Don't take a chance

Don't you feel more secure already?

Double protection

Easy and safe to operate

Ensure your safety

Equipment protection

Excellent protection

Extra effective. Extra protective.

Feel more secure

Feel safe. Be secure.

For added strength and safety

For low-cost security

For safety's sake

For the peace of mind you want

Gives you security in an insecure world

Handles with care

Helps prevent injuries

Here's a safer way to _____

High-speed performance safety

Holds and protects

In the safety of your own home

Introducing the safe way to _____

Is your home safe?

It's safe. It's effective. It's fast.

It's the safe choice

Make sure your home (yard, office, etc.) is hazard-free

Nontoxic formula

Offers powerful insurance against _____

On-the-job protection

Play it safe

Practical and safe

Prestige and protection, all in one

Prevents costly accidents

Protect your investment

Protects and organizes

Protects you and your (equipment, family, home, etc.)

Provides maximum protection

Real-life testing

Safe and easy to use

Safe, strong, and versatile

Safety features include:

Safety, security, and protection

Safety-tested

Security should never be optional

Standard safety features included

Take no chances

Takes the danger out of _____

The key to your peace of mind

The most durable protection

The protection you need

The safe way to _____

The top choice of law-enforcement
professionals

The ultimate weapon in the war on
_____

There's no risk involved

Think safety, think _____

To protect and watch over you

_____ to the rescue

Vandals have met their match with
_____

We believe in safety first

We're always there to protect you

We've got you covered

Why take any chances?

Without worry

Your choice of custom security features

Your safety is our responsibility

You're covered from every possible
angle

Sensory Delights

A burst of flavor

A _____ by any other name would never (taste, smell, look, feel) the same

A celebration of the senses

A delicious indulgence

A difference you can feel

A feast for your eyes

A fragrant hint of _____

A glorious bouquet

A gourmet treat

A luminous effect

A luscious combination of flavors

A magical scent that goes beyond the senses

A sensational feeling

A sensual feast

A sight to behold

A soft luster

A sunny sensation

A temptation of treats

A ten on the olfactory scale

A triple treat

A vivid aroma

A whole new freshness

A whole new standard of soft

An especially appealing scent

An eye-catching accent

And it smells nice, too

Another epicurean delight

As appealing to the eye as to the touch

Bone-tingling

Buttery soft

Caresses your palette

Close your eyes and it's _____

Close your eyes and you're in _____

Concert-quality sound

Cooked to perfection

Cool, refreshing taste

Delicious flavor

Deliciously sumptuous

Delightful aroma

Dripping with _____

Easy on the eyes

Endlessly fresh and inviting

Ever fresh

Exceptionally soothing

Exquisitely soft

Farm-fresh

Feast your eyes on _____

Feel the difference

Feel the mystery

Feels as good as it looks

Feels so good to the touch

Flavor and aroma

Flavor-enhancing

Flavor you just can't hide

For a softer feel

For extra taste

For your sensory pleasure

Forever fresh

Fresh and flavorful

Freshness guaranteed

Full-flavored and 99 percent fat-free

Gastronomic ecstasy

Gentle as an ocean breeze

Gives you a sensational feeling

Goes to the greatest length to pamper you

Great texture

Have a spoonful of summer

Indulge your senses

Instantly refreshing

It will tempt your palate

It's hot, hot, hot!

Just heat and serve

Kissed by the sun

Lends a rich aura

Lick your lips

Light. Pure. Refreshing.

Like a breath of fresh air

Lilting tones

Long-lasting aroma

Love at first bite

Lush texture

Luxurious in feel

Moist and succulent

Moist. Easy. Irresistible.

Mouthwatering

Music to your ears

Natural scents

Nice to be next to

No artificial flavors

Not only looks better, but _____ better

Nothing feels better than _____

Nothing pleases all your senses like _____

Offers that one-of-a-kind feeling

One-of-a-kind taste

One of life's greatest pleasures

Outstanding taste

Pamper yourself with softness

Petal soft

Picture-perfect results

Pleasures meant to be savored

Plush details

Polished to perfection

Preserves freshness

Rich and flavorful

Rich to the touch

Rich, warm patina

Savor the rainbow of color
See, hear, and feel the difference
Sensory satisfaction
Sensual. Tactile. Irresistible.
Sets hearts and minds racing
Sets the mood
Silky smooth
Smooth and mild
Smooth as silk
Smooth to the touch
So satisfying
Soft and inviting
Soft and supple
Soft as a baby's bottom
Soft enough for her
Soft, satiny finish
Soft, silky, touchable
Soft-to-the-touch
Softer than ever
Soothes and softens
Soothes the soul
Soothing to the touch
Spice up your table with _____
Spicy scent of _____
Stimulates the senses
Stirs the senses
Sumptuously enriched
Sunset-kissed
Superior flavor

Surprisingly good taste
Sweet temptations
Sweetly scented
Taste it all
Taste it and see
Taste tantalizers
Tastes as good as it looks
Tastes great!
_____ tastes so good, it's addictive
Tastes too good to be good for you
Texture and warmth
The feel of luxury
The heady fragrance of _____
The rustic allure of metal
The sweet smell of success
The tangy taste of _____
The taste that _____
The warmth of wood
They feel even better than they look
To delight the senses
Tropically fragrant
Velvety softness
Very soft. Very sensuous. Very sexy.
Wakes up all your taste buds
Warm and toasty
Warm, inviting glow
We bring you good taste
What a feeling!
Where the flavor is

Whet their appetite right from the start

Whimsical images

Whisper quiet

Will instantly add a touch of warmth to any _____

Will stir your soul

Wonderfully scented

Worth savoring

You have to taste it

You'll hear (see, smell, taste) the difference

You'll want to pump up the volume

Your senses will smile

At Your **Service**

A commitment to service

A phone call away

All night long

Available around the clock

Available to meet with you day or night

Call our product specialists

Call today, _____ tomorrow

Complete with a smile

Continuing assistance

Courteous service

Don't expect the usual service. Expect more.

Easy to order—guaranteed to please

Effort-free exchange

Exceptional amenities

Extended-service plans

For year-round flawless service

Free immediate exchanges

Friendly service

Full service

Full service. All the time.

Full-Service Shop

Go up a level in service

Guaranteed service

Hands-on personal attention

House calls available

If you don't see it, ask. We can probably get it for you.

Impeccable service

Impress your customers in a way they'll never forget

In stock and ready to go

Incomparable service

Individualized service

It's no fun to _____, but we can help

Just ask. We'll do the rest.

Just tell us what you want

Just the way you like it

Knowledgeable, friendly service

Let us do it for you

Let us help you

Long dependable service

Need a sample?

No appointments necessary

No job too big or too small

No matter what your needs

No-problem purchasing

No strings attached

Nobody understands _____ like we do

Now what can we do for you?

Only a phone call away

Open seven days a week

Open to the public

Order anytime, day or night

Ordering is easy

Other companies may offer the same deal, but not the same service

Our customer service is unmatched

Our customers always come first

Our customers are our #1 priority

Our expert staff will help you

Our products deliver what they promise

Our quality and service know no boundaries

Our representatives are waiting for your call

Our specialty is your satisfaction

Personal attention

Personalized service

Place yourself in our hands

Professional, courteous, and personal attention

Professional packing

Prompt service

Prompt turnaround and guaranteed workmanship

Quick turnaround on all orders

Reserve yours today

Return privileges

Returns at no cost, and no bother

Returns made easy

Schedule an appointment today

Send no money now, take no risk

Service begins the moment you place your order

Service hotline—24 hours a day

Service with a smile

Services that really help

Spa-like pampering

Special orders don't upset us

Taking service a step further

Thank you for your support

The best service in town

The service you deserve

Toll-free hotline

24 hours a day, seven days a week

Unrivaled services and amenities

Voted #1 in Customer Service

We appreciate your business

We bring you the world

We can help

We care about your _____ as much as you do

We cater to special needs

We cater to you

We do that too!

We don't just do it, we do it better

We give you the service and respect you deserve

We install anywhere

We just wanted to say thank you

We know how you feel

We know the value of a customer

We know what you really want

We know you want it now

We make house calls

We may be your only source

We stand behind the quality of our products

We stock every product

We take care of the hard part

We take it personally!

We'll be there

We'll work with you every step of the way

We're all you need

We're always there to help

We're experts so you don't have to be

We're old hands at helping companies like yours

We're passionate about _____ and it shows

We're the pros to call

We're there for you at a moment's notice

We're waiting for your call

We're with you all the way

We're working hard for you

We've got it!

What can we do for you?

When four-star service is a must

When our customers speak, we listen

Whenever you need us

White-glove service

Year-round flawless service

You asked for it, you got it

You can also order via the Internet

You deserve it, we'll find it

You won't feel alone

You'll always be our #1 concern

You'll always get professional, courteous service

You'll get special attention

Your complete satisfaction, nothing less

Your patronage is our most valuable asset

Your satisfaction always comes first

Your satisfaction is our business

Your wish is our command

You're entitled to _____

You're meant to be pampered

Just the Right **Size**

A blockbuster event

A bounty of _____

A little goes a long way

A miniature interpretation

A scaled-down version

A smaller version

About the size of a deck of cards

Almost life-size

America's fastest-growing _____

And there's more where that came from

Any size, any shape

Appropriately sized

Big and beautiful

Big enough to hold everything

Big style on a small scale

Bigger and better

Chock-full

Don't let the compact size fool you

Dramatically sized

Extralong cut

Fits into the palm of your hand

Fits into those hard-to-reach places

Fits perfectly anywhere

For getting into small or tight spaces

Generous proportions

Generously cut for comfort

Generously sized

Gives you a lot of room

Good things come in small packages

High capacity

Huge portions

Impressively large

In all shapes and sizes

In two great lengths

It may be small but _____

It's big!

Just the right size for your little ones

Large capacity

Larger than life

Lavished with _____

Lavishly sized

Little things mean a lot

Make the most of limited space

More than just a _____

New fuller cut

Nicely sized and well proportioned

No job is too small

Not enough room

Not just bigger but better

Often the smallest touches make the biggest impact

One size fits all

Our large capacity

Oversized to suit a variety of needs

Palm-size perfection

Perfect for the challenge of a limited living space

Popularly oversized

Room to grow with you

Roomy enough for all

Scaled-down version

Short and sweet

Size does matter

Sized to fit any location

Slim enough to slip into your pocket

Small and intimate

Small but mighty

Space-efficient

Spacesavers

Substantially proportioned

Tall and majestic

The biggest and best

The daintiest

The perfect size

The sky's the limit

The smallest _____ we've ever seen

The world's biggest _____ just got bigger

The world's largest

There's strength in numbers

Think big!

Tight spaces require creative answers

True to size

Twelve great reasons to _____

Ultracompact

Wallet-sized

We make more types of _____ than anyone else in the world

We're the biggest

While quantities last

Yes, we have your size

You can never have too many _____

You'll have the biggest on your block

Snob Appeal

A distinctive address for premier shopping

A gift to enhance your lifestyle

A polished look

A premier offering

A prized property

A rare experience you can't afford to miss

A reflection of your impeccable taste

A significant piece

A subtle sign of success

All the accoutrements of life at its best

An assured future asset

As close to heaven as you can be

Create a designer look

Defines luxury

Discriminating people all over the world are _____

Do it in luxury

Emulating the masters

Enjoy the special luxury of _____

Enjoyed by connoisseurs everywhere

Exclusively ours

Extraordinary _____ for extraordinary people

Fit for a king

Fit for a queen

For a discriminating clientele

For discriminating individuals

For owners with impeccable taste

For the collector

For the person who has everything

For those at the top

For those who appreciate excellence

For those who are worldly-wise

For those who demand the finest things in life

For those who recognize true magnificence

From around the world

Gives you the royal treatment

Ideal for the connoisseur

If money's no object

If you can afford the very best

Impeccable detailing

Individually hand-numbered

Instant heirloom

It's an original

Let's talk about luxury

Limited quantities

Luxury at its best

Luxury without limits

Museum quality

Oh-so luxurious

Only the finest

Own a masterpiece

Provides a thoughtful bit of pampering

Rare, never-before-seen masterpieces

Richly furnished

Signed by the artist

Simply the finest in the world

Sleek lines

Standout status

Step into our very special world

That's luxury!

The best in the world

The crème de la crème

The enduring expression of your personal values and taste

The luxury and ease of _____

The modern-day status symbol

The name that says it all

The perfect accoutrements of success

The ultimate gift

The undisputed status classic

The very glamour of Hollywood

The world's finest

Top of the line

Treat him or her to the outright luxury of _____

Treat yourself like a queen

Treat yourself to a little luxury

Uniquely luxurious

Unmistakable luxury

Unparalleled sophistication

Upward mobility

Virtually identical to some of the world's finest _____

We cater to an elite set of clientele

We take it to a new level of sophistication

We're dedicated to excellence

When nothing less will do

World-class standard of luxury

You deserve it!

You deserve the best

You don't have to be an heiress to enjoy luxuries like these

You'll get noticed when you _____

You're worth it!

Socially Conscious

A generous portion of the proceeds will be donated to . . .

Be kind to the environment by _____

Because we believe the environment matters

Better for the environment

Conserves energy

Domestically made

Earth-friendly products

Ecologically-friendly

Environmentally-friendly

Environmentally-responsible

Environmentally-safe

Every time you buy from us, you give something back to the earth

For a better planet

Give something back

Have a more peaceful, simpler life

It's good for you and for the planet

It's great for the environment

Made from recycled materials

Made in the USA

100 percent recyclable

Organically-grown

Our uncompromising commitment to the environment

Preserve our planet

Promotes conservation of _____

Protect our planet

Safely and humanely

The best elements in design and ecology converge

The company with a heart

We recycle

We use recycled materials

We're sensitive to the balance of nature

Without the chemicals

You give back to the planet when you _____

Superior **Solutions**

A dream realized

A perfect companion piece to _____

A perfect complement to _____

A perfect match

A promise fulfilled

A safe, lasting solution

A simple solution

All you need is _____

An attractive solution to an unsightly problem

Announcing the long-term solution you've been looking for

Another problem solved

Effective solutions for busy people

Everything you could wish for

Everything you need to get the job done

Everything you'll ever need

Everything you've ever wanted from a _____

Exactly what you've been looking for

Expert solutions for _____

Find the answer you need today

For your busy lifestyle

Gives you peace of mind

_____ has the answer

Here's the place for _____

Here's the solution!

How to get from here to there

Ideal for _____

If you're worried about _____

If you've been on the lookout for _____

Imagine never having to think about _____ again!

It's all right here

It's the only way to go

Just-right solutions

Just the right amount

Just the right tool for the job

Look no further

Looking for that special something?

Need a _____?

Perfect for adults who want to be babied

Perfect for beginners and old pros who thought they had everything

Perfect for today's lifestyles

Perfect to mix and match

Provides weeks of relief

Quality, customized solutions

Sure to satisfy even the connoisseur

The answer is "Yes!"

The answer you've been looking for

The civilized answer to _____

The first place to go for _____

The ideal alternative

The key to _____
The next logical addition
The one source for all your needs
The only one you'll ever need
The perfect accent
The perfect accompaniment
The perfect accoutrement
The perfect answer
The perfect background for _____
The perfect complement to _____
The perfect environment for _____
The perfect keepsake
The perfect note on which to _____
The perfect partner
The perfect solution
The perfect way to express your refined taste
The smartest way we know to _____
The versatile, inexpensive solution
The watchword for this season is _____

There's a better way
To meet the demands of a challenging world
Try it and you'll see
We can solve it. Together.
We have a better solution
We have the solution
We meet your needs
We provide special care for special people
We'll tell you what you can do about it
We're the one
We've got one that's just right for you
We've got the answer
What could be more appropriate
Will make your wishes come true
You'll be prepared
Your dream come true
Your search for the perfect _____ is over
You've come to the right place

Up to **Speed**

A real shortcut
And it's fast, fast, fast!
At a moment's notice
At your own pace
Before you can say _____
Before you know it
Breakthrough speed
Fast, efficient, and reliable
Fast. Faster. Fastest.
Faster than ever
Faster than the speed of light
For executives on the go
Get a head start
Gets you up to speed right away
Hotfoot it to _____
Immediate relief
In a flash
In a snap!
In an instant

In minutes
In no time at all
In the blink of an eye
It's fast!
Just a minute to _____
Makes quick work of even the toughest jobs
Nonstop action
Quickly and quietly
Ready at a moment's notice
Ready in no time
Screaming-fast performance
See results right away
Sets up in seconds
Starts working instantly
Takes just seconds
The fastest _____ just got faster
The quickest way to _____
What used to take a full weekend can be done in an hour
Works instantly!
You're six hours away from a more beautiful _____

Modern **Technology**

A breakthrough formula

A marvel of the space age

A new level of performance technology

A tool for creating solutions

Advanced computer technology

Advanced engineering

Advanced technology for a variety of applications

Amazing technology! Amazingly affordable

An ingenious device

Authorized reseller

Born of advanced technology

Brand-new technology in a familiar package

Breakthrough products

Brings world-renowned engineering into your home

Brought together art and high technology

Call for a demo disk

Combines technical expertise with sensitivity

Design wizardry

Designed from years of research

Designed to prolong the life of your _____

Discover a fortune hidden in your computer

Easy to install

Easy to program

Free technical support

Free upgrades

Get _____ and get serious about the quality of your work

Get the support you need when you need it

Gives you control

Greater precision

Increase your productivity

In-depth systems knowledge

Ingenious technology

Join the technological revolution

Latest technology on the market today

Leading-edge technology

Never-before-seen technology

100 percent guaranteed compatibility

Ongoing support available

Our technical advisers are standing by to answer your questions

Patented technology

Revolutionary technology

Scientific breakthrough

State-of-the-art technology

Support. By phone. By fax. Online.

Technical-help hotline

Technically advanced

Technological know-how

Technological mastery combined with uncommon elegance

Technologically advanced

Technologically unique

Technology you can trust

The cutting edge

The _____ of the future

The precision of modern technology

The productivity-boosting edge only we can give you

The result of years of research

The 21st century today

Toll-Free Technical Support

Tomorrow's technology today

Turn your computer into a cash cow

Turnkey systems

Unlimited expansion available

Unlimited technical assistance

Visit us on the Internet

Will help your customers find the answers they need

World-class technology

It's **Time**

A blast from the past

A contemporary vision

A delightful step back in time

A luxury with timeless elegance

A 1940s-inspired sensation

A once-a-year event

A real time-saver

A specially-cherished time

A time-honored tradition

A time-wise solution

A time-worn presence

A turn-of-the-millennium _____

Act now!

All day long

All in one week or your money back

All year round

Always ready to go, no matter what time it is

As soon as possible

At a time like this

At home, in your own time

Be the first

Before it's too late

Born of centuries of experience

Borrows from a multitude of traditions

Built to withstand the test of time

Call us today. It's time!

Changes to suit your needs over the years

Clean, timeless styling

Coming soon

Don't be a lady-in-waiting

Don't put it off

Don't waste another moment

Ends today!

Flexible time commitment

For more than 100 years

For now and for always

For treasured moments

Get an early start

Get in touch with us right away

Gives you a brighter future

How timely!

If you agree that it's time for a change

Improves over time

In half the time

In just two short years

Isn't it about time?

Isn't it time you found out about _____

It's the future today

It's time to discover

It's time to take matters into your own hands

It's time you gave us a call

It's your future

Just in time

Just takes minutes

Let us offer you a glimpse of the future

Long-awaited

Long-term strategies

Looks to the future

Make every minute count

Manages your time

Maybe it's time to _____

Never again waste your valuable time

Now is the moment to _____

Now is the perfect time to _____

Now more than ever

Now open

Once a day

One minute of ours equals _____ hours of theirs

Our vision of the future

Perfect for any occasion

Prepare for the 21st century

Rare beauty that will last generations

Reflect on a time very long ago

Reward her with the gift of time

Ride the wave of the future

Right now!

Right on time for _____

Say "yes" today

Shaping the future

Stands the test of time

Start right now

Step into the future with _____

Stop wasting your time

Take a moment right now

The art of timeless style

The event you've been waiting for

The future has arrived

The future is _____

The moment has arrived

The time has come. Are you ready?

The time is right for _____

There's never enough time

There's no better time than right now

This is the moment you've been waiting for

Thoroughly modern

Time after time

Time for _____

Time stands still with _____

Timeless and always appropriate

Timeless and treasured

Timeless beauty, uncompromising quality

Timeless, hand-crafted

Timeless in their appeal

Timeless motifs

Timeless styling

Timelessly appealing

Time-saving

Time-tested

Timing is everything

Today (tomorrow, this weekend, Wednesday, etc.) only

Tomorrow's _____ today

Transport yourself back to a time of grandeur and elegance

Try it today

User-friendly technology

We know your time is valuable

We see into your future

We'll prepare you today for tomorrow

We'll take you into the 21st century

We're shaping the future

What a time-saver!

What are you waiting for?

When every second counts

When was the last time you _____?

While they last

Why wait another minute?

Will keep you on time

With the elegance of timeless masterpieces

You must act now

Your future is on the line

Your future is too valuable to risk

Travel Savvy

A faithful traveling companion

A natural-born traveler

A travel necessity for your peace of mind

An enchanted landscape

Breathtaking views

Closer to paradise

Easily portable

Easy to carry

Easy to pack

Exactly what every traveler needs

For the armchair traveler

For your protection and peace of mind while traveling

Gets you there and back

Goes anywhere

In the mood to travel?

It's a great travel accessory

Just right for the road

Just the right size for any trip

Let us put our travel savvy to work for you

Make us part of your travel plans

Makes travel more comfortable

Makes travel more organized and less stressful

Naturally packable and portable

On the move

Pack and go

Perfect for people on the move

Perfect for the weary traveler

Perfect for travel

Protect your _____ from the rigors of travel

The art of travel

The least-expensive way to go

The ultimate destination

The ultimate sanctuary

The ultimate traveling companion

The ultimate vacation

There's no place like _____

Travel in comfort

Travel in style

Travel the world with _____

Trust us to get you there

Unexpected. Unspoiled. Undisturbed.

We put the world at your fingertips

We'll get you there and back

You can take it with you

Your travel companion

It's **Unique**

A handmade original
A unique blend of _____
A unique formula
An original collection inspired by

_____

An original masterpiece
An uncommon accent
Available nowhere else in the world
Be different, be better
Be the only _____
Designed especially for you
Develop your own style
Don't let yours get lost in the crowd
Don't settle for the ordinary
Each is unique
Escape the ordinary
Hard to find
Has the look and feel of _____ made
    right here in America
If unique is what you seek
In a class of its own
Individually designed
It's ours and ours alone
_____ like no other
Limited edition
Made for this day alone
Made one at a time, by hand

No two are exactly alike
Nobody else can do it
Not just another _____
Not your ordinary _____
Offers a customized fit
One in a million
One of a kind
Ours is no ordinary _____
Say farewell to the ordinary
Separate yourself from the ordinary
Sets ours apart from all the rest
Specially blended for you
Step out of the ordinary
Suddenly you stand out
The art of being unique
The difference between the ordinary
    and the extraordinary
The first and only
The last of a disappearing breed
The most unique source anywhere
The one and only
The only one of its kind
The ordinary becomes extraordinary
The rarest of the rare
The single source for _____
There's never been anything quite
    like it
There's no other like it
There's only one!
These are no ordinary _____

They broke the mold

Unique helpers

Uniquely packaged

Unlike all others

We searched the world over for these

We'll create the perfect _____ just for you

We're the only one who _____

What makes this _____ unlike any other in the world?

What sets ours apart

You'll be the only one in the neighborhood to _____

You'll find but once in a lifetime

You'll never see another like it

Yours alone

You've got to see it to believe it

You've never experienced anything like it before

Versatile and Useful

A brilliant blend of traditional and contemporary

A _____ for all seasons

A must-have for people on the go

A myriad of imaginative uses

A perfect companion to _____

A seasonless basic

Adapts to any job

Adds a new dimension to flexibility

Adjusts to fit you perfectly

All a busy person could hope for

All-in-one

All-purpose

All-season

All-weather

All you need for the job

An indispensable tool

An ingenious dual purpose

And a host of other uses

And much, much more!

As functional as it is fun

As indispensable as it is good-looking

At home anywhere

At home indoors and out

At once decorative and practical

Available individually or as a set

Beauty, strength, and durability

Blends into any decor

Blends with every style

By day, _____. By night, _____.

Can be worn in several different ways

Certain to satisfy anyone's taste

Combines beauty and utility

Combines style and function

Combining the simplicity of functional design with _____

Crosses the line between _____ and _____

Custom _____ at noncustom prices

Day in and day out

Decorative and functional

Does double duty around the home

_____ does it all

Doubles as a _____

Doubly beautiful. Doubly useful.

Eliminates waste

Everyone needs one

Everything you're looking for in a _____

Fills so many needs

Fills your every need

Fits into any decor

Focus on functionality

For country or city

For day to dinner

For every day

Formal to informal

Fully coordinated

Functional pieces get a stylish update

Get the most out of _____

Go everywhere. Do everything.

Great for every day

Great for work or play

Has unlimited uses

Highly adaptable

Ideal for dozens of jobs

Indoor and outdoor use

Infinitely wearable

It's a winning combination

Looks good and works hard

Matches any decor

More than good-looking, it's very useful

Multifunctional

Multipurpose

Not just for holiday use

Not only functional but fabulous

Not only looks great but _____

Offers true versatility

1,001 uses

Perfect for just hanging out or going somewhere special

Perfect for most any use

Perfect for today's global _____

Practical and pleasing

Practical, versatile, economical

Serves a very useful purpose

So very versatile

Space-saving and functional

Spans generations and decors

Spectacular for day or evening

Start with a solid foundation

Styled to please weekday through weekend

Suitable for all ages

Suitable for children

Suitable for everyday use

Suitable for framing

Take it anywhere

That's what we're here for

The most widely used

The perfect combination of form and function

The perfect companion for _____

The possibilities go on and on

The question is . . . what *can't* it do?

To fit all your needs

To use and live with every day

To wear to work or through the weekend

Two _____ in one

Uniquely functional

Unisex appeal

Unisex styling
Utilitarian chic
Utterly indispensable
Versatile and varied
Versatility times three
Very adaptable

Welcome in any setting
Why you should use _____?
Will look at home in any setting
Year-round appeal
You'll find many uses for this _____

Descriptive Qualities/ People and Personalities

Communicative

A team player

Able to express feelings

Able to translate thought to action

Asks for what he or she wants

Clear-thinking

Clearly articulates thoughts

Communicates clearly

Easily resolves differences of opinion

Expresses oneself clearly

Gets the point across

Good listener

Is an effective communicator

Negotiates skillfully

Offers constructive criticism

Opens your heart

Opens your mind

Well-spoken

Competent

Able to anticipate and respond quickly
    to problems

Able to take control

Assesses objectively

Can be counted on

Can create what he or she wants in life

Does a superb job

Finishes what he or she starts

Follows directions

Follows up

Gives it his or her all

Goal-oriented

Good at handling details

Has all the necessary skills

Is more successful at achieving goals

Problem solver

Shows competency

Superior concentration

Dedicated

Gives of oneself

Goes beneath the surface

Has stick-to-itiveness

Meets every challenge

Shows perseverance

Willing to make personal sacrifices

Works overtime

Enthusiastic

An irrepressible spirit

Be inspired

Comes to life

Full of energy

Joyful and inspiring

Never runs out of steam

Participates fully

Self-motivated

Unceasing energy

Expert

A working knowledge
Can do the job
Has impeccable credentials
Has _____ years of experience

In-depth knowledge
Well-informed
Well-prepared
Will make you an expert

Hardworking

A competent decision maker
A real go-getter
Always does his or her best
Become more productive
Does not procrastinate
Gets more done

Goes the extra mile
High-powered
Is equipped with all the right skills
Makes an important contribution
Ready to pitch in
Seeks increased responsibility

Improved

A tool for self-discovery
Able to inspire others
Changes your life for the better
Develop compassion for yourself
Eager to learn
Enhance your prestige
Enhances intimacy with your inner self
Forward-thinking

Get your needs met
Helps you manage difficult change
Increase your mental abilities
Lets go of old negative belief systems
Lets go of the past
Open to new ideas and approaches
Path to personal enrichment
Upgrade your skills

Miscellaneous

Deserving of _____

Discover your strengths and weaknesses

_____ for your soul

Get to know yourself better

Get your needs met

Has let go of the past

Knows the fine points

Lives life with passion

See yourself as you really are

Sets clear and healthy boundaries

Shoot for the stars

Show compassion for yourself

Stop procrastinating

Take control of your life

Trusts the future

Welcomes life's adventures

Mood-Related

A unifying spirit

Able to manage anger

Copes well with anger

Creates a mood that's both serene and exciting

Creates an enchanting mood

Give your mood a lift

_____ got you down?

Inner contentment

It's magic

Mood-elevating

Perfect for someone who's feeling low

The essence of freedom

To help smooth out the rough edges of your busy days

Will warm your heart

Personal Qualities

A sense of refinement
Able-bodied
Bighearted
Brings out the best in others
Caring and sharing
Develop mutual respect
Down to earth
Easy to get along with
Easygoing
Enhanced focus
Enjoys oneself
Feel good about yourself
Feels completely at ease
Gets along well with others
Has plenty of character

Improved alertness
Is compassionate
Is very perceptive
Keeps his or her word
Leaves a lasting impression
Makes a positive impression
Personally dynamic
Ready for anything
Strong-minded
Strong-willed
Strongly ambitious
Superior memory
Warmhearted
Well-liked
Well-respected

Positive

A sunny disposition
A sunny spirit
Add some sunshine to your life
An instant spirit raiser
Approaches conflict directly and positively
Be positive
Become happier
Boundless optimist
Bright and bouncy
Bright and cheerful
Brighten your outlook with _____

Builds self-confidence
Create what you want in your life
Fill every day with positive energy
Has a positive impact
Make everyone happy
Perk up your spirits
Ready for anything
Sees the glass as half full
Start off your day on the right note
The sunny energy of _____
When you want to feel really good

Professional

A seasoned professional

Always on the lookout for new opportunities

Checks work carefully

Computer-literate

Does whatever it takes

Effectively manages time

Follows through

Gets the job done

Goal-oriented

Has the spirit of teamwork

Has top credentials

Highly trained

In high regard

Is a skilled worker

Leadership abilities

Maintains complete and accurate records

Management skills

Open to new approaches

Pays close attention to details

Performs conscientiously

Remains on course

Resolves differences of opinion

Respected by his or her peers

Shows pride in workmanship

Single-mindedly pursues goals

Takes whatever steps are necessary

The professional edge you need

Troubleshooter

Works well independently

You'll think it was done professionally

Relationship-Related

A trustworthy individual you can rely
on
Achieve a more socially rewarding life
Attractive to the opposite sex
Creates a sense of community
Deals tactfully with difficult people
Improve all your relationships
Is open with others

Leaves a lasting impression
Lends a hand to others
Meets others head-on
Preserves and maintains relationships
Promotes cooperation
Puts others at ease
Respects others' opinions

Self-Confident

Achieve a winner's attitude
Banish _____ forever
Be the envy of all your friends
Builds confidence
Cool and confident
Go ahead. Make a statement.
Has it changed your life yet?
If you've had enough of being alone
No more lonely Saturday nights
Now you'll be able to get any guy you
want

Overcome self-doubt
Quiet confidence
Reassures and inspires
Risk taker
Self-disciplined
Self-reliant
Stands up for his or her beliefs
Takes the worry out of _____
You'll be the loveliest one
You'll never feel self-conscious again
Why not you?

Successful

Able to motivate others

Be a total winner

Clearheaded

Clear-sighted

Committed to achieving excellence

Demands excellence

Full of character

Get more of what you want in your life

Gets you noticed

Has good judgment

Has it all

Have a wonderful stress-free life

Highly perceptive

Lives up to his or her potential

Mentally sharp

Motivated to achieve

Overcomes obstacles

Performs effectively

Personal transformation

Quick-witted

Reach any goal you want

Reaching new heights

Sets and achieves goals

Sets high standards

Stays on track

Strives for perfection

Strives to excel

Takes a leadership role

Takes the initiative

Tranquil

Add a dose of tranquility to your life

Become more relaxed

Calms your emotions

Create balance and harmony

Creates inner tranquility

Deals effectively with stress

Enhances your inner peace

Experience nirvana

Feeds your soul

Feel calmer

Feel more in control

Feel soothed and relaxed

Helps you relax

Keep your cool

Learn to manage your anger

Reduce stress with _____

Relaxed. Refreshed. Renewed.

Think of it as portable tranquility

Unknots your nerves

When serenity feels just right

You'll never be in a more relaxed state

Key Word Index

Building the CUSTOM
HOME OFFICE

Building the CUSTOM HOME OFFICE

Projects for the Complete Work Space

NIALL BARRETT

The Taunton Press

The Taunton Press
Inspiration for hands-on living™

The Taunton Press, Inc., 63 South Main Street, PO Box 5506, Newtown, CT 06470-5506
e-mail: tp@taunton.com

Distributed by Publishers Group West

COVER DESIGN: Ann Marie Manca
INTERIOR DESIGN AND LAYOUT: Lori Wendin
ILLUSTRATORS: Michael Gellatly, Ron Carboni, and Rosalie Vaccaro
COVER AND INTERIOR PHOTOGRAPHER: Chris Holden

LIBRARY OF CONGRESS CATALOGING-IN-PUBLICATION DATA:
Barrett, Niall.
    Building the custom home office : projects for the complete work space / Niall Barrett.
       p. cm.
    ISBN 1-56158-421-5   2811 6290 6/03
    1. Home offices--Design and construction. 2. Dwellings--Remodeling. I. Title.

TH4816.3.O34 B37 2002
643'.58--dc21   2001044580

Printed in the United States of America
10 9 8 7 6 5 4 3 2 1

SAFETY NOTE: Working with wood is inherently dangerous. Using hand or power tools improperly or ignoring standard safety practices can lead to permanent injury or even death. Don't try to perform operations you learn about here (or elsewhere) unless you're certain they are safe for you. If something about an operation doesn't feel right, don't do it. Look for another way. We want you to enjoy the craft, so please keep safety foremost in your mind whenever you're working with wood.

To Alice Barrett, for creating the adventure that is my life, and to the memory of Cornelius Barrett— so much has happened lately!

ACKNOWLEDGMENTS

I MUST FIRST ACKNOWLEDGE my family and friends for their unlimited enthusiasm and encouragement for whatever I choose to do in my life.

For producing, yet again, a book alive with rich, wonderfully precise photography—"Cheers" to my friend Chris Holden.

I would also like to thank Accuride International, Inc.; Alienware Corporation; Bessy Corporation; Festool USA; Häfele America Company; Herman Miller, Inc.; Lie-Nielsen Toolworks, Inc.; One Tech, LLC; Psion USA; R & R Clamp, Inc.; and Rockler Woodworking and Hardware for the thoughtful assistance with this book.

As always, thanks to all the folks at The Taunton Press who contributed their knowledge and efforts to produce this book. Their professionalism and attention to detail are apparent throughout.

Contents

Introduction

ARTISTS, SCHOLARS, SCIENTISTS, and writers all traditionally worked at home, so the home office has existed in our society for a long time. It could be called the first professional work environment. The studio, library, study, and den, now thought of as living spaces, all evolved from work spaces.

Almost all of us have some kind of work space in our homes. Often it's nothing more than a corner of the kitchen where bills pile up and phone calls are answered, but just as often a small room or portion of a room is devoted to the normal paperwork generated from running a household. For the self-employed, this space does double duty as a location for home and business paperwork.

There is also a growing trend toward telecommuting, or working in traditional office jobs from home. What used to be a utopian ideal realized only by a talented few has now become commonplace. New technology, systematization of working practices, and demands for a better quality of life have pushed many people into home offices. Today some 20 million people in the United States work from home, and it is estimated that worldwide the figure is around 40 million and growing.

Working in the home is practical primarily because of the technology that makes communication so easy and inexpensive. Telephone and data transmission between the home and almost any place in the world is common and easy to arrange.

Many companies now consider the traditional nine-to-five approach to working in commercial offices to be outdated. Increasingly sophisticated computer and communication systems have made it possible for them to allow staff to work either full time or part time at home.

Working at home is as much a lifestyle choice as a business decision. Your own home office is the ultimate expression of personal choice, embodying personal autonomy and the power to create an environment specially designed to meet your individual requirements, peculiarities, and tastes. It can radically alter how you view your work and leisure time. Working at home gives you the flexibility and freedom to work from 11 A.M. to 8 P.M. or to work in your bathrobe if that is how and when you are most creative and productive.

Manufacturers are flooding the market with home-office equipment such as computers, printers, copiers, modems, fax machines, and telephones that can do things I never knew needed doing. Even furniture manufacturers see an opportunity to market desks and cabinets that are uniquely designed to fit efficiently into the home.

Part of the fun of working at home is deciding how you want your office to look, especially because there is no need to re-create the look of a commercial office. Magazines and books provide plenty of information on how to organize and start up a business and there are books on various aspects of the home office, but there is precious little material on the nuts and bolts of building your own home office.

In this book, I deal with the practical issues you need to consider when you're setting up a home office. I've included guidelines for design, layout, and ergonomics as well as information on wiring, lighting, computer equipment, and more. The guidelines are followed by step-by-step instructions on how to build a modular suite of office furniture. The project chapters show you how to create a pleasing, integrated, coordinated office that can be adapted to almost any space and style. Enjoy building your office, but be careful that you don't end up with such a wonderful space you won't want to leave it.

PART ONE

Office Design Guide

CHAPTER 1

Designing Your Home Office

YOU HAVE A LOT OF DECISIONS to make in setting up your home office. It's best to make as many of them as you can before you start any construction. Some of the decisions depend solely on your personal preferences—for example, the color of the room and the window treatment. I can't help you with these except to advise you to make the room as comfortable and cheerful as you can and leave space for personal items. Family photos on your desk and artwork on the wall can make a space much more pleasant to work in.

Some of your design decisions will be based on the kind of work you plan to do in the office. For example, if you're highly computerized, you'll need to make room for all of your computer equipment. Your budget will also influence your decisions, but remember that it's better to start with a few high-quality items and add to them later than to outfit your entire office with things you will have to replace very soon.

Before you start compromising, make a wish list. Write down everything you would

like to have in your ideal home office. After you've decided what you want, think about the limiting factors that are keeping you from building the ideal office. Then you can start making adjustments to your wish list. You may be surprised to see how close you can get with a little compromise and common sense.

You'll find that it's a treat to plan a home office tailor-made just for you, one that reflects your style and personality, caters to your work requirements, and dovetails with your other commitments. Pamper yourself with at least one luxury item, whether it's a leather chair or an espresso machine. And don't rush your decisions—you may be living with the results for a long time. Enjoy the process; it's an exciting challenge.

Space Planning

First things first: Where will you put your office? How will you fit what you need into this space?

Throughout this book you will see color illustrations of our virtual office. They represent our virtual person's spare bedroom. In the unlikely event that your spare bedroom is identical to this one, you will have very little work to do to plan your office. Most likely, though, you will have to design your own space. In this chapter, I will lead you through a step-by-step process that will facilitate planning and allow you to start thinking now about the projects discussed in later chapters.

Choosing the right space for your home office is most important if you plan to work at home full time, since you will be spending a great deal of time there. The location will, of course, be constrained by what spaces you have available. Still, try not to choose a space just because it is available. We all have spaces

that are available because they aren't useful for anything. These are not necessarily the best choices for a home office.

A home office can be located in an outbuilding, attic, or basement. However, these spaces often require substantial renovation before you can begin to furnish them. Also, basements can be damp, attics can be very hot, and neither one typically has good natural light. Outbuildings, though, can be effective home offices since they are more likely to be quiet, well lit, and isolated from interruptions.

The most practical space for your home office is an existing room or portion of a room inside your home. Such a space will require little, if any, renovation—even if you

want to separate a portion of a room from the remainder, you can do this by using a freestanding screen. The most you will have to do to ready the space is add some extra electrical capacity for office machines and lighting. In this book, I generally assume that you've chosen to locate your office in a spare room of your house.

If possible, choose a space that can be made attractive and inviting. A quiet, well-ventilated space with plenty of natural light is ideal, although I would try to position the main work area so that you are not directly in front of a window. A view is nice, but if it's right there every time you look up it can be a distraction.

Floor Plan

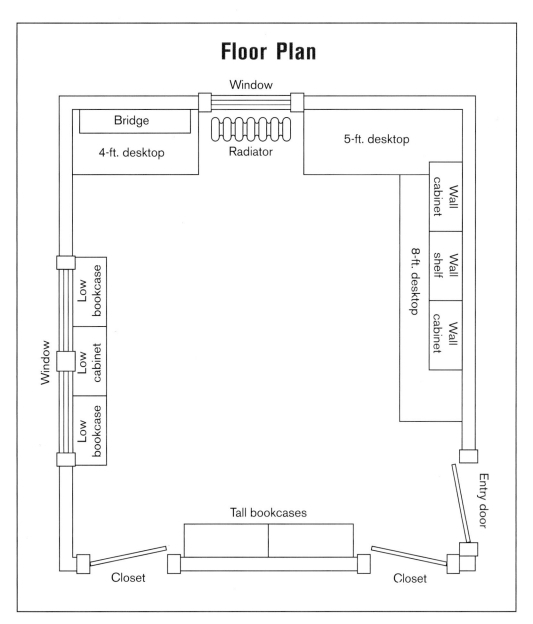

Window

Bridge

4-ft. desktop

Radiator

5-ft. desktop

Wall cabinet

Wall shelf

Wall cabinet

8-ft. desktop

Window

Low bookcase

Low cabinet

Low bookcase

Entry door

Tall bookcases

Closet

Closet

This attractive room with plenty of natural light is an ideal work space.

Creating the Plan

Once you have decided on a location, you can choose a layout. To do this, you will need to create some simple drawings. They don't have to be fancy, but they do have to be drawn to scale. The easiest way to do this is to use graph paper. But first you will have to map out your room, so you will need a notepad, a pencil with an eraser, and a tape measure.

Taking dimensions

Start with the floor plan and elevations. Once you finish them you can transfer your measurements to graph paper to create accurate scale drawings.

Measure the length, width, and height of each wall in the room.

Be sure to map all the architectural features such as doors, windows, and heating appliances.

Draw a rough sketch of the floor plan of the room, including doors, windows, and any odd corners the room may have. Measure all of the features you have drawn and note the dimensions on the sketch. Accuracy is critical, so double-check all of your measurements. Also note on the sketch any other details that will affect the placement of your office furniture—the size of the molding, which way the doors swing. Note the locations of all of the light switches, electrical outlets, and heat sources.

Next, sketch an elevation view of each wall. Draw in the doors, windows, and other features. Measure these items and record their dimensions on the sketches. Also check the ceiling height on the off chance that it will limit the height of the shelving.

Making scale drawings

Using the information and dimensions in the rough sketches, create accurate scale drawings of your room—one floor plan and an elevation for each wall. You will need some Imperial graph paper (1:24), a drafting triangle, a ruler, a pencil, an eraser, and a pen. Refer to the drawings you just made for precise measurements and transfer them to the graph paper. Be sure to add the locations of electrical outlets, switches, and heating sources. You should also illustrate the swing of any doors since this can affect the placement of furniture.

Office Layout

At this point you are ready to determine the furniture layout for your office. Photocopy

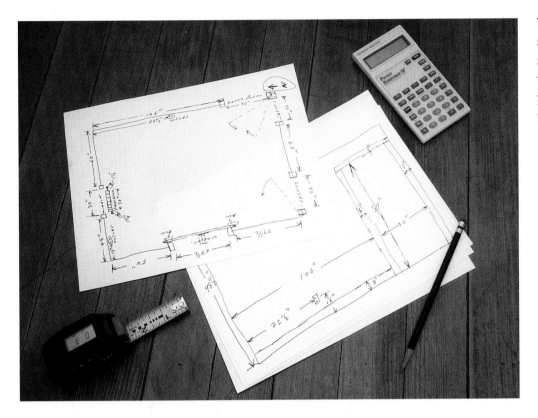

Your finished sketches should look something like these. Double-check your measurements for accuracy.

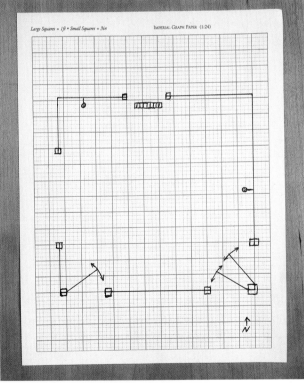

Plot all the features of your room on the floor plan. Include electrical outlets, heat sources, and the swings of the doors.

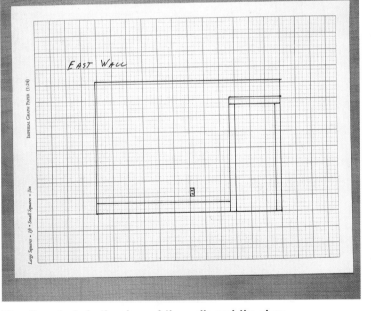

Elevations include the sizes of the walls and the sizes and locations of features such as doors and molding.

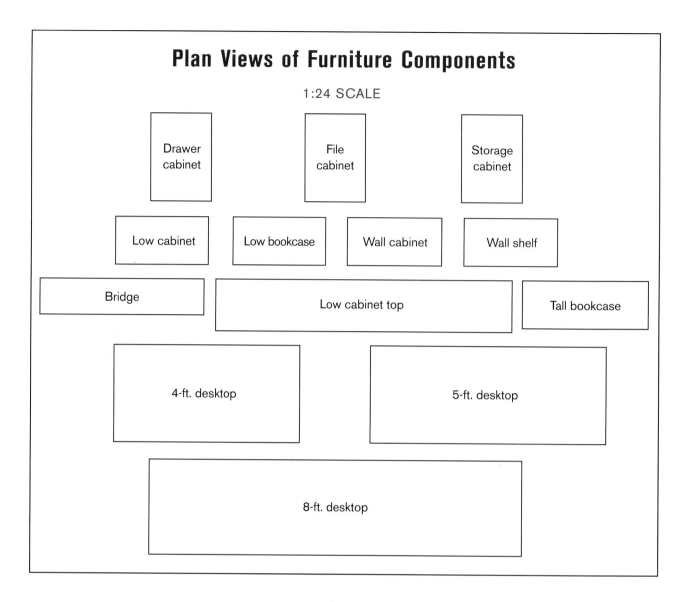

Plan Views of Furniture Components

1:24 SCALE

| Drawer cabinet | File cabinet | Storage cabinet |

| Low cabinet | Low bookcase | Wall cabinet | Wall shelf |

| Bridge | Low cabinet top | Tall bookcase |

| 4-ft. desktop | 5-ft. desktop |

| 8-ft. desktop |

the illustrations above and on the facing page, which are scaled for the graph paper you used, and carefully cut out the furniture components. Make copies of the components you might want to have more of. Next, arrange the components on the scale drawings you made to determine the best layout for your room. The furniture components are designed to be flexible, so you can decide how many of which pieces you will need. Remember that although the plan views of the desktops and low cabinet top are drawn to the default lengths used in this book, these pieces can be built to any length necessary for your space. Use the following information as a guide for deciding appropriate placement and, when done, you'll have your own plan and can begin sizing and building the individual components.

Ergonomics

Before you charge ahead with your plan, you should take ergonomics into consideration; it will almost certainly affect your final decisions on the layout of your home office.

Ergonomics is the study of the range of human movement and our physical interaction with the world around us. Ergonomic research allows us to set guidelines based on the average size and range of motion of a typical person. Ergonomic questions and the answers to them used to be relatively simple: How high should a chair or desk be? How much room does a person need to write

Elevations of Furniture Components

1:24 SCALE

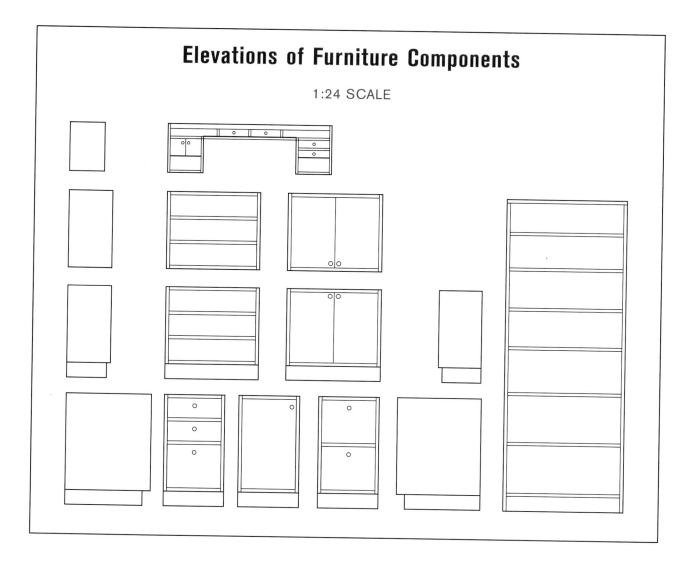

comfortably at a desk? Should a task chair be the same height as a side chair? I've designed the furniture for this office using the results of this sort of ergonomic research—for example, the desktop height and depth accommodate the average person's seating and reach.

Today, however, the issues are much more complex. A lot is going on in a home office, especially one with a computer and all its associated peripherals. Many of our spaces have to do double duty. We need space on our desks for a computer (or at least for the keyboard, mouse, and monitor), but we also need space for papers around the computer. Anyone who has ever had to copy something from paper into a computer knows what I mean. We seem to be perpetually crowded, and crowding doesn't make us healthy or efficient.

To make the home office functional, we must choose the right desk and chair and position the furniture and equipment to maximize efficiency and minimize physical effort and discomfort. Your home office should be designed with practicality as well as comfort in mind. This requires careful planning and analysis; in other words, the office needs to be designed ergonomically.

Before making any decisions, think about how you work and what your physical requirements are. Doing this now will not only save you time and expense but also, more importantly, will help you avoid long-term strains and injury from using badly designed or incorrectly positioned products. Think about the amount of time you'll spend in this space, how long you'll sit at your desk, how often you'll get up, and what items you need around you. What kind of equipment is

ERGONOMIC CHECKLIST FOR CHAIRS

True lumbar back support Maintains the natural curvature of the hollow of the back.

Waterfall edge Relieves pressure on the blood vessels of the mid-thigh and prevents numb legs, cold feet, and varicose veins. The forward edge of the seat should slope gently downward, and should not press against your thigh.

Padding Less is more. Too much padding makes getting in and out of your chair difficult and defeats the other ergonomic features.

Mobility The chair should roll effortlessly. Five-spoked bases make it safe.

Armrests Allow your chair rather than your upper back to support the weight of your arms while you work. Armrests are offered as an option on most office chairs. A well-designed armrest does not extend in front of the chair.

Depth Too deep a chair can be a problem for a small person. When you're sitting with your back well supported, there should be enough room for a closed fist between the edge of the chair and your knee.

Height Make sure the chair is just high enough so your thighs make a 90-degree angle with your lower legs while your feet make a 90-degree angle with the floor. Consider a footrest if the chair is too high.

Footrest This is an acceptable compromise when you're working at a high desk or on a chair that can't be lowered. Supporting your feet helps restore the natural curve of your back. Never let your feet dangle in the air. Since a footrest will limit your mobility, use a long one that permits healthy squirming.

Bargain task chairs will not provide the support you need for more than occasional use.

most important to you, and what can you afford to spend?

Seating

There is no clearer example of ergonomic design (good and bad) than chairs. I'm sure you have a nice, reasonably comfortable extra chair around your home that you may be tempted to use for your office. A dining room chair, for example, could certainly be used as an office chair for a short time. But if you intend to sit for many hours in front of your computer, you will be better off relegating this chair to visitors and purchasing a work or task chair.

A chair that adjusts to fit your body allows you to sit for hours in comfort. Unfortunately, most furniture is designed to match other furniture rather than your body, and making do with a poorly designed chair carries a price. The strain from sitting with a curved spine is approximately three times

greater than that from standing. To minimize strain, choose a chair whose back inclines inward to support your lumbar area and that moves as you stretch or lean back and forward. Ideally, the chair back should be high and wide enough to support your back and shoulders, and the chair should have armrests to take the weight off your neck and shoulders. Many office-supply stores sell very reasonably priced task chairs that look as if they will do the job, but you shouldn't be seduced by looks.

How do you feel at the end of the day? Are you exhausted and cranky or still fresh? Good ergonomics is what makes the difference. Your own body is the best measure of your needs; just allow yourself to feel what's right. You can adjust to poor working conditions for an hour or two, but in time the wrong chair, desk, or lighting will undermine even the healthiest lifestyle. The ergonomic choice is always the healthiest one.

Desks

In the virtual office, I have incorporated as much desktop area as possible. This is a good strategy because the desk is where you work and it fills up quickly. Since your desk is the center of your home office, any ergonomic improvement here will produce benefits for you all day long. Not long ago the desk was gloriously free of mechanical clutter. The only objects necessary were a small light, an inkwell, and a set of writing quills. These days, electronic office tools crowd the desktop. The personal computer vies for space with machines that copy, fax, dial and answer the telephone, and keep track of appointments.

The number of accessories grows every year. Scanners, shredders, and laser printers all claim to improve your efficiency and make your life easier. But where are they supposed to go?

Although it's expensive, a high-quality task chair (above right) will provide health and comfort benefits that more than justify the cost.

An ergonomically designed task chair (above left) is the ultimate treat you can give yourself.

Small office spaces are quickly taken over by equipment, leaving little work space and creating unproductive clutter.

Having enough room is essential if you're going to stay organized.

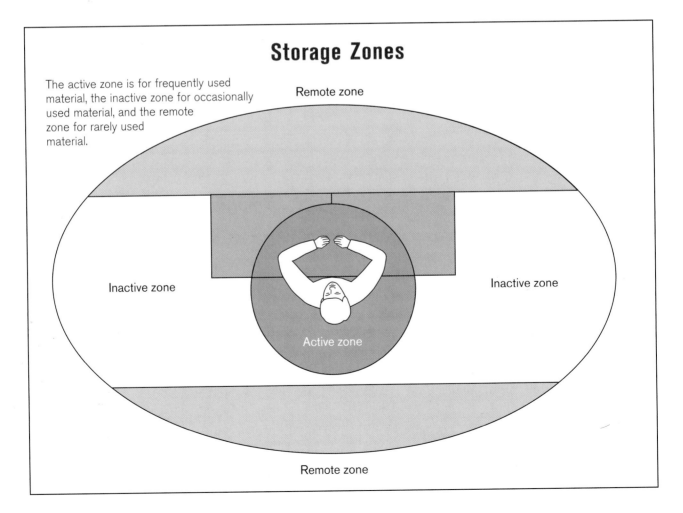

Storage Zones

The active zone is for frequently used material, the inactive zone for occasionally used material, and the remote zone for rarely used material.

Remote zone

Inactive zone

Inactive zone

Active zone

Remote zone

Organizing Your Work Space

In any office there is a constant struggle to maintain order. Proposals, letters, and invoices pile up day after day, faster than we can file them away. We strive to keep the desk clear so we can be more efficient, but sometimes we confuse efficiency with neatness. While most of us work better in neat offices, many creative and productive people seem to thrive in utter chaos. You may be one of those people who don't have to be perfectly neat to be functional. If you are, you have a right to your own clutter—that is, as long as it consists of things you need for work. Your storage system is not working if piles of junk dominate the office.

The ergonomic question is what kind of storage supports your work style? It's much easier to change your office than to change your behavior. Ergonomic storage planning requires only that you understand how you work. Begin by taking an inventory of what you actually need all the time to get your work done. Don't be surprised if you run out of space quickly. The trick is to find a way to keep these essential items from crowding you out of your office.

Computers can go a long way in solving storage problems in the home office by providing easy access to information without tedious storage and manual searching. They keep information out of sight (and out of mind) until the moment you need it. Storage alone is reason enough to have a computer.

Think of your work space as a series of storage zones (see the illustration on the facing page). The place where you sit is the active zone. Arrange things around the active zone in the order of their importance. Things you need most often should be kept visible so you can find them quickly and easily. You should be able to swivel and scoot around in your ergonomic chair to reach them. Less frequently used items can be stored in cabinets or on shelves, with light items on high shelves and heavier ones lower down. The floor is never a good storage space, and neither is your desktop. Instead of

letting small items accumulate on your desktop, find a place for them within easy reach but out of the way.

The many ergonomic issues concerning computers and their peripherals (printers, scanners, and so forth) are better dealt with separately. I will cover them more fully in chapter 2.

In a poorly organized work space, it's all too easy for papers and books to disappear. Searching for what you need isn't an efficient use of your time.

In an uncluttered work space, papers and books are clearly visible on shelves.

Lighting and Computers

NOW THAT YOU HAVE MAPPED out your physical space and planned a comfortable, efficient, and ergonomically sound environment, I'll take some time to explore lighting and computers in more depth. These two areas pose the greatest challenges in designing a healthy work environment. Work-space lighting has always been a problem, and most people know it requires attention—after all, we have to be able to see what we are doing. Computers arrived more recently on the office scene (even though the functions we use them for aren't new at all), so many people are less aware of their effect on the work environment. You'll be able to work much more comfortably and safely if you give careful thought to both of these subjects.

Your Eyes at Work

Proper lighting is essential for healthy eyes, and few things will affect your day-to-day health and productivity faster than poor lighting. Too little light can actually be dangerous to your health. Studies of regions with long, dark winters have demonstrated that light deprivation leads to health problems such as depression and weight gain, known collectively as seasonal affective disorder (SAD). The cheerful moods we associate with sunny weather are directly tied to light exposure. Natural light in your office can make a decisive difference in your mood. On the other hand, simply flooding a room with light will not automatically make it a healthy work environment.

Glare and shadow are surprisingly similar conditions. Shadow, or lack of light, causes eyestrain by reducing the contrast our eyes need to see objects. Glare or reflected light, such as daylight bouncing off a shiny desktop, also reduces contrast. As far as your eyes are concerned, it seems as if there is too little light instead of too much. You need to be able to control your light sources, whether they are natural or artificial.

To control glare, make sure no direct or reflected bright light can reach your eyes

while you're working. Eliminate large, glossy, highly reflective surfaces, and use diffused lights for general illumination. If you have north-facing windows, control the natural light in your room with semitransparent sun-reflective shades. Windows that face south, east, or west require opaque shades to block direct sun.

Shadows are usually caused by objects blocking a light source that is directly behind you. Smaller shadows may be caused by parts of your body. To prevent your hand from constantly shadowing your work, use a light that originates on the left if you're right-handed or on the right if you're left-handed.

A floor-standing torchère provides good ceiling-focused bounced light, but it takes up floor space.

standing, or wall- or ceiling-mounted adjustable lamp can provide task lighting. Your choice of ambient lighting depends on personal preference and the atmosphere you wish to create in your workplace.

If your work requires natural light but no window is nearby, consider a lamp with a halogen bulb.

Ambient lighting

Ambient lighting in commercial office spaces is typically supplied by ceiling lights (most often fluorescent) and sometimes by a combination of ceiling and natural light. In your home office, however, you have other choices. If you have good natural light available, you may be able to arrange your office to take advantage of it. Other options include floor lamps and wall sconces. A good lighting plan allows you to blend these sources or use them independently.

If you choose to install ceiling-based lighting, I would suggest not using fluorescent fixtures. They produce a harsh, cold, bluish light that is prone to flicker. However, if you already have fluorescent fixtures installed in your space, consider replacing the tubes with full-spectrum models. These produce a light that is more similar to daylight and, although they're more costly, they are significantly better than standard fluorescent tubes. Fluorescent fixtures should be shielded with louvers or other diffusers and, if possible, fitted with dimmers (most of the older fluorescent fixtures don't allow dimmer attachments).

If you already have incandescent ceiling fixtures or choose to install them, attach them to dimmers. If you have multiple light sources, set them up so that small groups of lights can be switched on independently. This is vital if you're a computer user. Each light should also be fitted with a diffuser, which is essential for glare-free illumination.

Ceiling lighting is not the only source of ambient light. Another option is a light that shines upward. Wall sconces or a floor-standing torchère can provide ceiling-focused, evenly diffused background light and make an attractive room feature. Be sure

Types of Lighting

Generally speaking, you need two kinds of lighting in any work environment: ambient lighting, which provides general illumination, and task lighting, which is for a specific task. You need to plan carefully to achieve the right lighting levels in your work area. Light that is either too strong or too weak can be counterproductive. Very low light levels impair efficiency and concentration, while excessive brightness tires your eyes, leading to eyestrain and headaches, and casts glare on the computer screen. The best lighting combines task lighting, which throws a directed beam onto your work area, with some form of diffused ambient light. A clip-on, free-to consider glare, as you would with any lighting choice, and try to avoid harsh light.

Uplighters are not suitable for rooms with dark ceilings. Floor lamps shining down can provide warmer ambient light and usually do not cause glare since they are shaded. Either the lamp itself or the outlet it is connected to should be supplied with a dimmer.

A freestanding lamp that illuminates both above and below is a good, flexible, portable source of general diffused light. This is an option if you do not want to go to the expense and inconvenience of altering your electrical wiring to install ceiling- or wall-mounted lights.

Task lighting

Trying to make do with ambient lighting alone is a sure recipe for frustration. True task lighting is adjustable both in direction and intensity. Natural light is not suitable for task light because it's difficult to control. Although artificial lighting can spread glare as easily as unfiltered sunlight, it's much easier to configure to specific tasks. Don't confuse

ERGONOMIC LAMPS

MOST ADJUSTABLE LAMPS fight back when you adjust them. Pull the lamp head 2 ft. across your desk and it moves back 2 in. And no matter where the lamp is positioned, every attempt to illuminate your work seems to create serious glare. To further complicate matters, in less than five minutes the lamp becomes too hot to touch. You then push it out of your way, "adapt" to a single setting, and press on with light in your face.

For a lamp to be ergonomically sound, adjusting it must be effortless and utterly predictable; the lamp head should remain cool after hours of use. Look for strong, evenly distributed light that can be directed precisely where it's needed. The light should not shine directly in your eyes, and there should be no annoying glare. An ergonomic desk lamp has a way of banishing headaches and eyestrain; the moment you turn one on, you can feel the difference.

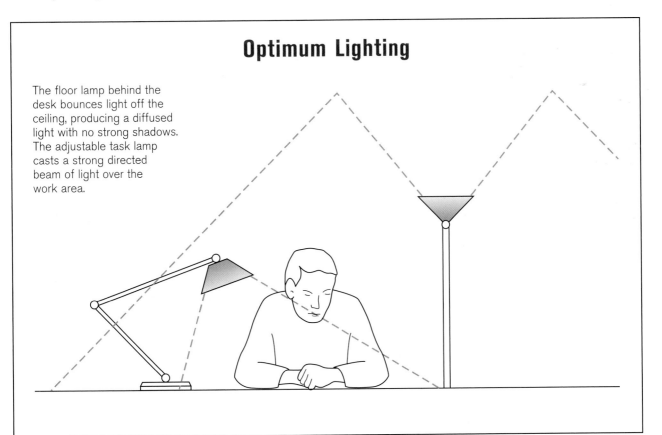

Optimum Lighting

The floor lamp behind the desk bounces light off the ceiling, producing a diffused light with no strong shadows. The adjustable task lamp casts a strong directed beam of light over the work area.

TASK LIGHTING OPTIONS

EFFECTIVE LIGHTING can help make the difference between efficient all-day production and early afternoon fatigue. For best overall results, mix focused task lighting with plenty of ambient light.

SPECIALTY LAMP: Single-purpose lights like this ECLIPSE Computer Light work extremely well for their intended tasks. However, be sure the light you choose is what you need and will perform as expected, or it will just add to desk clutter.

DOWNLIGHTER: A floor-standing or ceiling-mounted lamp provides medium light distribution and removes a cord from the desktop. Floor models are portable but take up floor space and can be easily knocked over. Ceiling-mounted lights are less flexible since their position is usually fixed.

DESK LAMP: A flexible-arm desk lamp casts a strong, directed, easily adjusted light onto the immediate work area with no direct glare from the light source. However, it can take up valuable desktop space and can be unstable if it sits on a base. Desk lamps are best attached or clamped to the desktop.

TABLE LAMP: As a source of soft, diffused lighting, a traditional table lamp can soften the office atmosphere with its domestic look. Table lamps are less expensive than floor lamps and can be easily moved around. They don't cause glare because their bulbs are not exposed. However, they are smaller and less robust than other office lights and may illuminate a very small area. They may also look too homey for the workplace.

CLIP-ON SPOTLIGHT: A cost-effective and easily movable clip-on spotlight provides a strong, directed beam. When it's attached to a shelf, it takes up no desktop space and cannot be knocked over. However, it lacks the flexibility of a desk light and must be unclipped to change light direction. The trailing cord can be unsightly.

task lights, which are designed to illuminate a specific job, with movable lamps, decorative wall lights, or general ceiling lights. A good task light has an opaque shade to prevent direct light from reaching your eyes and will illuminate your work and little else.

While ambient light sets the mood in your office, task lighting can be controlled more precisely and makes detailed work easier. No matter how brightly lit your office is, you will benefit greatly from task lighting.

Balanced Lighting

Most commercial office spaces provide too much ambient lighting and little or no task lighting. But simply substituting a desk lamp for those annoying ceiling fluorescents won't do much for your eyes. The pupil of the eye dilates in low light and contracts in bright light. The constant dilating and contracting of the pupil caused by putting a single task light in a dim room is a major cause of serious eye fatigue. Make sure the light on your work area is balanced elsewhere in the room. Task lighting should be no more than five times as bright as the overall room light.

Here are some points to consider:
- Place your task light on the opposite side from your writing hand to prevent shadows falling on your work as you write.
- If you regularly suffer from eyestrain and headaches while working, the level of light in your work area may be insufficient.
- Inadequate lighting can lead to bad posture if, for example, you have to sit hunched up in front of a computer screen to see it. This, in turn, may result in neck, shoulder, and back strain.
- When you're choosing lamps and fixtures, be aware of the kind of light generated from different bulbs. Traditional tungsten lighting casts warm-colored light but generates a lot of heat. Also, the bulbs require frequent replacement. Many modern light fixtures are fitted with compact fluorescent tubes, which are miniaturized versions of the lighting commonly used in offices. These consume 20 percent less energy and throw out less heat than tungsten bulbs,

A desktop covered with equipment is the downside of the computer revolution.

but the light is cool and somewhat harsh. Halogen bulbs provide the most natural color balance and have the advantage of supplying a great deal of light from a relatively small source.

To prevent eye fatigue, combine lamps that provide generalized, indirect illumination with adjustable desktop lighting. Light should be strongest in your work area and weaker and diffused elsewhere. Try to achieve a gradation in light contrast levels from the

PROBLEM LIGHTING CHECKLIST

IF YOU CAN ANSWER "yes" to any of these questions, you may need to adjust your office lighting.

- While you're working, is the light source visible to your naked eye?
- Is the light source reflected into your eyes?
- Does the light cause a visible reflection on your work surface?
- Are shadows cast across your work area?

desk to the background, since this is easier on your eyes than an abrupt change or none at all. Eliminate bright or shiny desk surfaces and repaint walls that reflect too much light. Light-colored ceilings, matte walls, medium-colored furniture, and dark floors control glare best.

Personal Computers

The pundits who promised that the computer would bring about the "paperless office" were wrong. In fact, we generate more paper with our computers than we ever could without them. E-mail, for example, allows us to send documents to dozens of people with one click of a mouse—and all these people seem strangely compelled to print out the documents and file them away. Any space that we *have* managed to save by reducing paper files has been taken up by the rows of computer equipment and accessories marching along our desktops. Though the computer has made us more productive and efficient, it is definitely a mixed blessing.

Buying a computer can be the realization of a dream or the beginning of a nightmare. Few endeavors are as frustrating or depend so much on an accurate understanding of ergonomics. First, the dream: You have a tireless servant. The computer can be your proofreader, librarian, financial advisor, stockbroker, project coordinator, and newscaster. Using it, you acquire a sense of independence and confidence. Every day you are able to explore new worlds. It adds little freedoms, too: Your spelling is corrected, your address files are updated, and your checkbook is balanced. At its best, the computer can transform your life by replacing the post office, eliminating the daily commute, and creating flexible work hours.

But the same computer can turn your job into a distressing ordeal, and the technology can take a physical toll. To minimize the physical costs of computer ownership, you need to pay attention to a few facts and listen to your body.

Whether you work on a personal computer in the office or at home, the essential ergonomic question is how does it feel to

A friendly user interface is as important as speed, power, and performance in a desktop computer.

work with this machine and its peripherals all day? Think first about the way the computer itself feels, and then deal with the peripherals.

Computer ads, like automobile ads, emphasize speed, power, and performance while ignoring the fact that human beings must operate the machines. Forget power and speed for the moment and ask, simply, how hard is the machine to use? (Or, in computerese, how friendly is the user interface?) Software designers have made their interfaces much friendlier by allowing users to point to icons instead of typing strings of arcane commands. However, you interface with the hardware as well as the software. Friendly

hardware interfaces can make the difference between success and frustration in your office. You can't mistake the feel of an ergonomic interface; it allows the beginner to feel confident, the casual user to get up to speed quickly, and the experienced user to access the full power of a computer efficiently.

Computer Ergonomics

In addition to the user interface, consider your physical interactions with your computer. I have divided these into two rough categories: input devices and screens.

An ergonomic keyboard can reduce the incidence of hand and wrist injuries.

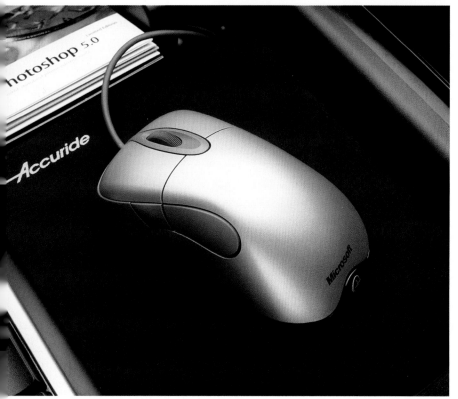

An ergonomic mouse helps keep your hand in a natural position.

THE CONVENTIONAL WISDOM

THE ONLY CONSTANT in the science of ergonomics is change. Much of the position advice of five years ago is obsolete now. Turf battles are raging among physical therapists, ergonomic experts, and orthopedists over who can give the most authoritative advice on matters of body position. So, get your medical advice from medical professionals, but realize that even they may not know the latest. Stay fluid, keep moving, and don't sit or stand still.

Input devices

These include keyboards, mice, and their alternatives, such as trackballs and tablets. Many new keyboard designs offer significant ergonomic benefits over the standard design. You should preview the input devices when you're purchasing a new computer and also consider upgrading the ones you have if you already own a computer. How they feel, especially during repeated use, is extremely important. Don't shortchange yourself here; many of these items are inexpensive and can make you much more comfortable while you're using your computer.

Many accessories are available to help you use keyboards and mice repetitively without injuring yourself. Wrist rests and arm supports are helpful, and keyboard support arms and trays can position the keyboard to conform better to your individual posture.

Screens and lighting

Since the advent of television, we have been warned that prolonged viewing of illuminated screens is hazardous to our eyes. The pervasiveness of computers in our work and private lives has made matters worse. We now have a documented illness (computer vision syndrome, or CVS) associated with the use of computer screens. Strictly speaking, CVS is a repetitive stress injury caused by the act of refocusing the eyes on a computer screen image again and again. (Experts compare the repetitive refocusing required of computing to squeezing your hand hard 30,000 times a day.)

Even worse, the blink reflex, one of the fastest in the body, is brought to a standstill when you stare into a computer monitor. On average, you blink 22 times per minute. When you're reading a book, the blink rate decreases to 12 times per minute. At the computer, it falls to just four times per minute, increasing tear evaporation, doubling the exposure of your sensitive corneas, and resulting in drier, more irritated eyes. The vast majority of computers are used for word processing or manipulation of text or numbers. Most of us would not read a book for hours in an uncomfortable chair without proper light, yet this is essentially what many of us do when we work at our computers.

Larger screens or monitors are easier to view than older, smaller computer screens.

KEYBOARDS: QWERTY VERSUS DVORAK

FOR MORE THAN A CENTURY, typists have been using the inefficient QWERTY keyboard (named after the row of letters on the top left-hand side of the keyboard) that was designed to work around the mechanical limitations of early typewriters.

To transfer a letter from keyboard to paper, mechanical typewriters relied on a complex network of cams and gears to propel metal spokes

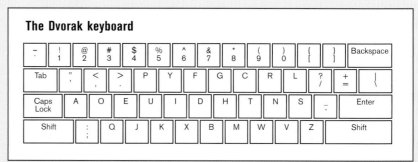

The QWERTY keyboard

with tiny characters fastened to their ends against a narrow fabric ribbon. With so many intricately linked moving parts, a fast typist could easily outpace the flailing spokes, bringing on massive key jams.

These typewriters were also a maintenance nightmare. Spokes had to be untangled and straightened, ribbons adjusted, tiny pieces of type cleaned, and the whole network of gears and levers needed regular oiling and fine-tuning. The faster a person typed, the more maintenance was required and the more often parts failed. Given the limited technology of the time, the simplest solution seemed to be a compromise. Manufacturers realized that the only way to save typewriters was to slow down typists. The QWERTY keyboard was born. It was one of the slowest possible keyboard layouts.

The QWERTY keyboard persists even though the manual typewriter has all but disappeared. Manufacturers of computers, which have no moving parts between keyboard and printer, have so far refused to abandon the unwieldy QWERTY system. Since millions of QWERTY touch typists have made it the standard, most people simply learn the keyboard that's supplied with the computer. But you don't have to. If you're still a hunt-and-peck typist, it's worth considering converting your keyboard to the Dvorak system. Typically this means pasting new key caps onto your keyboard and installing software that is readily available for most computers.

The Dvorak keyboard, named for its inventor, Dr. August Dvorak, maximizes typing efficiency. The

The Dvorak keyboard

keyboard is designed so that the most common digraphs (two-letter combinations, such as "ed") in English occur with a minimum of "hurdling" (jumping over keys) and makes use of stronger fingers rather than weaker ones. Dvorak estimated that the fingers of an average typist travel between 12 and 20 miles a day on a QWERTY keyboard, while the same text on his keyboard would require only about one mile of travel. Hurdling and awkward keystroke combinations are responsible for most of the common errors typists make.

As I have already discussed, proper room lighting is essential, but computer monitor screens present specific problems. Screen size is possibly the easiest to overcome. Early computer screens were quite small, but now there are many more screen options. The state of the art in monitors today is generally superb, and the cost of large monitors and flat-screen LCD monitors (which are typically easier to view) continues to drop. There is now less of a reason to lean forward and squint to see a screen that is too small or to settle for a poor-quality screen.

Because computer screens are backlit, you may assume that you can view them in darkened rooms, but this extreme contrast is very taxing on the eyes. Computers are best viewed in well-lit rooms. Also, many monitor manufacturers' default settings for contrast and brightness are much too harsh. These values are adjustable and the correct settings depend on room and task lighting and on your personal comfort preferences.

Glare is another common problem. If you're experiencing glare on the computer screen, check the location and position of the monitor as well as the room lighting. If the lighting can't be changed, try moving the

monitor. Most monitors swivel and tilt, and sometimes this is all that is needed. There are also lighting fixtures such as the ECLIPSE Computer Light especially designed to deal with glare (see p. 22).

Remember that not only your eyes are affected by poor lighting and screens that are too bright, too dark, too small, or poorly placed. Awkward or tense environments of any kind always affect posture. Solving a lighting problem will minimize not only eyestrain but also the neck and back pain associated with it, resulting in a more ergonomically correct workplace.

Computer Accessories

The marketplace is full of computer peripherals and accessories that manufacturers would like you to believe are indispensable. Look at your needs, research the products well, and choose the ones that make sense for you. Above all, choose equipment that is user-friendly. Consider how you will interact with this equipment. Is it easy to use and understand? Once you purchase it, consider carefully where you're going to place it. Try to place the telephone, fax, printer, and other

Three of the most common pieces of peripheral equipment are the fax, printer, and scanner.

This combination machine, replacing printer, fax, scanner, and copier, could free up space in your office.

This CPU holder frees up desk space. It fits under the desktop and slides out and swivels for access.

machines so you aren't craning your neck or twisting your back to use them. Arrange and rearrange them until you're happy with their placement. Since it isn't good for you to sit in one position too long, you may want to put some equipment where you will have to get out of your chair to use it.

Once you determine what equipment you need, you may wonder where you are going to put it all and still leave room to work. Research your choices. Think about multifunction machines—the one pictured above, for example, combines printer, fax, copy, and scan functions in one relatively small machine. Or if all you need is, say, a printer and a scanner, try to find small machines. Their size is limited only by the size of the paper you choose to use.

You can also place many of these components, as well as your computer's CPU (the main case to which your keyboard, mouse, and monitor are connected), somewhere other than your desktop. The major limitation is the length of the connecting cords. Some components require the use of relatively short cords, but others can be located quite far from your computer. Placing a CPU under the desktop or a printer inside a base cabinet can free up a great deal of work space.

MOBILE COMPUTING

AT FIRST GLANCE, the diminutive laptop or notebook computer seems an ideal solution for freeing up space. It's light, thin, compact, and portable, and it has a small footprint. But whether or not a laptop will work for you depends on how you plan to use it.

Some of its most attractive features have distinct ergonomic drawbacks: The small LCD screen becomes difficult to read during long sessions. The cramped keyboard attached to the screen recalls the inflexibility of the first one-piece desktop computers, which forced users to bend and squint while they worked. Finally, the fixed-position pointing device, while handy for short sessions, reduces flexibility. Think of a laptop as a traveling computer and you will appreciate its convenience. However, if you also plan to use it as your main machine, consider adding a larger screen, a detached ergonomic keyboard, and a separate pointing device such as a mouse or trackball. All of these accessories can be easily disconnected for travel.

But maybe even a laptop is more than you need. Today even smaller traveling devices are available. PDAs (personal digital assistants) are perfect for storing addresses and phone num-

bers, notes, and even games to while away spare moments at the airport. If they don't have enough computing power for you, take a look at the tiny palm-type computers, some of which are barely bigger than a PDA (see the photo below). Although they are somewhat limited, palmtops provide many of the features of a full-sized desktop computer. Most of them can link and communicate with your home computer and will fit easily in your pocket.

Laptop computers are great for travel but don't fully replace desktop computers.

Palm-type computers provide many of the features of a full-sized computer or laptop in a pocket-sized package.

CHAPTER 3

Materials, Hardware, and Accessories

ALTHOUGH YOU HAVE NOW made a great deal of progress in planning your home office, several practical issues still remain to be addressed before you start building. I've made some choices in the project chapters about materials and hardware to be used for construction, and you could, of course, simply follow these. However, since I could not have possibly anticipated all the distinctive features of your office, you may find it helpful to look first at the options presented in this chapter. While these options don't exhaust all the possibilities, they should at least point you in the right direction. You don't want to build a beautiful suite of furniture only to find that the glare on your desktop is intolerable or that you can't run a wire from point A to point B without mangling it.

Materials

Is your desktop giving you a headache? Furniture stores are bursting with inexpensive, prefabricated white desktops intended to complement white bookcases, file cabinets, and chairs. Look at a white desktop next to a matte gray one, and note the relief you feel when your eyes shift from the bright white to the soothing gray. Desk surfaces were less of a problem a century ago when natural woods were the only choice. Medium-tone, natural wood colors are close to ideal as long as the final finish isn't high gloss.

The warm, natural-finished cherry used for all the projects in this book is, in my opinion, close to perfect. It is dark enough to be fairly nonreflective but not so dark that it affects the lighting in the room. Other good choices would be oak or butternut. I prefer to avoid woods that are too dark (such as walnut) or too light (such as maple), but you may disagree. There's plenty of room for personal preference, and room lighting also plays a role. If you choose a laminated surface, stick to medium colors and matte finishes.

I've used mainly cabinet-grade plywood to construct the project pieces, along with

High-quality plywood has a decorative face veneer covering a stable
core made of veneer layers. Each layer has grain running at right
angles to the grain of the layers above and below.

solid wood for desktop edges and other small
parts. Plywood is a good choice for several
reasons. It comes in large sheets, eliminating
the need to glue up boards for parts such as
cabinet sides. It is a stable material, so there
are no wood movement issues to deal with,
and it's attractive enough, especially when
you consider that much of the furniture will
be hidden beneath desktops where no one
will see it. Finally, some of the construction
techniques presented (for the desktops, for
example) will not work using solid wood. If
you want to use solid wood, restrict it to
doors (see "Style Option: Frame-and-Panel
Doors" on pp. 88–89) and perhaps some
frame-and-panel add-ons to dress up the
show sides of certain cabinets.

Functional Hardware

The subject of hardware could easily fill a
book by itself, but I've limited the discussion
to the types of hardware used in the project
chapters. For our purposes, hardware can be
divided into two categories: functional and
decorative. I'll start with the functional side.

Drawer glides

There are many types and brands of drawer glides to choose from. A high-quality drawer glide from a reputable manufacturer is your best choice. Choose a glide that has a smooth, accurate, and quiet extension. For file drawers, you will need a glide with a load rating of at least 75 lb. (100 lb. is preferable). Glides for accessory drawers can be lighter weight. In all cases, however, I recommend full-extension glides, which provide better access to the interior of the drawer, rather than three-quarter-extension glides. This is especially critical when you have an over-hanging top, which makes getting to the back of the top drawer even more difficult. Extension is also important with inset drawers, which I've used for the projects in this book. Since the drawer glide starts behind the drawer front, you have to subtract the thickness of the drawer front from the amount of extension.

The Accuride glides I've used in the projects (see Sources of Supply on p. 152) are over-travel glides. These glides allow the drawer to extend out more than the length of the drawer. They are generally more expensive since they are more mechanically complicated. They are also less compact than most regular full-extension glides, so they may not fit on shallow drawers. Nearly all drawer glides take up ½ in. of space between the drawer and the cabinet side, so your drawer box will be 1 in. narrower than the inside of the cabinet. If you plan on using drawer glides of a different size, be sure to take this into account when building the projects.

One last suggestion—this is a personal preference, so take it for what it's worth. I like glides with a black finish. Not too long ago glides came only in bare metal or zinc finish, neither of which is very attractive. Then came the Euro glides, which were available in almond or white. These colors look fine with kitchen cabinets but not with more formal furniture. Most major manufacturers now have glides available in black. I think black is much more professional looking and worth seeking out.

Hanging file systems

A number of hanging file systems are commercially available, and I have even made my own by setting metal or plastic strips into grooves in the tops of the drawer sides. But in my opinion the two easiest to install and most readily available hanging file systems are Pendaflex and Slip-On Folder hangers. Both of these systems will fit into the project furniture. Although the hanging file system may seem like a trivial part of the project, it can dictate the size of your drawers and consequently the size of the cabinets they fit into (see "File Drawers" on p. 60–61). If you buy a system other than the two I've mentioned, be sure to take this into account before you start building.

The Pendaflex system, which is available in any office-supply store, is a metal frame that slips into the drawer box. The Pendaflex frame comes in both letter and legal sizes, and the rails can be cut to fit either the depth

The Pendaflex hanging file system uses rods to support the tabs of hanging files.

or the width of your drawer, depending on how you wish to hang your files. This is important if you wish to store legal files in the drawers in the project cabinets. Since the width of these cabinets is designed for letter-size files, you will have to place legal files side to side rather than front to back.

The Slip-On Folder hangers (see Sources of Supply on p. 152) are plastic extrusions that are cut to length and slipped over the sides of the drawers. The file folders rest and slide on these extrusions. As an option, you can buy small clips that attach to the extrusions and hold thin metal bars. As in the Pendaflex system, this lets you fit legal files in the drawers side to side.

Keyboard trays and slides

Keyboard trays and slides are often viewed as a way to keep the mouse and keyboard off the desktop, but they do much more than

The Slip-On Folder hanging file system uses a plastic extrusion that fits over the drawer sides.

The Slip-On Folder is also sold with accessory bars that allow you to fit legal-size files into narrow drawers.

that. While there is nothing wrong with placing the mouse and keyboard on the desktop (as long as the desktop is at an appropriate height or within the adjustment range of your chair), a properly chosen, installed, and adjusted keyboard tray or slide can make a huge difference to your health and comfort. It can improve your posture, help reduce repetitive stress injuries, and provide a better viewing arrangement by positioning you further back from the computer screen.

You have a choice between keyboard trays and keyboard slides (see the photos at right). The best way to choose one of these products is to try it out. Go to an office-supply store or consult your friends and co-workers who are using them. The tray or slide you choose should feel stable and allow adjustments to the height and angle of the keyboard and mouse. It should also provide a wrist rest that is adjustable, and, ideally, independent of the keyboard. Keep in mind that most keyboard trays and slides reduce knee clearance, some of them significantly.

Hinges

There are hundreds of hinges on the market. I chose Lamello Duplex hinges for the projects (see Sources of Supply on p. 152) because they are relatively easy to install and have a traditional look. But any standard butt hinge will work as well.

You may also wish to use a European or concealed hinge (shown in the top photo on p. 38) for a more contemporary look. These hinges are fairly simple to install and they're adjustable, which makes it easy to correct the hang of the door. They've become very popular and, as a result, they are now easy to find (see Sources of Supply). Be aware, however, that concealed hinges are somewhat more difficult to install on inset doors (the kind we're building in the projects) than on standard overlay doors. Sometimes you need to use rather large hinges or hinge bases, which can take up room inside the cabinet. So think ahead and consider how your choice of hinges might affect the construction or use of your cabinets.

Keyboard trays are like drawers for your keyboard. They are generally more stable but less adjustable than keyboard slides.

Keyboard slides pivot from a single mounting point and have flexible adjustments. They can interfere with your knees, however, and feel less stable than keyboard trays.

Knockdown fasteners

Many different types of knockdown (KD) fasteners are available, but for the sake of brevity, I will discuss only the fasteners used in this book and one variant. KD fasteners such as the connector bolts and Euro screw (sometimes called Confirmat screw) can be invaluable when you want to securely connect two cases and still be able to separate them for moving.

Screws of all types could be considered KD fasteners—after all, they connect parts and can be removed and reinserted. However, some fasteners are designed specifically for this purpose. The Euro screw (shown at the bottom of the photo below) is one of them. When used in a properly drilled hole (a special bit is needed), it can be removed and reinserted many times without losing its holding strength. This screw is used in the projects to connect most of the bases to their respective cabinets.

European hinges are extremely adjustable but are not suitable for a traditional look.

The connector bolt and cap nut (top) can be seen from both sides; the connector bolt/threaded insert combination (center) is visible from only one side; and the deep threads on the Euro screw (bottom) allow it to be reused many times without loss of holding strength.

Connector bolts are exactly what their name implies. They are used with either cap nuts (shown at the top of the bottom photo on the facing page) or threaded inserts (shown in the center of the bottom photo on the facing page) to connect two parts together. In the projects in this book, I used the bolts with threaded inserts for all the connections that don't use the Euro screw. I've chosen the threaded inserts because only one side of the connection shows, making the bolt easier to hide. However, the connector bolt is much stronger with the cap nut, so you can use that if you don't mind seeing it.

Adjustable shelf supports

The method I use most often for adjustable shelves is line boring with shelf pins. It's very discreet and reasonably elegant. In the projects in this book, I used simple, straight 5mm pins, but there are many other options. Most differ only in looks, but some are made for special applications, such as glass shelves.

You will need a jig to allow you to space and bore the holes evenly. You can choose one of the many commercially available jigs (one is shown in photo A on p. 74) or you can make your own. Shopmade jigs wear and get sloppy after a few uses, but for occasional use they are fine. Line boring is easy. If you are careful with your layout, the process is very fast. Once the holes are bored (standard hole diameter choices are ¼ in. and 5mm), you need only insert the shelf pins of your choice.

Decorative Hardware

Think of decorative hardware—those eye-catching bits of hardware that set off your furniture—as jewelry for your cabinets. Knobs, pulls, and handles are the most common types of decorative hardware, but hinges may be decorative as well. In the projects, I used the same chrome pulls on all of the pieces for two reasons: They look good with the Lamello Duplex hinges shown in photo D on p. 76, and they're simple and generic. You can choose among tens of thousands of decorative pulls; some of the more

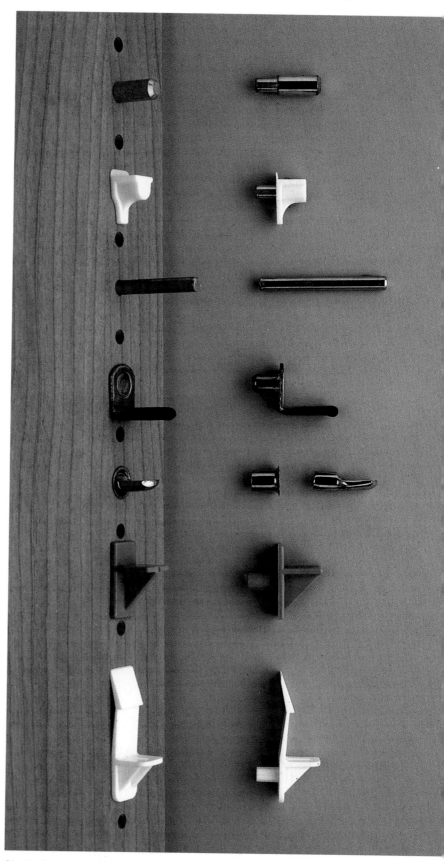

Shelf pins are available in many shapes, styles, and finishes.

contemporary styles available from Häfele Furniture Hardware (see Sources of Supply on p. 152) are shown in the photo at left.

The variation among hinges isn't nearly so wide. Aside from size differences, one butt hinge looks pretty much like another. However, you do want to make sure the era and finish of the hardware you use is consistent. Look at the example in the photo below of an antique finished, Mission-style hinge next to a Craftsman-style pull (both available from Rockler Woodworking and Hardware; see Sources of Supply). While these two pieces of hardware complement each other, the hinge would look out of place next to a shiny contemporary pull, just as the pull would look out of place next to the hinges in our projects.

This collection of contemporary hardware is just a small sampling of the thousands of decorative pulls and handles available.

Substituting period hardware for contemporary can greatly alter the look of your cabinets.

Accessories

So many well-designed, easy-to-add accessories are available from woodworking suppliers that I question whether it's worth the time it would take to build them. For this reason, I haven't customized the drawers and cabinets in the project chapters or presented projects such as CD holders. Besides, planning and building your home office is a big enough project without constructing your own accessories. Also, you may not know at the outset which accessories you'll want or need.

It is much easier to add accessories as you become aware of the need for them. You can purchase a small accessory or pencil drawer such as the one shown in the top photo at right and install it where you need it in a few minutes. The same is true for CD holders. Many commercially available CD holders are modular (see the photo below), so you can add to them as the need arises. Inexpensive organizers for the small items you want close at hand are cleverly designed to fit in out-of-the-way places and would be extremely difficult to construct yourself (see the bottom photo at right).

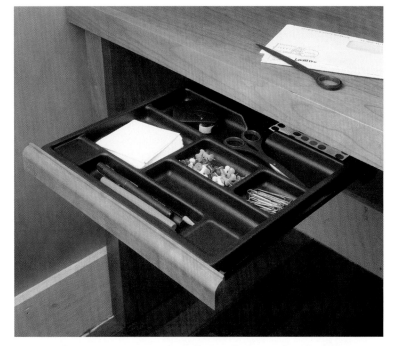

This small accessory drawer installs in minutes under a counter or desktop and takes a wood front for an attractive appearance.

This swiveling radius organizer is designed to fit in out-of-the-way places.

Modular CD holders can grow with your CD collection and can hold other items as well.

Wire channels and troughs give easy access to wires while containing them neatly, preventing the unsightly curtain of wires below a desk.

Wire grommets protect wires while neatly trimming unsightly holes in the desktop. They are available in a wide assortment of sizes and in several colors.

Managing Wiring

Computers and associated equipment create a tangle of wiring. While bringing equipment—computers, phones, printers, fax machines, and so forth—into your home office is relatively easy, preparing the space for this invasion is another problem. Most home office equipment requires little power and fits comfortably in limited space. However, the many connections from one piece of equipment to another, as well as from the equipment to the telephone system, can create a wiring nightmare.

You almost certainly have at least one phone line in your home already, but your computer will include a modem for connecting to the Internet, and you'll probably also need a fax machine. You could allow the fax to share your voice line, but that prohibits talking on the line and sending or receiving faxes at the same time. You could also do your faxing through your data modem using fax software, but then you couldn't connect to the Internet and send or receive faxes at the same time. To run your office comfortably, you will need a minimum of two phone lines in addition to the telephone line you started out with.

For your computer to function properly, it must be connected (obviously) to a keyboard and a mouse; that's two wires. The modem connection and printer connection require two more wires, and I haven't even mentioned the power cords for each component. The situation becomes more complicated as you add a scanner, a second printer, and so on. And things will only get worse in the future as you add high-speed data modems and all the peripherals that haven't been dreamed of yet but will be indispensable in two or three years.

Try to keep cords and wires as short as possible and routed as neatly as possible. You can find a wide variety of products designed to organize and retain wiring. These include wire channels and troughs (see the top photo at left) that contain wires en route to their destinations; cable ties and organizers (see the top photo on the facing page) that collect and restrain wires neatly; and grommets (see the bottom photo on the facing page) that dress up the holes you've created in the desktops to allow the wires through and keep the wires from chafing on the rough openings. All these products are well worth their minimal costs.

While a detailed discussion of the wiring is beyond the scope of this book (and beyond the expertise of the author) the subject deserves a brief mention. Your equipment and lighting need adequate power supplies. If your chosen office space doesn't have enough electrical outlets or if the outlets are not conveniently located, address these issues before you start building your furniture and bringing in equipment. Don't be tempted to take the easy way out and just run extension cords everywhere. Not only is this unsightly, but also trailing cords are a hazard and overloaded outlets are extremely dangerous.

Electronic equipment, and especially their connections to telephone lines, can be easily damaged by power surges such as lightning strikes. To protect against surges and against large fluctuations in the power lines them-

Neatly placed wiring not only looks better but also is safer. A surge protector is essential to protect expensive equipment.

Don't take shortcuts! Trailing cords are a hazard, and overloaded outlets are extremely dangerous.

selves, you need a surge protector (see the photo above). Surge protectors are often incorporated into outlet strips that provide fused AC power for up to six pieces of equipment along with one or more protected phone line connections and an on/off switch. These should not be confused with ordinary power strips and extension cords, which do not provide any protection.

Promoting the use of surge-protector strips may seem to contradict what I just said about "taking the easy way out." But keep in mind that not only do surge protectors provide protection, but they also are designed specifically for use with computer equipment, which draws only a small amount of power per component. Also, surge protectors aren't a substitute for adding outlets or power; it's still important to have enough of both.

Office Building Projects

CHAPTER 4

Drawer Cabinets

TO BE FUNCTIONAL, AN OFFICE or work space must be organized. Every item should be stored in its own place, close at hand when you need it. Drawers are perfect storage places, particularly for small items that tend to migrate and scatter themselves over every horizontal surface. You can store items in drawers close to their associated tasks, reducing clutter by keeping them out of sight when they aren't needed.

A wide choice of drawer configurations is available, from large file drawers to tiny pencil trays. Taking inventory of your materials will help you decide what size drawers you need and where they should be located. You can also purchase accessories to personalize your drawer storage—holders for computer discs and CDs, compartments for pens and paper clips, and so forth. With a little imagination you can customize your drawers even further. Shopmade inserts and dividers are easy to build and allow you to partition your drawer space in the way that best meets your needs.

This chapter features two of the most common drawer sizes and cabinet configurations. One unit has two file drawers, and the other unit has a file drawer with two smaller drawers above. If these aren't right for you, you can easily build drawers of different sizes to fit into the same cabinet. My sample office shown above contains two of each type of drawer cabinet, but you can build as many of these units as you need.

File Drawer Pedestal

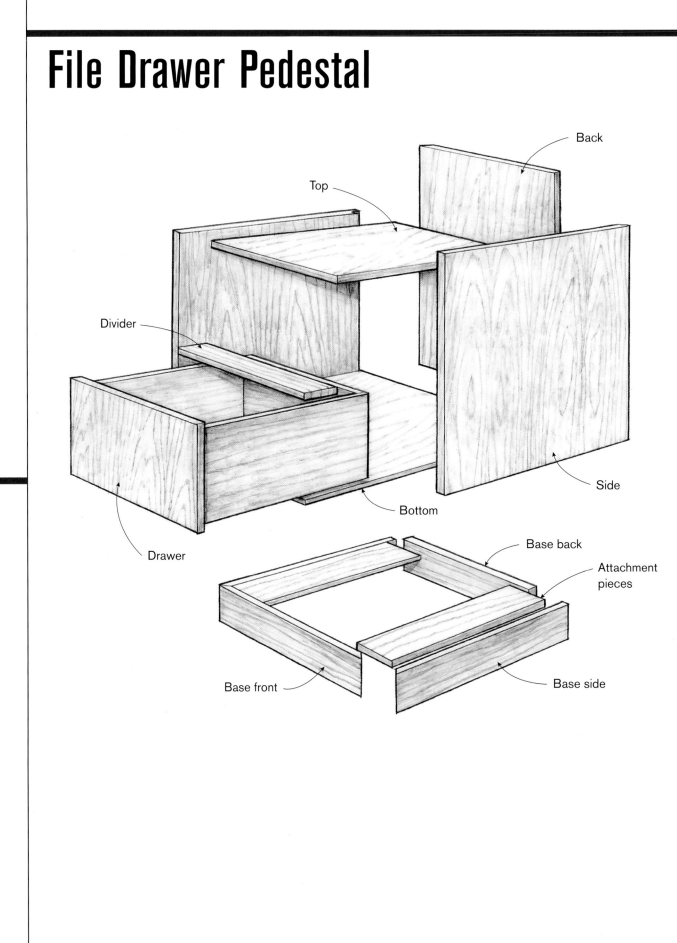

Back

Top

Divider

Side

Drawer

Bottom

Base back

Attachment
pieces

Base front

Base side

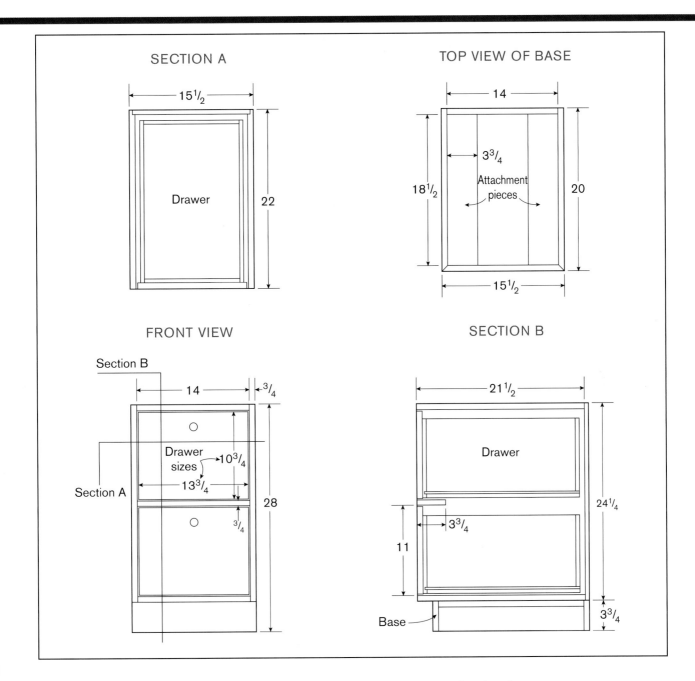

SECTION A

FRONT VIEW

TOP VIEW OF BASE

SECTION B

Construction and Assembly

THE MOST IMPORTANT ITEMS stored in offices are typically files. Two file sizes are in common use in the United States: letter size (8½ in. by 11 in.) and legal size (8½ in. by 14 in.). In a home office, most files will be letter size. With this in mind, I've designed the file drawers in this pedestal unit to be wide enough to fit letter-size files. However, you can fit legal-size files in the drawers if you store them side to side rather than front to back (see pp. 35–36 for an example of how to fit legal-size files into a narrow drawer).

Layout

All of the projects in this book are constructed primarily of cherry veneer plywood, a relatively expensive material that is normally sold in 4x8 sheets. You don't want to waste material. On the other hand, you can't let material size drive all your decisions. I've

CUT LIST FOR FILE DRAWER PEDESTAL

Base

1	Front	15½ in. x 3¾ in.	¾-in. cherry plywood
1	Back	14 in. x 3¾ in.	¾-in. cherry plywood
2	Sides	20 in. x 3¾ in.	¾-in. cherry plywood
2	Attachment pieces	18½ in. x 3¾ in.	¾-in. cherry plywood

Cabinet Box

1	Top	21½ in. x 14 in.	¾-in. cherry plywood
1	Bottom	21½ in. x 14 in.	¾-in. cherry plywood
1	Divider	14 in. x 3¾ in.	¾-in. cherry plywood
2	Sides	24¼ in. x 22 in.	¾-in. cherry plywood
1	Back	24¼ in. x 14¾ in.	½-in. cherry plywood

Drawers

4	Sides	20 in. x 9½ in.	½-in. Baltic birch plywood
2	Fronts	12 in. x 9½ in.	½-in. Baltic birch plywood
2	Backs	12 in. x 8⅞ in.	½-in. Baltic birch plywood
2	Bottoms	19¾ in. x 12½ in.	¼-in. Baltic birch plywood
2	Drawer fronts	13¾ in. x 10¾ in.	¾-in. cherry plywood

Other Materials

Approximately 20 linear ft. edge tape	cherry
2 Pair drawer glides	
2 Drawer pulls	
4 Confirmat screws	
#20 biscuits	
#10 biscuits	
Finish	

tried to design most of the parts so they can be cut from sheets of this size without undue waste.

Sometimes I couldn't avoid having material left over. For example, the sides of the cabinets in this chapter are 24¼ in. high, so you can cut only three of them from an 8-ft. length of plywood. If I'd shortened the cabinet so you could cut all four pieces from a single length, it wouldn't have had room for two file drawers. Even in this case, you'll find you can use the leftover pieces of plywood in other parts of these cabinets or in other projects in this book.

Before you decide how to divide up the material, you should also consider wood grain. Just cutting up the sheets into usable sizes may not produce the most attractive grain pattern on all of the pieces. By this time you should already have planned out your space and decided how many cabinets you need and of what kind. Take the time to think about your office as a whole, and lay out your materials carefully so you can make the best and most attractive use of them.

One last thing to keep in mind when laying out your materials is that you need to cut the parts slightly larger than their finished dimensions. The saw is going to remove material, and you'll lose additional

PHOTO A: A careful layout will ensure efficient use of your material.

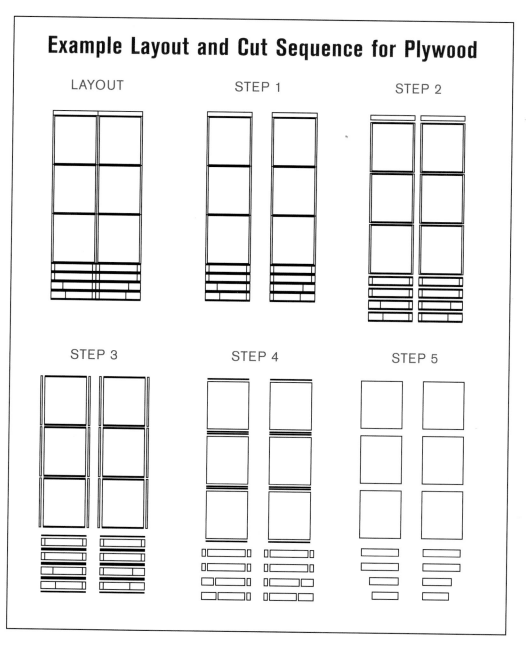

Example Layout and Cut Sequence for Plywood

LAYOUT   STEP 1   STEP 2

STEP 3   STEP 4   STEP 5

material in truing and squaring the edges (see **photo A**).

Cabinet Boxes

Once your material is layed out, cut all of the cherry plywood for the cabinet boxes and drawer fronts to size. The dimensions of the drawer fronts include the edgebanding, so you will have to take into account the actual thickness of the tape you are planning to use and subtract twice that thickness from each dimension when you size the drawer fronts.

The dimensions in the cut list give you the finished sizes, but to assure clean, square parts when sizing plywood I suggest cutting the plywood in the following sequence:

1. Following the illustration above, lay out the parts on the sheet of plywood. Add at least ¾ in. to the length and width of each part, plus the waste from the thickness of your sawblade.

2. Make any rip cuts on a table saw (see **photo B** on p. 52). In this case the only rip cut is down the center of the sheet.

3. Make the crosscuts using a circular saw with an edge guide (see the sidebar on the facing page) or using a radial-arm saw (see photo C).

4. Returning to the table saw, rip the parts to their finished dimensions in two passes. First remove half the waste from one edge to produce a straight, clean edge. Then with this edge against the fence, cut the parts to their finished dimensions. Be sure to cut all like-dimensioned parts one after the other, without resetting the fence, so that they will be identical.

5. Returning to the circular saw or the radial-arm saw, repeat this process to cut the parts to finished length.

PHOTO B: Ripping the plywood sheet in half first will make subsequent cuts more manageable.

PHOTO C: A radial-arm saw makes short work of cutting the cabinet parts, but you can also use a circular saw and edge guide as shown in the sidebar on the facing page.

THE TABLE SAW/RADIAL-ARM SAW combination is probably the most common method for cutting plywood and other sheet goods. However, you can cut sheet goods accurately without either of these machines—it just takes more time and requires more careful measuring and setup. You can easily build your own system out of plywood and a cleat used as a guide for the saw shoe. Alternatively, you can rough-cut close to your layout lines using a circular saw or jigsaw and clean up the cuts by routing to the lines using a straightedge and a router fitted with a flush trim bit. There are also commercially available guide rail/saw setups. Some work with their own integrated saw; others work with a standard circular saw.

A circular saw and guide can be used instead of a table saw and radial-arm saw to cut cabinet parts to size.

Shop-Built Methods

CIRCULAR SAW AND GUIDE

1. Build the guide and rail to fit your saw and as long as necessary. Screw and glue the guide to the rail. Be sure that the width of the rail is greater than the width of the saw base when it is against the rail.

2. With the saw base against the guide, cut the excess off the edge of the rail. This will become the line of the cut.

3. Clamp the guide/rail to the workpiece with the cut edge of the rail along the layout line.

4. Place the saw on the rail with the base against the guide and make your cut.

JIGSAW, STRAIGHTEDGE, AND ROUTER

1. Cut close to the layout line with a jigsaw.

2. Clamp the straightedge to the workpiece along the layout line.

3. Rout off the remaining waste to the layout line.

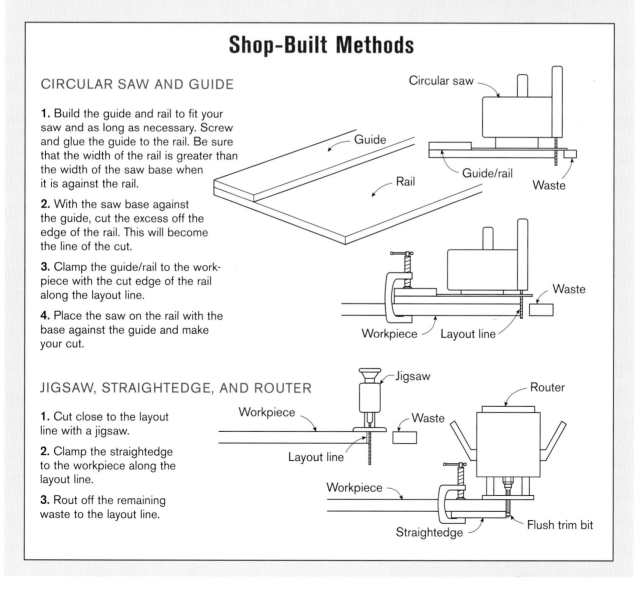

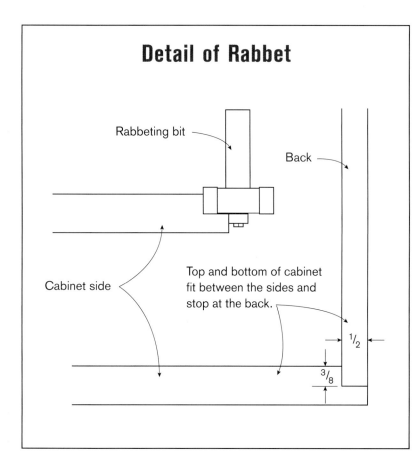

Detail of Rabbet

Rabbeting bit

Back

Cabinet side

Top and bottom of cabinet fit between the sides and stop at the back.

$\frac{1}{2}$

$\frac{3}{8}$

Cutting the rabbets

Once all of the parts for this cabinet box are sized, it's time to cut the rabbets that the back will fit into. For this cabinet, you'll cut rabbets only in the inside back edges of the cabinet sides, since these are the only places that show. You don't need to hide the back in rabbets at the top and bottom of the cabinet, since these can't be seen in the finished office—the bottom of the cabinet sits on the base and the top will be covered by the desktop. To accommodate the back, the top and bottom of the cabinet are cut ½ in. shorter than the sides, front to back.

1. To cut the rabbets, install a sharp, piloted rabbeting bit in your router. I recommend using a ½-in. collet router with at least 1½ hp. Set the bit to cut a ½-in.-wide rabbet, ⅜ in. deep (half the thickness of the plywood).

2. Clamp the workpiece so its edge overhangs your workbench.

3. Rout the rabbet, taking care at the beginning and the end of the cut not to let the

PHOTO D: A large router and a sharp bit are necessary for a cleanly cut rabbet.

BISCUIT JOINTS will produce accurate, easy-to-cut, super strong joints. However, laying out the slots can be confusing, especially in projects with many parts. You need a clear head, a methodical approach, and a good visualization of the way the parts connect. Take your time and think about what you are trying to accomplish.

Three different types of cuts can be made with biscuit joiners as follows.

Slots along the edge of a board This is the simplest type of biscuit slot to cut. Set the fence at 90 degrees and hold it flat against the face of the board, then plunge the cutter into the edge.

Slots along the face of a board, next to the edge Here the orientation of the joiner is the reverse of what it was in the edge slots—the fence registers against the edge, while the joiner cuts into the face. This is the most difficult type of slot to cut because the fence doesn't have much to register against. Make sure the face of the joiner lies flat on the workpiece, and hold it there as steadily as you can while you make the cut. You can make the joiner more stable by clamping a square block to the opposite side of the board, flush with the edge of the workpiece. But be careful; if the block is slightly off or out of square, your slot will be as well.

Slots in the middle of a board's face These types of slots are easily cut, and the fence is stable when it is set at 90 degrees flat on the workpiece. But since the slots are registered from the base of the machine and not the fence, a temporary fence or stop is needed to register the machine.

The tricky part about cutting slots in the middle of the board is remembering to use a consistent reference edge. The back of the base and the underside of the fence on my biscuit joiner are

Types of Biscuit Slot Cuts

Workpiece

Slots on the edges of a board

Workpiece

Slots along the face of a board, next to the edge

Workpiece

Temporary fence

Slots in the middle of a board's face

both ⅜ in. from the center of the cutter, which would be very helpful if I were working with material exactly ¾ in. thick. However, ¾-in. plywood is not actually ¾ in. thick; it's slightly less.

Suppose you are using a similar joiner to join the center divider to the side in this project. If you cut slots in the end of the divider by registering the machine from the top of the divider and then cut the mating slots in the side by registering from the bottom of where the divider will join, the divider will end up too high by twice the difference between ¾ in. and the actual thickness of the shelf. This may not sound like much, but if you did the opposite on the other side, your divider would be off horizontal by *four* times the difference, or as much as ¼ in.

PHOTO E: A temporary plywood stop is used to position the biscuit joiner for cuts in the field of a board.

[tip] It is always important to make cabinets square, but with these cabinets it is especially important. The most accurate way to check a cabinet for square is to measure corner to corner across the diagonals. If the two measurements are equal, the cabinet opening must be square.

bearing roll around either corner (see **photo D** on p. 54).

Cutting the biscuit slots

The corner joints and the joints for the drawer section divider are configured so as to put the sides of the cabinet on the outside and the top, bottom, and divider between the sides.

1. Lay out and cut three biscuit slots for each of the corner joints: one in the center and one 2 in. in from each of the front and back edges. Be sure to take into account that the top and bottom are ½ in. shorter front to back than the sides, with the shortfall at the back.

2. Lay out and cut one biscuit slot in the center of each end of the divider and a mating slot halfway down each side (see **photo E**).

Edgebanding

Before assembling the cabinet boxes, apply iron-on cherry edgebanding to cover the exposed plywood edges on the front of the sides, top, bottom, and divider. Iron-on edgebanding is available from many woodworking suppliers (see Sources of Supply on p. 152) and is easy to apply. It comes in many different species of wood and has hot-melt glue on the back.

1. Break off a piece of edgebanding a little longer than you will need.

2. Set an ordinary household iron to high temperature and no steam. Using the iron to apply the edgebanding, move it along the edge bit by bit and soften the glue as you go until the edging sticks (see **photo F**).

3. Trim off the excess length by scoring the edgebanding lightly on the glue side and snapping it off.

PHOTO F: Hot-melt adhesive-backed edgebanding is easily applied using an ordinary household iron.

4. Since the edgebanding is slightly wider than the plywood, sand it flush with the sides of the plywood.

5. Finish-sand all of the insides of the cabinets, including both sides of the divider, to 150 grit.

Assembly

1. After clearing a suitable space and gathering all the clamps, glue, and biscuits you'll need for the glue-up, lay the two sides down with their insides facing up. Glue biscuits into all of the slots in their faces.

2. Apply glue to the slots in the ends of the top, bottom, and divider.

3. Position the top, bottom, and divider onto their respective biscuits on one of the sides, making sure all of the front edges are flush, and press down firmly.

4. Next, turn over the other side piece and position it on the ends of the top, bottom,

PHOTO G: Placing a clamp at each biscuit location will ensure that the joints close up tight.

Base Construction and Attachment

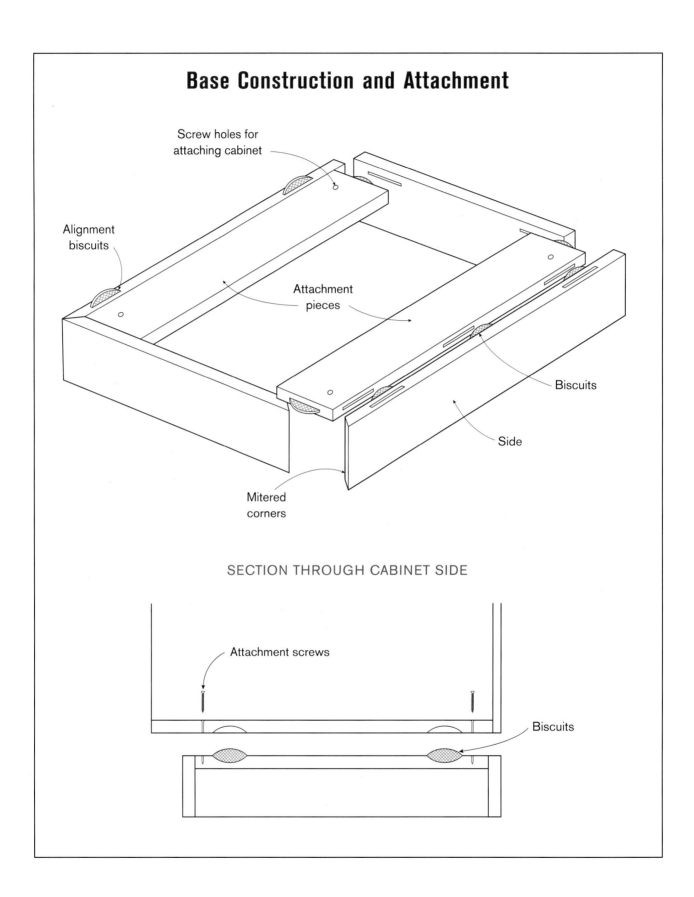

Screw holes for attaching cabinet

Alignment biscuits

Attachment pieces

Biscuits

Side

Mitered corners

SECTION THROUGH CABINET SIDE

Attachment screws

Biscuits

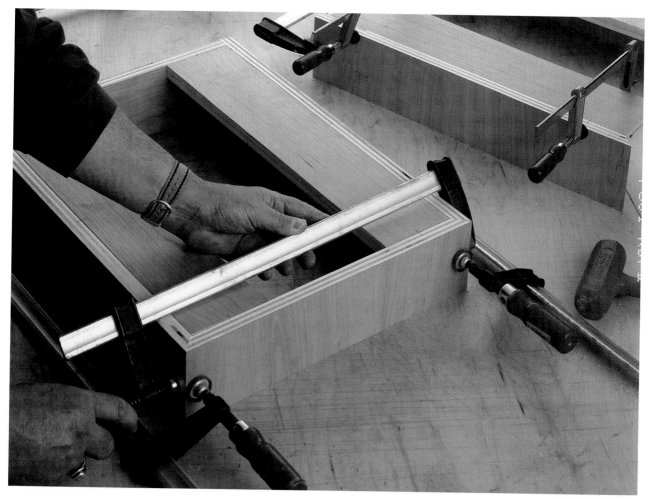

and divider, again making sure all of the front edges are flush, and press down firmly.

5. Clamp at each biscuit location. The clamps will go across the case at the top and bottom and across the front at the divider (see **photo G** on p. 57).

6. Check the cabinet box for square, adjust the clamps if necessary, and set the box aside to dry.

7. When the glue is dry, finish-sand the outside of the cabinet to 150 grit.

8. Cut two biscuit slots on the bottom edge of each side of the cabinet, positioned as shown in the illustration on the facing page. These will mate with slots cut in the base later.

9. Finish-sand the ½-in. plywood back, slip it into its rabbets, and screw it in place.

Making the Base

The base for this cabinet has front corners that are mitered together, which avoids the necessity of edge-banding raw plywood edges. Edgebanding wouldn't look attractive on the front of the base, and if it were placed on the sides its thickness would have to be factored into the construction.

1. After cutting the cherry plywood for the cabinet base to size, make two subassemblies of the two attachment pieces and the two sides. Glue, biscuit, and clamp these pieces together.

2. Once the glue is dry, complete the assembly by gluing, biscuiting, and clamping the front and back to the subassemblies. The mitered corners do not require any biscuits, just careful alignment and clamping (see **photo H**).

PHOTO H: The mitered corners must be aligned and clamped carefully, but they don't require any biscuits.

PHOTO I: The cabinet is screwed to the base with Euro screws.

3. When the glue from the front and back pieces is dry, finish-sand the outside of the base to 150 grit.

4. Cut two biscuit slots in the top edge of each of the base sides to mate with the slots you cut in the bottom of the cabinet. Position the slots in the base so the back of the base will be flush with the back of the cabinet.

5. To attach the base, place biscuits into the slots in the top of the base. No glue is required, since these are for alignment only.

6. Position the cabinet onto these biscuits, making sure the back of the cabinet is flush with the back of the base, and push down until the cabinet sits flat on the base. Use clamps if necessary.

7. Lay out and drill a hole in each corner through the bottom of the cabinets and into the attachment pieces of the base. The fasteners you choose will determine the size of the holes. I used Confirmat or Euro screws, shown in **photo I** (see Sources of Supply on p. 152).

8. Screw the cabinet to the base.

File Drawers

The details of constructing and installing the file drawers are covered in the accessory drawer pedestal section on pp. 62–67. However, since the file drawers affected other elements of the design, I thought it would be interesting to use them as an example of how design decisions are interrelated.

Whenever you design a cabinet to house a particular object, start with that object and design around it. In this case, the object is a hanging file folder, which is 11¾ in. wide with metal hanging bars extending ½ in. on each side. The bars are notched to fit over rails that are attached to the drawer tops. (Two of the more common rail systems are shown in the photos on pp. 35–36.) To give the file folders a little wiggle room, the inside of the file drawer should be about 12 in. wide. (Actually, the rails, which extend upward from the inside edges of the drawer sides, can be spaced apart anywhere from 12 in. to 12⅜ in., but 12 in. is the easiest measurement to work with.) Since the sides are ½ in. thick, the drawer box should be 13 in. wide on the outside.

Hanging file folders are 9⅛ in. high. They extend over the top of the rail by ⅜ in., but they're raised off the drawer bottom ⅛ in., so the drawer sides need to be 8⅞ in. high on the inside. Adding the thickness of the drawer bottom (¼ in.) and the amount of material needed under the drawer bottom to support it (⅜ in.) gives a total of 9½ in. outside height.

The depth of the drawer box is based on the length of a standard drawer glide. Drawer glides come in several sizes, but the most appropriate size for this purpose is 20 in., which becomes the depth of my drawer box. You'll see later why I couldn't use a longer drawer glide.

Once you have the outside dimensions of the drawer box, you can design the cabinet itself. The drawer glides add ½ in. to the width on each side, and the cabinet sides are each ¾ in. thick, so the total outside width of the cabinet is 15½ in.

To calculate height, take the drawer heights (9½ in. each) and add the ¾-in. thicknesses of the cabinet's top, bottom, and divider boards. In addition, each of the two drawers needs clearance inside the cabinet— ⅜ in. for the folder rails, ⅞ in. for folder tabs, and ¼ in. at the bottom. Adding all these numbers gives us a cabinet box that is 24¼ in. high.

To the 20-in. drawer depth, add ½ in. for the cabinet back and ¾ in. for the inset drawer fronts to obtain a depth of at least 21¼ in. However, you also have to take the desktop into account. The desktop is 24 in.

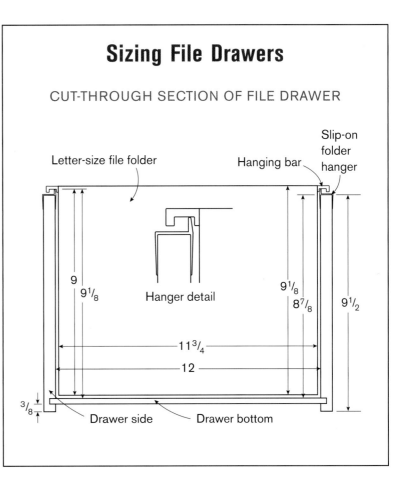

Sizing File Drawers

CUT-THROUGH SECTION OF FILE DRAWER

Letter-size file folder   Hanging bar   Slip-on folder hanger

Hanger detail

Drawer side   Drawer bottom

9 9⅛   9⅛ 8⅞   9½

11¾   12   ⅜

deep, a dimension I chose mainly to save material, since I used 4x8 plywood. The cabinet can't take up all the space under the desk; it needs at least 1¼ in. of clearance behind it for baseboard as well as wiring, and it's more attractive with a ¾-in. overhang in front. Thus, the cabinet can't be more than 22 in. deep. I could have made the cabinet any depth from 21¼ in. to 22 in. I chose 22 in.

I've also sized the cabinet base so that the cabinet will fit snugly under the desktop. The desktop is 30 in. high—a height most people find comfortable—and 2 in. thick, with a space of 28 in. underneath. Since the cabinet box is 24¼ in. high, this leaves 3¾ in. for the height of the base.

Finally, since I had decided to make this office project as modular as possible, I designed the second cabinet with dimensions identical to the file drawer cabinet but with a different drawer configuration, which I'll address next.

Accessory Drawer Pedestal

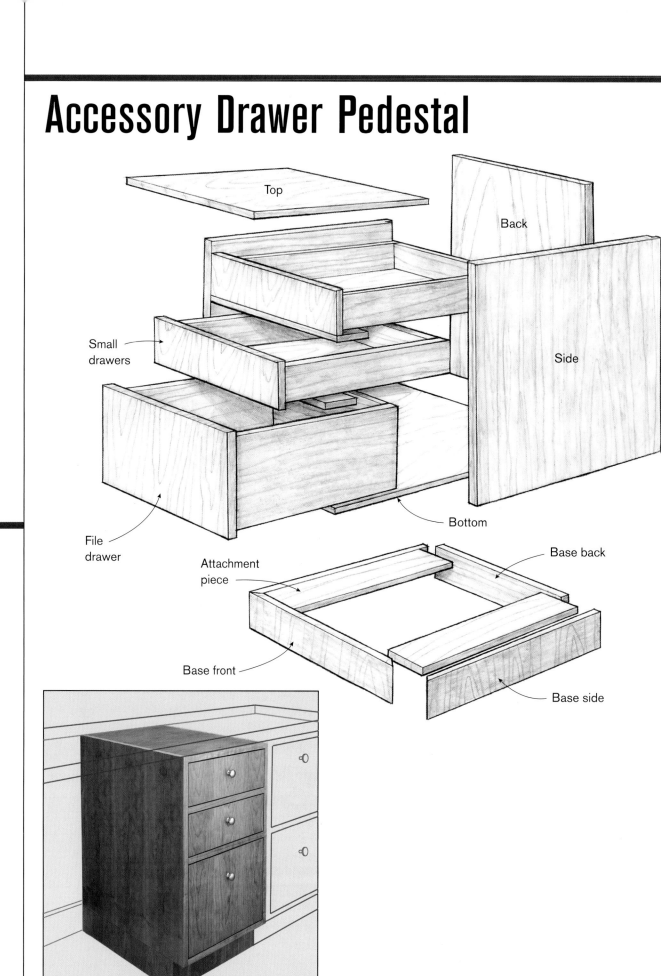

Top

Back

Side

Small drawers

File drawer

Bottom

Attachment piece

Base back

Base front

Base side

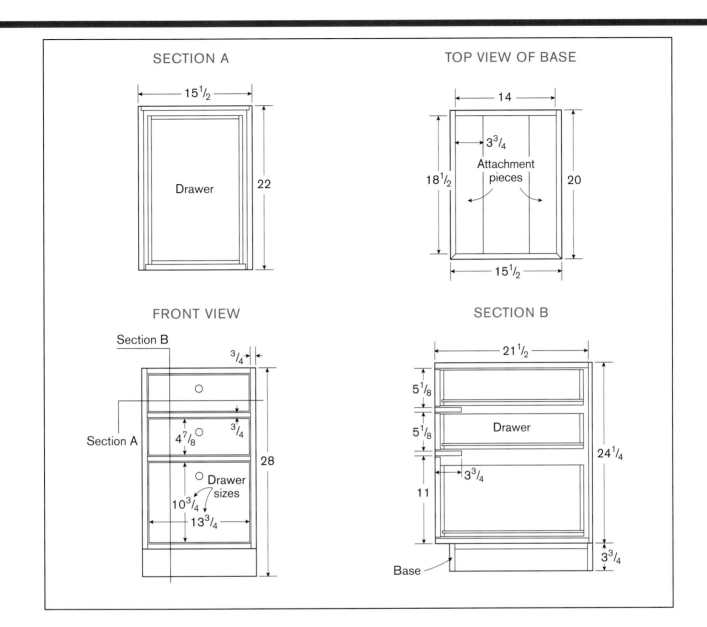

SECTION A

15 1/2

Drawer

22

TOP VIEW OF BASE

14

3 3/4

Attachment pieces

18 1/2

20

15 1/2

FRONT VIEW

Section B

3/4

Section A

4 7/8

3/4

28

Drawer sizes

10 3/4

13 3/4

SECTION B

21 1/2

5 1/8

5 1/8

Drawer

24 1/4

11

3 3/4

Base

3 3/4

Construction and Assembly

THE CABINET AND BASE of this unit are identical to the file drawer pedestal, except that two smaller accessory drawers replace the top file drawer. I have found this drawer arrangement works well, but you may want to change it to suit your needs. With only minor changes, you could build this cabinet with four drawers or with any combination of drawer sizes that will fit in this cabinet box.

You can build and assemble this cabinet by following the instructions on pp. 48–60 for the file drawer pedestal and the instructions below for building the drawers.

Drawer Construction and Installation

The drawers are constructed of 12mm (½-in.) Baltic birch plywood biscuited together. They also have a second, decorative front of cherry plywood that matches the rest of the cabinet. If you prefer, you can use solid wood for the inside of the drawers without changing the construction.

Plywood boxes are slightly stronger because the orientation of the plies allows

CUT LIST FOR ACCESSORY DRAWER PEDESTAL

Base			
1	Front	15½ in. x 3¾ in.	¾-in. cherry plywood
1	Back	14 in. x 3¾ in.	¾-in. cherry plywood
2	Sides	20 in. x 3¾ in.	¾-in. cherry plywood
2	Attachment pieces	18½ in. x 3¾ in.	¾-in. cherry plywood
Cabinet Box			
1	Top	21½ in. x 14 in.	¾-in. cherry plywood
1	Bottom	21½ in. x 14 in.	¾-in. cherry plywood
2	Dividers	14 in. x 3¾ in.	¾-in. cherry plywood
2	Sides	24¼ in. x 22 in.	¾-in. cherry plywood
1	Back	24¼ in. x 14¾ in.	½-in. cherry plywood
Drawers			
4	Sides	20 in. x 4⅝ in.	½-in. Baltic birch plywood
2	Sides	20 in. x 9½ in.	½-in. Baltic birch plywood
2	Fronts	12 in. x 4⅝ in.	½-in. Baltic birch plywood
1	Front	12 in. x 9½ in.	½-in. Baltic birch plywood
2	Backs	12 in. x 4 in.	½-in. Baltic birch plywood
1	Back	12 in. x 8⅞ in.	½-in. Baltic birch plywood
3	Bottoms	19¾ in. x 12½ in.	¼-in. Baltic birch plywood
2	Drawer fronts	13¾ in. x 4⅞ in.	¾-in. cherry plywood
1	Drawer front	13¾ in. x 10¾ in.	¾-in. cherry plywood
Other Materials			
Approximately 20 linear ft. edge tape			cherry
3	Pair drawer glides		
3	Drawer pulls		
4	Confirmat screws		
#20 biscuits			
#10 biscuits			
Finish			

more gluing of side grain to side grain, which forms a strong glue joint even without the biscuits. The solid-wood joints, which are end grain to side grain, rely primarily on the biscuits for strength. However, I have built many drawers out of both plywood and solid wood, and I find they both work well in normal use. Unlike drawers made in the days before drawer glides, these drawers will be put under very little stress. Modern drawer glides such as the Accuride glides I've used work extremely well. The drawers open and close with almost no force, making elaborate joinery such as dovetails unnecessary.

1. Rip plywood for the drawer sides, fronts, and backs, then crosscut the pieces to length.

2. Choose the pieces for the backs of the drawers and rip them to ⅝ in. narrower than the fronts. Making the backs of the drawers shallower will allow you to slide the drawer bottoms into the completed drawer boxes.

3. On a table saw, install a ¼-in. dado blade and adjust the height to ¼ in. Cut a groove in the bottom inside edge of the drawer fronts and sides ⅜ in. in from the edge. This groove will house the ¼-in. drawer bottoms. Test the fit first with a scrap piece of drawer material and a piece of the drawer bottom material. The bottom should fit snugly into the groove, but hand pressure should be enough to push it in. Sanding the drawer bottoms will remove enough material to allow you to slide them into the groove easily.

4. Next, cut slots for as many #10 biscuits as will fit in each corner joint, positioning them so that the fronts and backs of the drawers will fit between the sides.

5. Finish-sand the insides of all of the parts to 150 grit, then glue, biscuit, and clamp the drawer boxes together. Make sure that the top edges of all parts are flush and that the boxes are square (see **photo J**).

6. When the glue is dry, finish-sand the outsides of the drawers.

7. Cut the bottoms to fit, finish-sand them, and slide them into their grooves. Fasten them in place with a couple of small screws along the back edge.

8. Remove the back of the cabinet, then mount the drawer glides and install the drawers in their openings, as shown in **photo K**. Don't reattach the back of the cabinet yet. I used Accuride 7434 glides (see Sources of Supply on p. 152), which have a 100-lb. load rating. Heavy glides are needed for the file drawers, which can accumulate quite a bit of weight, but you could use lighter glides for the accessory drawers. I've used over-extension glides, which pull out a little more than full-extension glides. This is useful when you have an overhanging desktop and inset drawers that start off ¾ in. inside the cabinet. However, many different kinds and styles of drawer glides are available, and your choice will determine the exact installation positioning and technique.

Attaching the drawer fronts

The drawer fronts are easy to install, but holding everything in place can be a little tricky, so enlist a helper for this task if you can.

1. Cut a few ³⁄₃₂-in. spacers. I like to use small strips of ⅛-in. luan plywood, since for some reason they actually measure about ³⁄₃₂ in.

2. With the drawers in place, put a spacer on the bottom of the cabinet or the divider, depending on which drawer you are working on. These spacers will help assure the correct spacing around the drawer fronts.

3. Position the first drawer front on its spacer, centered side to side in the opening (see **photo L** on p. 67).

4. Placing the palm of one hand on the back of the drawer box (the cabinet back should still be off) and the palm of your other hand on the drawer front, squeeze tightly as you open the drawer. While you're holding the drawer front in place, have your helper place

PHOTO J: Strong, attractive drawer boxes can be made from Baltic birch plywood and biscuit joints.

PHOTO K: Choose high-quality drawer glides that will support the anticipated load.

[tip] If you don't have a second pair of hands, you can use double-sided carpet tape to temporarily hold the drawer front onto the box.

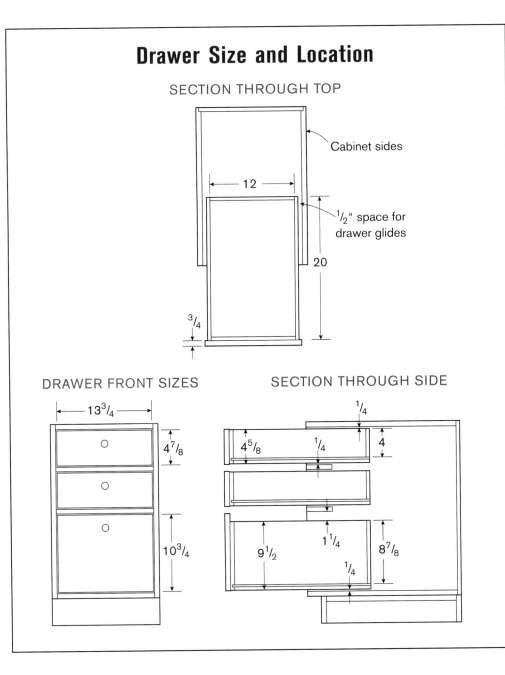

Drawer Size and Location

SECTION THROUGH TOP

Cabinet sides

12

$1/2$" space for drawer glides

20

$3/4$

DRAWER FRONT SIZES

$13^3/4$

$4^7/8$

$10^3/4$

SECTION THROUGH SIDE

$1/4$

$4^5/8$ $1/4$ 4

$9^1/2$ $1^1/4$ $8^7/8$

$1/4$

a couple of spring clamps on the drawer to hold the front in place.

5. From the inside of the drawer, drill four holes for the screws that attach the drawer front to the drawer box. If the drawer front needs a little adjustment, remove the front and enlarge the holes in the drawer box. This gives you a little room to move the drawer front around. Special screws with extra large heads are available for this application, but a screw and washer will work just as well.

6. Repeat the process for each of the other drawers, then reattach the cabinet back.

7. Install the decorative drawer pulls you have chosen.

Finishing

I finished these pieces using a spray-on lacquer but several other finishing methods would work equally well (see the appendix on p. 151 for details on finishing).

PHOTO L: Installing a drawer front can be tricky without help.

Drawer Construction

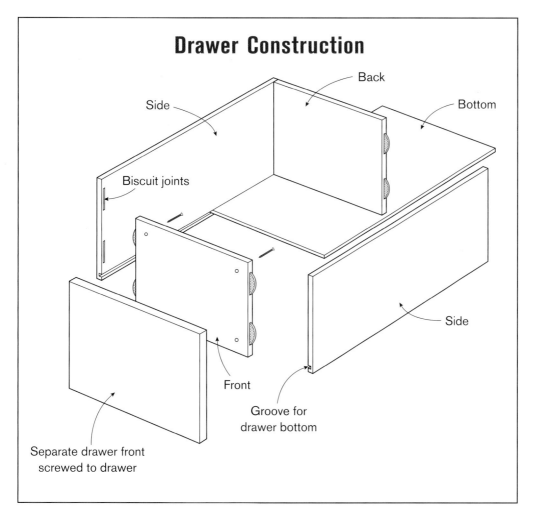

Side

Back

Bottom

Biscuit joints

Side

Front

Groove for
drawer bottom

Separate drawer front
screwed to drawer

I CHOSE A RATHER GENERIC STYLE for this suite of office furniture so it would be suitable for almost any room. However, with small, simple changes you can personalize these pieces to fit your tastes. Just substituting a different species of wood could make a dramatic change. Red oak or maple, for example, would completely alter the feeling of this furniture. You can also change the look of these pieces by modifying small details. I've included suggestions for changes in each section.

These are not meant to limit your choices but rather to get you thinking about the possibilities.

If you substitute the feet shown in the illustration below for the plinth base, these pedestal cabinets suddenly become more Shaker-like. The feet shown here are simple and only take a few minutes apiece to make—certainly less time than the plinth bases.

1. Joint and plane a piece of 8/4 solid cherry as close to 2 in. square as possible. I was able to finish mine out at a heavy 1$\frac{15}{16}$ in.

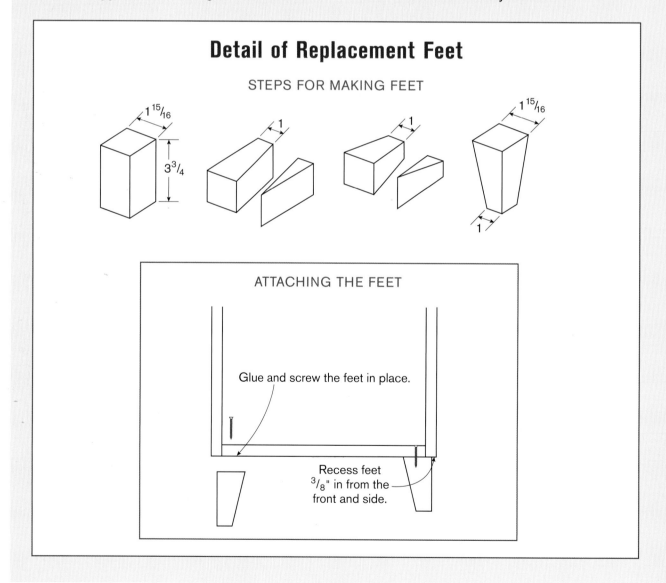

Detail of Replacement Feet

STEPS FOR MAKING FEET

ATTACHING THE FEET

Glue and screw the feet in place.

Recess feet $\frac{3}{8}$" in from the front and side.

2. Cut the stock into 3¾-in.-long blanks.

3. Measure in 1 in. along one bottom edge and draw a line connecting this point diagonally to the opposite top corner, creating a wedge-shaped piece of waste ¹⁵⁄₁₆ in. thick at one end and tapering to a point at the other. Remove this waste using a bandsaw (see the photo below left).

4. Repeat steps 1 to 3, but this time draw the line on the sloped face. The sloped face should face up for the second cut.

5. Finish-sand the feet to 150 grit.

6. Next, drill and countersink two holes for the front feet in the bottom of the cabinet, ⅝ in. from the insides of the sides and 1⅝ in. from the front edge. Then drill and countersink two holes for the back feet ⅝ in. from the insides of the sides and 1⅛ in. from the back edge.

7. Line up the feet so they are recessed ⅜ in. from the side and ⅜ in. from the front or back, respectively.

8. Drill a pilot hole in each foot, then glue and screw the feet to the bottom of the cabinet (see the photo below right).

The feet are quickly and easily cut using a bandsaw.

The feet are attached with screws and a little glue.

CHAPTER 5

Closed Storage Cabinets

SOME ITEMS IN YOUR OFFICE—reams of
paper, for example—don't belong in drawers, either because they won't fit or because
they aren't used every day and don't need to
be at your fingertips. Closed storage cabinets, or cabinets with doors, are just the ticket for this kind of
item. This office suite includes three closed storage
cabinets: a pedestal cabinet, a low cabinet, and a wall-
hung version of the low cabinet. As with the drawer
cabinets, you can build as many or as few of these
units as you need.

Since this office suite is modular, I designed the
pedestal cabinet to be exactly the same size and
construction as the drawer pedestal cabinets in
chapter 4, except that it has a door and shelves

instead of drawers. In addition, the wall-hung cabinet and the low cabinet are essentially identical to
each other, except that the wall-hung version doesn't
have a base or top. These two cabinets are themselves
identical to the wall-hung shelves and low shelves
that you'll find in chapter 6, except that the shelves
don't have doors.

Organizing the projects in this way allows you to
pick the components that you wish to include in
your office and turn directly to those projects. You
may have to flip back and forth in the book, since I
have tried not to repeat similar instructions from
chapter to chapter, but the issues relating directly to
any particular project should be easy to find and
clearly laid out.

Pedestal Cabinet

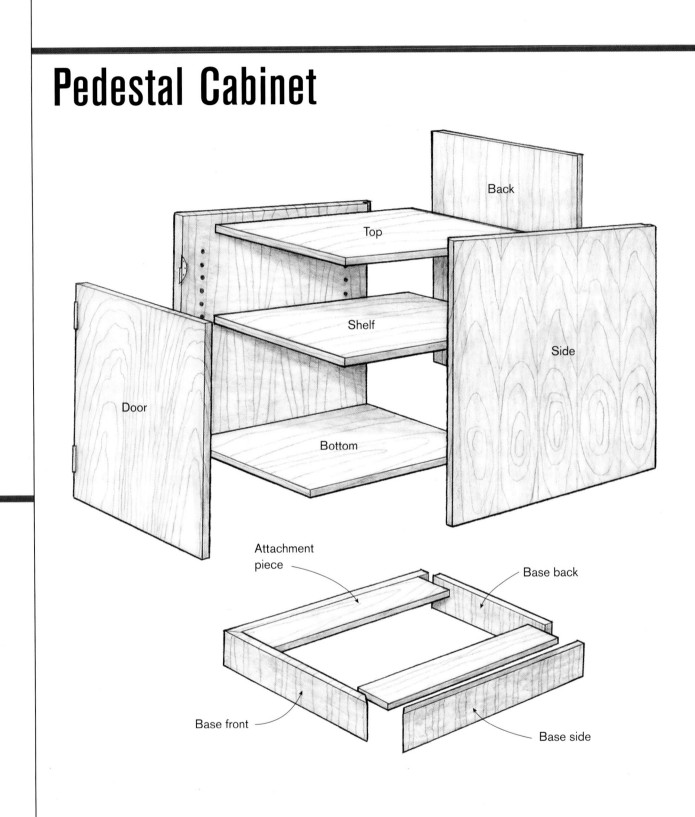

Back

Top

Side

Shelf

Door

Bottom

Attachment
piece

Base back

Base front

Base side

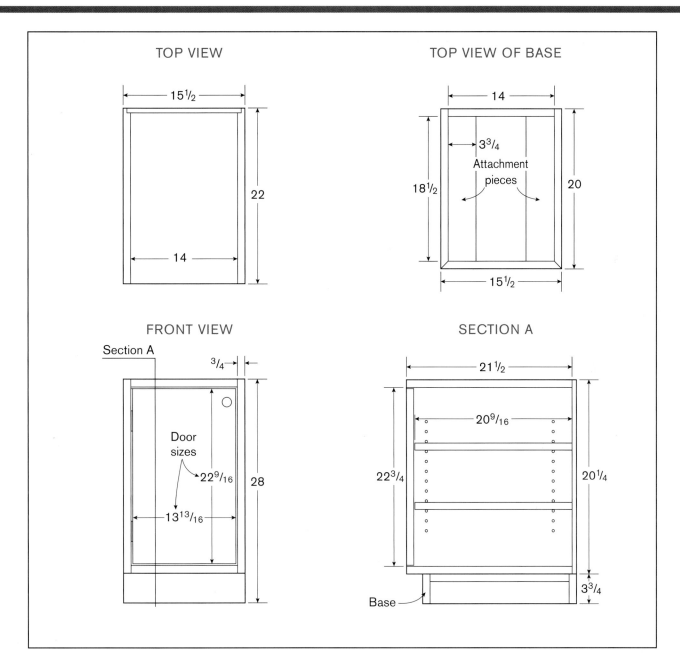

TOP VIEW

15½

22

14

TOP VIEW OF BASE

14

3¾

Attachment
pieces

18½

20

15½

FRONT VIEW

Section A

¾

Door
sizes

22⁹⁄₁₆

28

13¹³⁄₁₆

SECTION A

21½

20⁹⁄₁₆

22¾

20¼

Base

3¾

Construction and Assembly

ALTHOUGH THIS CABINET and base are identical to those used in the drawer pedestals in chapter 4, the drawers have been replaced with a door and adjustable shelves.

1. Following the detailed instructions on pp. 48–54, lay out and cut all of the parts for the cabinet and base, omitting the drawers, drawer fronts, and dividers and adding the

door and as many shelves as you need. The door should be about ³⁄₃₂ in. smaller all around than the opening it fits into. (Remember that these dimensions include edgebanding, so take into account the thickness of the tape when you size the doors.) Shelves should be about ³⁄₃₂ in. less than the width of the inside of the cabinet and ⅛ in. shorter front to back.

2. Cut all of the biscuit slots as described on p. 56.

[tip] A good rule of thumb for locating shelf pin holes is to measure one-sixth the total depth in from the front and back edges.

CUT LIST FOR PEDESTAL CABINET

Base

1	Front	15½ in. x 3¾ in.	¾-in. cherry plywood
1	Back	14 in. x 3¾ in.	¾-in. cherry plywood
2	Sides	20 in. x 3¾ in.	¾-in. cherry plywood
2	Attachment pieces	18½ in. x 3¾ in.	¾-in. cherry plywood

Cabinet Box

1	Top	21½ in. x 14 in.	¾-in. cherry plywood
1	Bottom	21½ in. x 14 in.	¾-in. cherry plywood
2	Sides	24¼ in. x 22 in.	¾-in. cherry plywood
2	Shelves	20⁹⁄₁₆ in. x 13⅞ in.	¾-in. cherry plywood
1	Back	24¼ in. x 14¾ in.	½-in. cherry plywood

Door

1	Door	22⁹⁄₁₆ in. x 13¹³⁄₁₆ in.	¾-in. cherry plywood

Other Materials

	Approximately 20 linear ft. edge tape	cherry
1	Door knob	
4	Confirmat screws	
8	Shelf pins	
2	Duplex hinges	
	#20 biscuits	
	Finish	

3. Using iron-on edgebanding, edge-band the exposed raw plywood edges on the front of the sides, top, and bottom, and on all of the edges of the door.

Shelf pin holes

Before continuing with the assembly, drill holes for the shelf pins that will be used to support the adjustable shelf or shelves. Since shelf pins come in various sizes—the most common fit into 5mm or ¼-in. holes—you should select your pins before you drill the holes.

Drill two rows of holes in the sides, one about 4 in. in from the front of the cabinet and the other about 3½ in. in from the back (see **photo A**). I use a commercial jig made by Festool, but many other jigs are available, and you can easily make your own by drilling a series of holes in a piece of plywood that fits the space. Even if the holes are not perfectly spaced, your shelves will lie flat as long as each row is the same (see **photo B**). Make sure you always register the jig from the same edge.

After drilling the holes for the shelf pins, finish assembling the cabinet and base, then attach the cabinet to the base.

PHOTO A: This commercial jig makes accurate shelf pin holes quickly.

PHOTO B: This simple straight pin is just one of many types of shelf supports available.

The Door

The two most common styles of cabinet door are inset and overlay. These names refer to the position of the door relative to the cabinet opening. Overlay doors, which are common on European cabinetry, overlay or cover the front of the cabinet. This is a very forgiving arrangement, since the door hides small, out-of-square errors in the cabinet. Inset doors have a more traditional look. They fit within the sides of the cabinet. The cabinet frames the door, and the gap between the door and the cabinet sides is small. Any irregularity or out-of-square construction in the cabinet is emphasized, and in severe cases a door may rub against the frame.

Since all the doors in this office are inset doors, pay particular attention to squareness when you cut and assemble your cabinets as well as when you cut and size the doors (see **photo C**). The stout, ½-in. backs will help square up the cabinets, but you can't rely on this alone.

Installing the hinges

Another difference between overlay and inset doors is the type of hinge used. Overlay doors are typically hung on European or

PHOTO C: The use of inset doors requires an absolutely square cabinet.

Door Installation

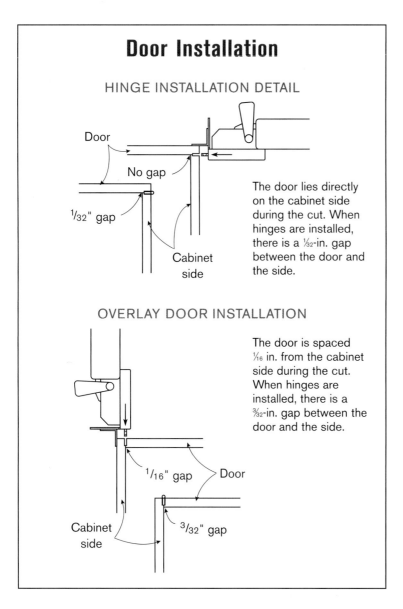

HINGE INSTALLATION DETAIL

Door

No gap

1/32" gap

Cabinet side

The door lies directly on the cabinet side during the cut. When hinges are installed, there is a 1/32-in. gap between the door and the side.

OVERLAY DOOR INSTALLATION

The door is spaced 1/16 in. from the cabinet side during the cut. When hinges are installed, there is a 3/32-in. gap between the door and the side.

1/16" gap

Door

Cabinet side

3/32" gap

concealed hinges, which have the advantage of being adjustable in four directions. Not only does this make the fit of the door less critical, but it also makes the installation of the hinge easier. Inset doors are typically hung with straight butt hinges, which are more difficult to install. These hinges must be fitted into mortises in the case as well as in the door. The mating of the two mortise locations and the fit of the hinge in its mortise is critical to the fit of the door.

For these cabinets, I chose a type of butt hinge called Duplex (see **photo D**) manufactured by Lamello (see Sources of Supply on p. 152), which fits into a biscuit slot. Interestingly, Duplex hinges are designed to be used with overlay doors and are very easy to install on those doors. Installing them on inset doors is a little trickier but is still much easier than installing regular butt hinges. However, I strongly recommend that you test this installation on some scrap pieces before you try it on a finished cabinet.

1. After laying the cabinet on its back, use some scrap plywood as temporary supports to prop up the door in its opening while you lay out and install the hinges. Cut a few pieces of scrap long enough to support the door in place, inset about 1/16 in. from the front of the cabinet, and place them upright

PHOTO D: Lamello Duplex hinges are designed to fit into biscuit slots.

PHOTO E: Wedges temporarily align the door for laying out and cutting slots for the hinges.

in the cabinet near the top and bottom. Place the door on the supports in the cabinet opening.

2. Place wedges in the spaces around the door so that the door is centered top to bottom and is just slightly closer to the hinge side of the cabinet (see **photo E**).

3. Mark the centerlines for the locations of the hinges.

4. Next, set the depth of the biscuit joiner to 15mm (approximately ⁹⁄₁₆ in.), and set the joiner's fence so the cutter will plunge equally into the cabinet side and the door edge.

5. Line up the centerline of the biscuit joiner with the hinge centerline and cut a biscuit slot for each hinge, as shown in **photo F**.

6. Separate the hinges and screw the leaves with the pins to the cabinet and the other leaves to the door.

PHOTO F: The biscuit joiner cutter is positioned to cut an equal amount from the door and cabinet.

CLOSED STORAGE CABINETS **77**

PHOTO G: These two-part hinges make hanging the door simple.

Hanging the door and installing the catch

Since these hinges separate, you don't have to hold the door in place while you screw on the hinges. Hanging the door is simply a matter of dropping the door with its hinge parts over the pin on the cabinet hinge parts (see **photo G**).

To latch the door, I used Bull Dog catches (see **photo H**) and Sources of Supply on p. 152). These may not be the most elegant catches on the market, but they latch so solidly and install so easily that I've gotten hooked on them.

1. Start by standing the cabinet upright again. Holding the door closed, reach in through the back of the cabinet (which has not yet been attached) and mark the location on the inside of the cabinet top where it meets the corner of the swing (unhinged) side of the door.

2. Line up the front of the bracket portion of the catch with the line you've just made, and mark the locations of the slotted holes in the bracket. Drill pilot holes in the center of these marks, then screw the bracket in place.

3. Insert the pin portion of the catch into the bracket and close the door firmly. The pin has a screw inserted in it, which will mark its location.

4. Drill a pilot hole on the mark made where the screw hits the door, and screw on the pin. You can microadjust the catch by sliding the bracket in or out.

PHOTO H: These Bull Dog catches latch firmly.

Low Cabinet

Top

Back

Side

Shelf

Bottom

Door

Base back

Attachment piece

Base front

Base side

Construction and Assembly

THIS CABINET IS SMALLER than the pedestal cabinet but since the construction is virtually identical, I've described it in less detail. For a fuller explanation of construction methods, refer to pp. 48–60.

1. Begin by laying out and rough-cutting all of the cherry plywood for the cabinet boxes.

2. Using a table saw and then a radial-arm saw, rip and crosscut the parts to their finished dimensions.

3. Cut the rabbets in the side pieces.

Low Cabinet Views

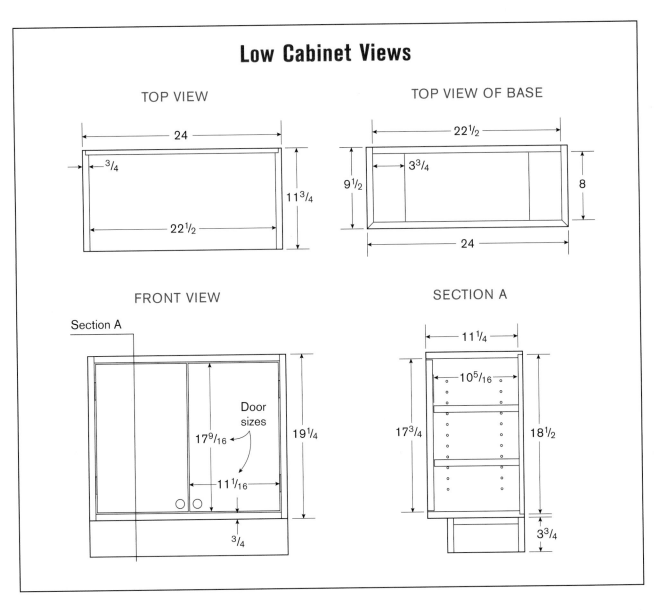

TOP VIEW

TOP VIEW OF BASE

FRONT VIEW

SECTION A

Section A

Door sizes

4. Cut biscuit slots for the corner joints so that the top and bottom will be between the sides and so that the front edges of all of the parts are flush.

5. In the sides of the cabinet, drill shelf pin holes. Since this cabinet is shallower than the pedestal cabinet, the rows of holes will be closer to the front and back edges of the sides. Remember that the rule of thumb is to measure one-sixth of the cabinet's depth in from the front and back.

6. Edge-band the front edges of all of the cabinet parts.

7. Cut, size, and edge-band the doors. Since this cabinet has two doors, you have to size

the doors to leave room for the space around and between the doors, as well as for the edgebanding around the outside of the doors. The space between the doors (after edgebanding is applied) should be ³⁄₃₂ in., just like the space around the doors.

8. Finish-sand the inside faces of all of the parts to 150 grit.

9. Glue, biscuit, and clamp the cabinet together.

10. When the glue is dry, finish-sand the outside of the cabinet.

11. Cut two biscuit slots on the bottom edge of each side of the cabinet in the positions

CUT LIST FOR LOW CABINET

Base

1	Front	24 in. x 3¾ in.	¾-in. cherry plywood
1	Back	22½ in. x 3¾ in.	¾-in. cherry plywood
2	Sides	9½ in. x 3¾ in.	¾-in. cherry plywood
2	Attachment pieces	8 in. x 3¾ in.	¾-in. cherry plywood

Cabinet Box

1	Top	22½ in. x 11¼ in.	¾-in. cherry plywood
1	Bottom	22½ in. x 11¼ in.	¾-in. cherry plywood
2	Sides	19¼ in. x 11¾ in.	¾-in. cherry plywood
2	Shelves	22⅜ in. x 10⁵⁄₁₆ in.	¾-in. cherry plywood
1	Back	23¼ in. x 18½ in.	½-in. cherry plywood

Doors

2	Doors	17⁹⁄₁₆ in. x 11¹⁄₁₆ in.	¾-in. cherry plywood

Top

1	Panel	74½ in. x 12 in.	¾-in. cherry plywood
1	Edge strip	76 in. x ¾ in. x ¾ in.	solid cherry
2	Edge strips	12¾ in. x ¾ in. x ¾ in.	solid cherry

Other Materials

Approximately 20 linear ft. edge tape	cherry
2	Door knobs
8	Shelf pins
4	Duplex hinges
#20 biscuits	
20 Hex-drive connector bolts and threaded sleeves	
Finish	

Base Construction

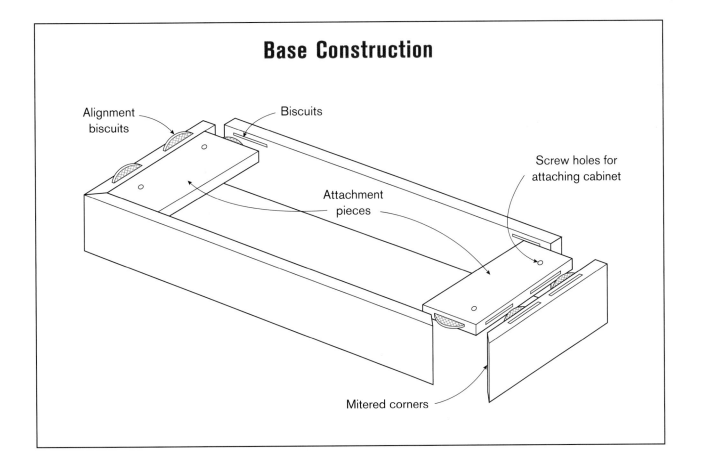

Alignment biscuits

Biscuits

Screw holes for attaching cabinet

Attachment pieces

Mitered corners

**PHOTO I: Dry-fitted
biscuits align the
base and cabinet.**

If you knew for certain that you would arrange these modules only as they are shown in this book, you might be better off building a single base to support all three pieces. However, you would then be locked into this arrangement, which could be a problem if you had to move your office. If you do decide to build a single base, you will have to change the grain orientation. The wood grain on the bases in all of these projects runs vertically, which is impossible to achieve with plywood construction if the base is more than 48 in. wide.

1. Lay out and cut to size all of the cherry plywood for the cabinet base.

2. Glue, biscuit, and clamp the base together.

3. When the glue is dry, finish-sand the outside of the base to 150 grit.

4. Cut two biscuit slots in the top edge of each of the base sides to mate with the slots you cut in the bottom of the cabinet. Position the slots so the base will be flush with the back of the cabinet (see **photo I**).

Don't screw the base to the cabinet yet. The shelving modules that will be joined to this cabinet are open, so any screws used to attach their bases would be visible. For this reason, their bases will be attached from underneath. To achieve a more unified look, I'll show how to connect the modules first, then attach all three bases at the same time with the attached units upside down (see "Attaching the Base" on p. 97).

marked in the illustration on p. 81. These will mate with slots cut in the base later.

12. Finish-sand the ½-in. plywood back, slide it into its rabbet, and screw it in place.

Making the Base

Although the base for the low cabinet is a different size, it is constructed like the base of the pedestal cabinet discussed in chapter 4. However, unlike the cabinets in chapter 4, which are simply placed next to each other under the desktop, this cabinet is designed to become a module. By combining this module with some of the shelving modules discussed in chapter 6, you can create what looks like a single, freestanding piece of furniture.

Making the Top

Like the pedestal cabinets, this cabinet has a top that is less than attractive. In this case, however, there is no desktop to slide the cabinet under. I could have built the cabinet in such a way that the top looked better but not without compromising the modular nature of the construction. The solution is to add a long top that covers the cabinet and the two low shelf units discussed in chapter 6. This will improve the appearance of all of these pieces and integrate them visually (see "Attaching the Top" on p. 98). This may

seem contradictory to my reason for building separate bases, but if you changed the configuration of these cabinets in the future it would be relatively simple to make a new top. Alternatively, you could build a separate top for each cabinet, but this might look less attractive. The top is constructed of the same plywood as the rest of the furniture, but for durability the front and sides are edged with solid wood rather than edge tape.

1. To make the top, cut a piece of ¾-in. cherry plywood 74½ in. long and 12 in. wide.

2. For the edging, mill solid cherry strips ¾ in. wide by approximately ¹³⁄₁₆ in. thick. Cut one length of approximately 78 in. and two lengths of approximately 15 in. each. These pieces are thicker and longer than you need but will be cut down. The ¹³⁄₁₆-in. face will be attached to the edge of the plywood and sanded down to the thickness of the plywood later.

3. Carefully miter one end of each of the three strips at 45 degrees across the ¾-in. face.

4. Line up the miter on the long strip at one end of the long edge of the plywood, using one of the short pieces as a guide to align it.

5. Next, clamp the strip in place and mark the other end where it extends past the plywood, then unclamp it and miter the marked end.

6. Apply glue to the strip, then carefully realign it and clamp it again to the edge of the plywood. Make sure the strip stands proud of the top and bottom faces of the plywood (see **photo J**).

7. Glue and carefully align the short strips and clamp them to the ends of the plywood.

8. After the glue dries, scrape off any excess and plane the edging flush with the face of the plywood using a sharp handplane, as shown in **photo K**. You could use a router but it would be difficult to control on the thin edge of the plywood.

9. Using a sharp handsaw, trim off the back ends of the edging, then finish-sand the top to 150 grit.

PHOTO J: A strip of solid cherry edge (above) hides the raw plywood edge of the top.

PHOTO K: The cherry edging is quickly and easily planed flush using a sharp handplane.

Wall-Hung Cabinet

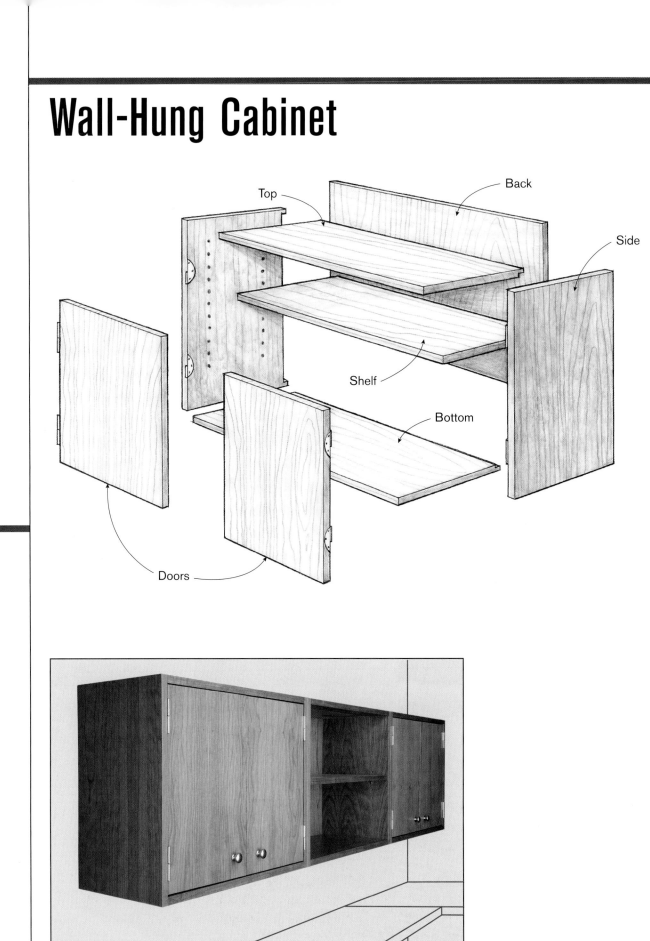

Top

Back

Side

Shelf

Bottom

Doors

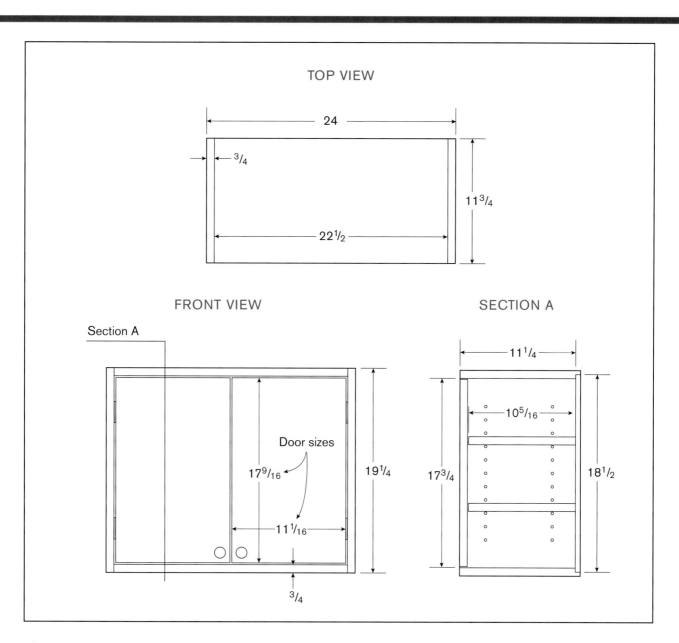

TOP VIEW

24

3/4

11³/4

22¹/2

FRONT VIEW

SECTION A

Section A

Door sizes

17⁹/16

19¹/4

11¹/16

11¹/4

10⁵/16

17³/4

18¹/2

3/4

Construction and Assembly

THIS CABINET IS NEARLY THE SAME as the low cabinet but without the base and top. Because there is no base or top, the back would be exposed at the bottom and top if the construction were identical. To avoid exposing the back, you will have to cut rabbets in the top and bottom pieces of this cabinet as well as in the sides. The rabbet on the bottom is especially important since the cabinet hangs on the wall and is seen from below. To give the cabinet a more finished

appearance from below, you'll also use stopped rabbets on the side pieces (see the illustration on p. 86) and edge-band the plywood edges on the bottoms of these pieces.

Cutting the rabbets

After you cut and size all of the plywood for the cabinet boxes and before you do anything else, cut the rabbets.

1. Install a piloted rabbeting bit in a router and mount it in a router table. Set the bit to cut a ½-in.-wide rabbet, ⅜ in. deep (half the thickness of the plywood).

[**tip**] Cutting stopped rabbets is easier when you mount the router in a router table. As long as you've set up the router table, you might as well use it to cut all the rabbets for this piece.

CUT LIST FOR WALL-HUNG CABINET

Cabinet Box

1	Top	22½ in. x 11¾ in.	¾-in. cherry plywood
1	Bottom	22½ in. x 11¾ in.	¾-in. cherry plywood
2	Sides	19¼ in. x 11¾ in.	¾-in. cherry plywood
2	Shelves	22⅜ in. x 10⁵⁄₁₆ in.	¾-in. cherry plywood
1	Back	23½ in. x 18½ in.	½-in. cherry plywood

Doors

2	Doors	17⁹⁄₁₆ in. x 11¹⁄₁₆ in.	¾-in. cherry plywood

Other Materials

	Approximately 20 linear ft. edge tape	cherry
2	Door knobs	
8	Shelf pins	
4	Duplex hinges	
	#20 biscuits	
8	Hex-drive connector bolts and threaded sleeves	
	Finish	

2. Clamp or hot-glue a small piece of scrap wood at each end of the edge to be rabbeted on both side pieces. Place these blocks so they will stop the bit about ⅜ in. from each end of the cut.

3. Next, rout the rabbet, rolling the bit carefully into the cut to make sure the bearing doesn't catch at the beginning.

4. Rout the rabbets in the top and bottom pieces all the way through from end to end.

The construction and assembly of this cabinet is the same as the previous cabinets (see pp. 48–60). However, be sure to edge-band the top and bottom edges of the sides as well as the fronts of the cabinet parts. Don't apply edgebanding until after you cut the biscuit slots. Cutting the biscuit slots in the sides after edge-banding their top and bottom edges increases the height of the cabinet by twice the thickness of the edge tape. If you have already cut the doors and back, they will no longer fit (see **photos L–N**).

Detail of a Stopped Rabbet

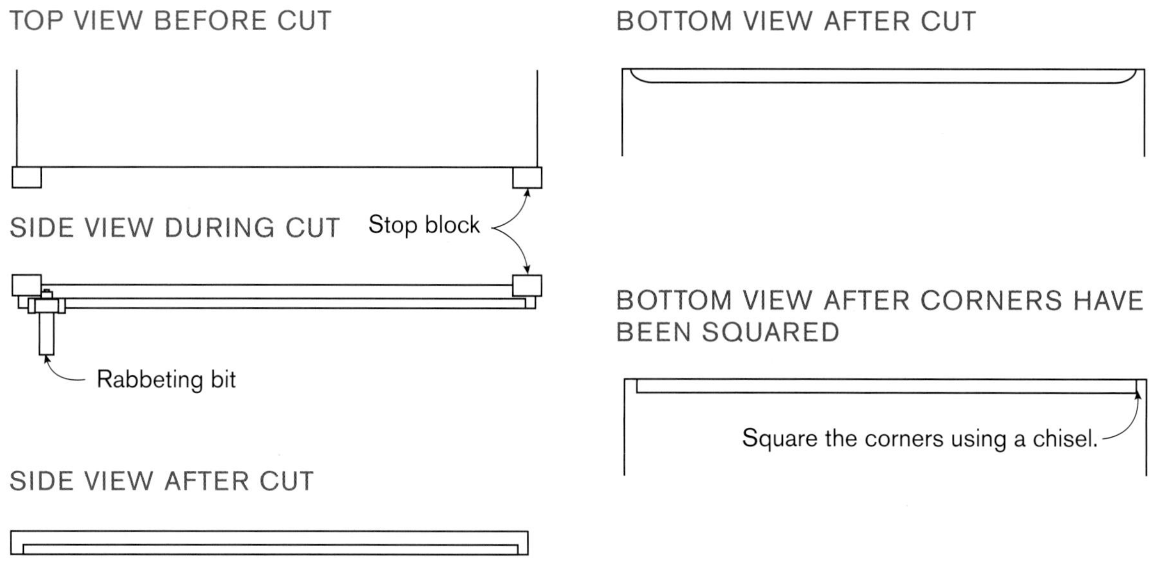

TOP VIEW BEFORE CUT

BOTTOM VIEW AFTER CUT

SIDE VIEW DURING CUT   Stop block

Rabbeting bit

BOTTOM VIEW AFTER CORNERS HAVE BEEN SQUARED

Square the corners using a chisel.

SIDE VIEW AFTER CUT

PHOTO L: Having all necessary materials on hand before glue-up and clamping will ensure a smooth procedure.

PHOTO M: The back is attached with small trim-head screws.

STYLE OPTION: FRAME-AND-PANEL DOORS

SUBSTITUTING frame-and-panel-doors for the flat doors would give these cabinets a more traditional look without greatly altering the construction. Frame-and-panel doors—especially raised-panel doors and doors that require coping and complicated joinery—are certainly more work than flat plywood doors. The door shown here is just one possibility, but it is relatively easy to build and will give the cabinet a more traditional look.

1. Joint, plane, and glue up enough ½-in.-thick solid cherry panel stock to make a panel longer and wider than the finished door (see the photo below). When the glue is dry, sand all of the glue joints flush.

2. To make the frame, joint and plane cherry stock to 2 in. by ¾ in. by whatever lengths you need to frame the door. Make each length a little oversized for now.

3. Using a table saw with a ¼-in. dado blade, cut a groove ¼ in. wide and ⅜ in. deep down the center of the inside edge of all of the frame pieces. This groove will accept the rabbeted edge of the panel.

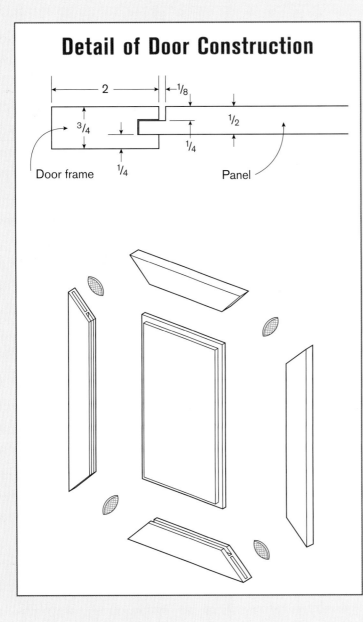

Detail of Door Construction

Gluing a number of narrow boards together will produce a board wide enough for the panel. This style of clamp uses a driver drill to close the jaws.

4. Using a table saw and miter gauge, carefully miter all of the frame pieces to their exact lengths.

5. Cut biscuit slots in all of the miters. Be careful in positioning them, since you don't have much room on these surfaces.

6. Size the panel to your frame (the panel should be slightly smaller to allow for seasonal wood movement), then rout a ¼-in. by ½-in. rabbet all around it.

7. Finish-sand the panel and the inside edges of the frame to 150 grit.

8. Glue, biscuit, and clamp the frame together around the panel. Since this can be a tricky glue-up, do a trial run first (see the photo below).

9. When the glue is dry, finish-sand the outside of the frame to 150 grit.

The frame is glued up around a floating panel.

PHOTO N: Finish-sand the outside of the cabinet after the glue has dried.

To assemble, follow the directions for the other cabinets (see pp. 57–59). The one special instruction for this cabinet is that you have to square up the round corners produced by routing the stopped rabbets in order to make the back sit into the rabbets (see the photo on p. 108).

Finishing

I finished these pieces using a spray-on lacquer but you can choose among several other finishing methods (see the appendix on p. 151 for details on finishing).

CHAPTER 6

Shelving

NO OFFICE WOULD BE COMPLETE without a place to store books. All kinds of books migrate into the office—reference books, computer manuals, and manuals for other office equipment and software. If you are anything like me, you have a lot of them and you want to find them easily when you need them, even if you need them only occasionally. You can't find them if they're stored one on top of the other in drawers or on their sides in cabinets. Bookcases are definitely the best place for books.

This office has three kinds of shelf units: a wall-hung shelf unit, a low shelf unit, and a simple, tall bookcase. As with the smaller cabinets discussed in chapter 5, the wall-hung shelf and the low shelf have only minor differences between them. The low shelf has a base and it shares a top with the low cabinets. Also, the rabbet for the back of the wall-hung shelf is slightly different. These two modules are the same size as the wall-hung cabinet and the low cabinet.

The tall bookcase is just what it sounds like: a workhorse meant to hold a lot of books. Though simple, it is not without style or charm. As with most of the furniture units in this office, you can build as many or as few as you need. If you have enough wall space and vast quantities of books, just keep on building. You might also find these bookcases useful in other rooms.

Low Shelf Unit

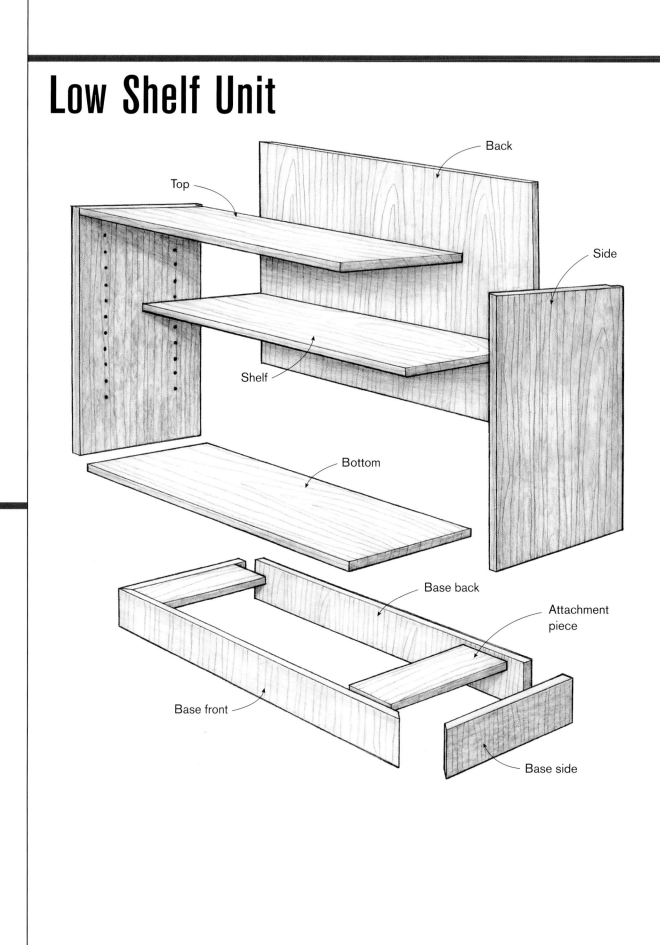

Back

Top

Side

Shelf

Bottom

Base back

Attachment piece

Base front

Base side

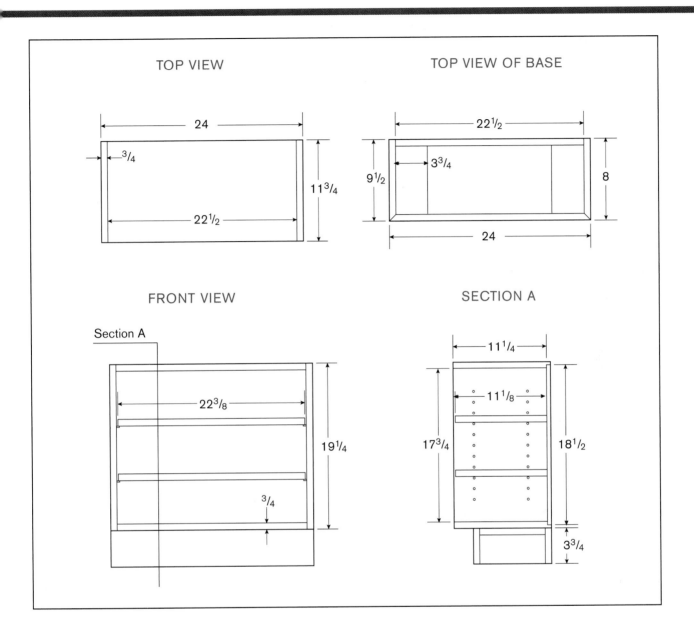

TOP VIEW

TOP VIEW OF BASE

FRONT VIEW

SECTION A

Construction and Assembly

THIS UNIT AND THE WALL-HUNG unit described after it are by far the simplest projects in this book. By now you should be able to build this type of plywood cabinet, top, and base without any problem, so I won't repeat the basic instructions (but see pp. 49–60 for details if you're building the shelves before tackling the cabinets). However, I do want to discuss a few issues related to connecting units together.

Connecting the units

The two low shelves and the low unit discussed in chapter 5 make up a single piece of furniture, so they will need to be fastened together securely. At the same time, since they are modular, you wouldn't want to give up the possibility of changing or adding to their arrangement. Also, it is handy to be able to break down larger pieces when you need to move them.

Various kinds of knockdown fasteners are available for exactly this purpose (see pp. 38–39). Some are difficult to install,

CUT LIST FOR LOW SHELF UNIT

Base

1	Front	24 in. x 3¾ in.	¾-in. cherry plywood
1	Back	22½ in. x 3¾ in.	¾-in. cherry plywood
2	Sides	9½ in. x 3¾ in.	¾-in. cherry plywood
2	Attachment pieces	8 in. x 3¾ in.	¾-in. cherry plywood

Cabinet Box

1	Top	22½ in. x 11¾ in.	¾-in. cherry plywood
1	Bottom	22½ in. x 11¾ in.	¾-in. cherry plywood
2	Sides	19¼ in. x 11¾ in.	¾-in. cherry plywood
2	Shelves	22⅜ in. x 11⅛ in.	¾-in. cherry plywood
1	Back	23½ in. x 18½ in.	½-in. cherry plywood

Other Materials

Approximately 20 linear ft. edge tape		cherry
8	Shelf pins	
#20 biscuits		
20	Hex-drive connector bolts and threaded sleeves	
Finish		

others require special tools, and many are just hard to find. For the projects in this book, I used special flat-head bolts, driven with a hex driver, that screw into threaded inserts (see Sources of Supply on p. 152). These are easy to install and use and are readily available. The disadvantage of these fasteners, unlike some of the more specialized fasteners on the market, is that they show on the surface. I think they look nice in the right situation, but in this project you will be keeping them out of sight when necessary and practical.

In this office, you'll connect the two low shelf units on either side of a closed cabinet unit discussed in chapter 5. The fasteners only have to show on one side of the walls they join together, so you'll keep the part that shows on the inside of the closed cabinet. To install and use the knockdown fasteners:

1. Start by lining up the cabinets to be joined and clamping them together. Mark the locations of the holes for the fasteners, placing one at each corner of the inside of the sides of the center cabinet (in this case, the closed cabinet).

PHOTO A: Threaded fasteners are installed to accept connector bolts.

Hole-Drilling Sequence for Fasteners

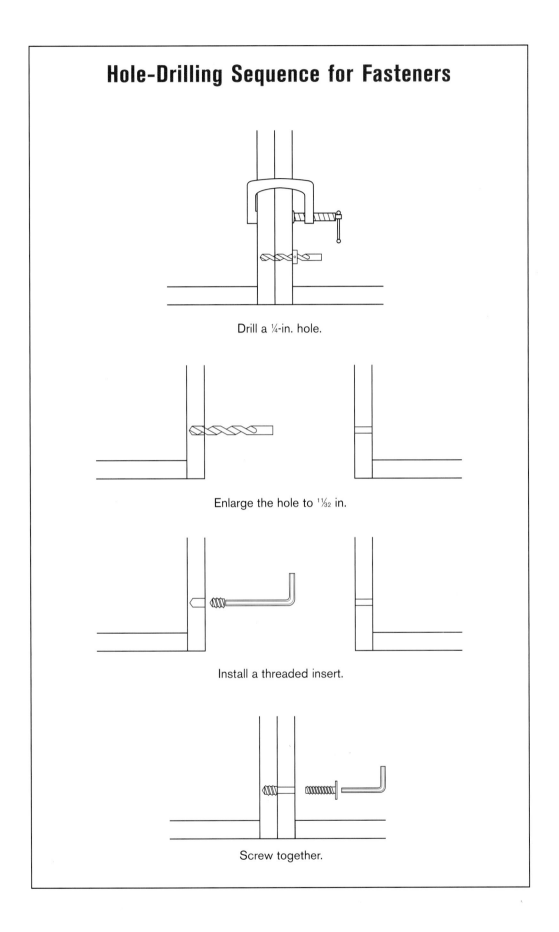

Drill a ¼-in. hole.

Enlarge the hole to $^{11}\!/_{32}$ in.

Install a threaded insert.

Screw together.

2. Drill a ¼-in. hole 1⅜ in. deep at each location (drilling through one cabinet and partly into the adjacent cabinet). To avoid drilling completely through and into the adjoining cabinet, use a depth stop on your drill bit.

3. Separate the cabinets and enlarge the holes in the outside cabinets using an ¹¹⁄₃₂-in. drill bit. (These are the holes that don't go all the way through.)

4. Install the threaded inserts into these holes. The drivers for installing the inserts are available from the suppliers of the inserts (see Sources of Supply on p. 152 and **photo A** on p. 94).

5. Line up the cabinets again (you don't need clamps this time) and screw the bolts through the ¼-in. holes and into the inserts, as shown in **photo B**. That's all there is to it.

PHOTO B: Once the threaded fasteners are installed, simply bolt the cabinets together.

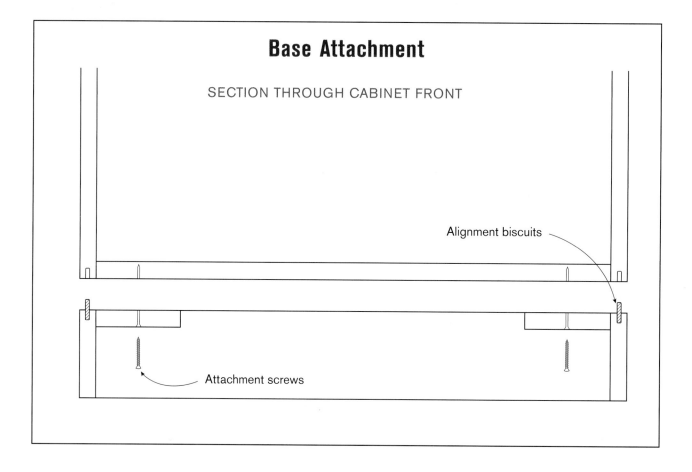

Base Attachment

SECTION THROUGH CABINET FRONT

Alignment biscuits

Attachment screws

Attaching the base

To hide the attachment fasteners, the base is attached from the underside.

1. Place the attached cabinets upside down on the floor and insert the alignment biscuits (without glue) into the bottoms.

2. One at a time, place the bases on the cabinet bottoms, aligning the biscuit slots so that the backs of the bases are flush with the backs of the cabinets. Press down until the bases are tight against the cabinets (see **photo C**).

3. Following the sequence described in "Connecting the Units" on pp. 93–96, install one fastener in each corner of each base, then attach the bases (see **photo D**).

PHOTO C: The bases are positioned on their alignment biscuits prior to drilling holes for fasteners.

PHOTO D: The bases are firmly fastened to the undersides of the cabinets.

PHOTO E: The top is fastened to the cabinet just as the base was.

Attaching the top

The top is attached using the same fasteners used to attach the base. The fasteners are inserted from inside the cabinets, so technically they show, but you won't see them unless you are lying on the floor.

1. Place the top upside down on a bench, using a blanket so you won't scratch the top.

2. Place the cabinet/base assembly you just created upside down on the top.

3. Aligning the backs of the cabinets flush with the back edge of the top, center the cabinets on the top. There should be a 2-in. overhang on each end and a 1-in. overhang in front.

4. Following the same sequence as when you attached the bases, install one fastener in each corner of the underside of the cabinet top and attach the top (see **photo E**).

Wall-Hung Shelf Unit

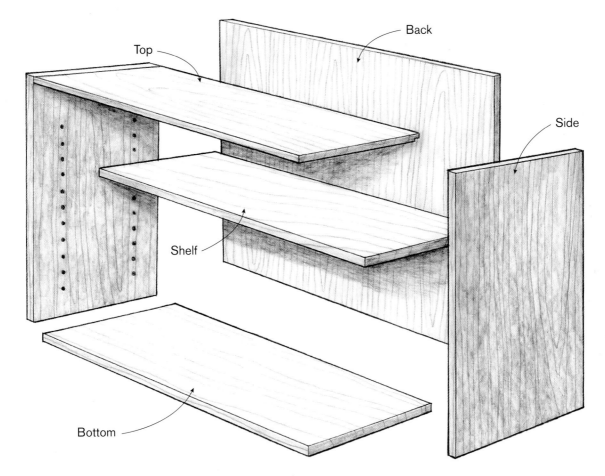

Back

Top

Side

Shelf

Bottom

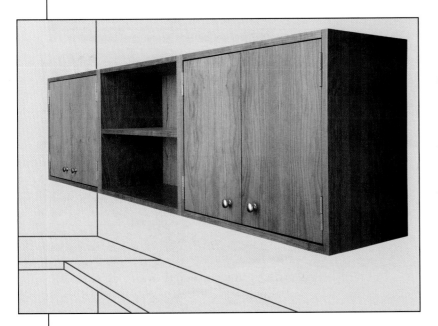

Construction and Assembly

THE WALL-HUNG SHELF unit is connected to the two wall-hung cabinet units that you made in chapter 5, which are the same size. Keep the fasteners from showing by installing them from the closed cabinets at the ends into the open cabinet in the middle, just the reverse of the way you connected the low cabinets and shelves (see **photo F** on p. 101). Otherwise, the process is the same.

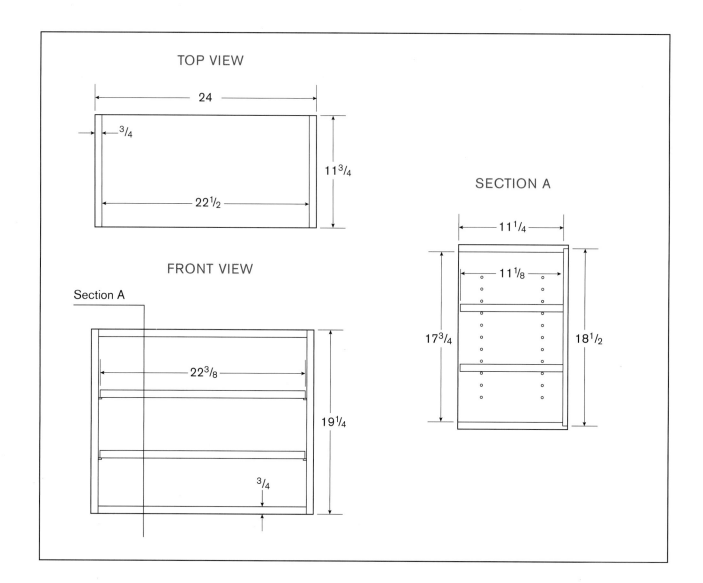

TOP VIEW

24

³/₄

11³/₄

22½

FRONT VIEW

Section A

22³/₈

19¼

³/₄

SECTION A

11¼

11⅛

17³/₄

18½

CUT LIST FOR WALL-HUNG SHELF UNIT

Cabinet Box

1	Top	22½ in. x 11¾ in.	¾-in. cherry plywood
1	Bottom	22½ in. x 11¾ in.	¾-in. cherry plywood
2	Sides	19¼ in. x 11¾ in.	¾-in. cherry plywood
2	Shelves	22⅜ in. x 11⅛ in.	¾-in. cherry plywood
1	Back	23½ in. x 18½ in.	½-in. cherry plywood

Other Materials

Approximately 20 linear ft. edge tape	cherry
8 Shelf pins	
#20 biscuits	
8 Hex-drive connector bolts and threaded sleeves	
Finish	

PHOTO F: Exact
alignment is critical
before drilling holes
for the fasteners.

STYLE OPTION: ATTACHED TOP

TO ME THE WALL-HUNG unit looks fine the
way it is. However, this option is so simple
and obvious that I would be failing in my duty as
an author if I didn't bring it to your attention on
the off-chance that you hadn't already thought of
it: Just build a top exactly like the one you built
for the low units. Attach the top from above,
inserting fasteners through the top and into the
cabinets. This will hide the fasteners where no
one can see them.

ABOVE: Fasten the top from above so the
fasteners won't be seen.

LEFT: Adding a decorative top gives some
style to these hanging cabinets.

Tall Bookcase

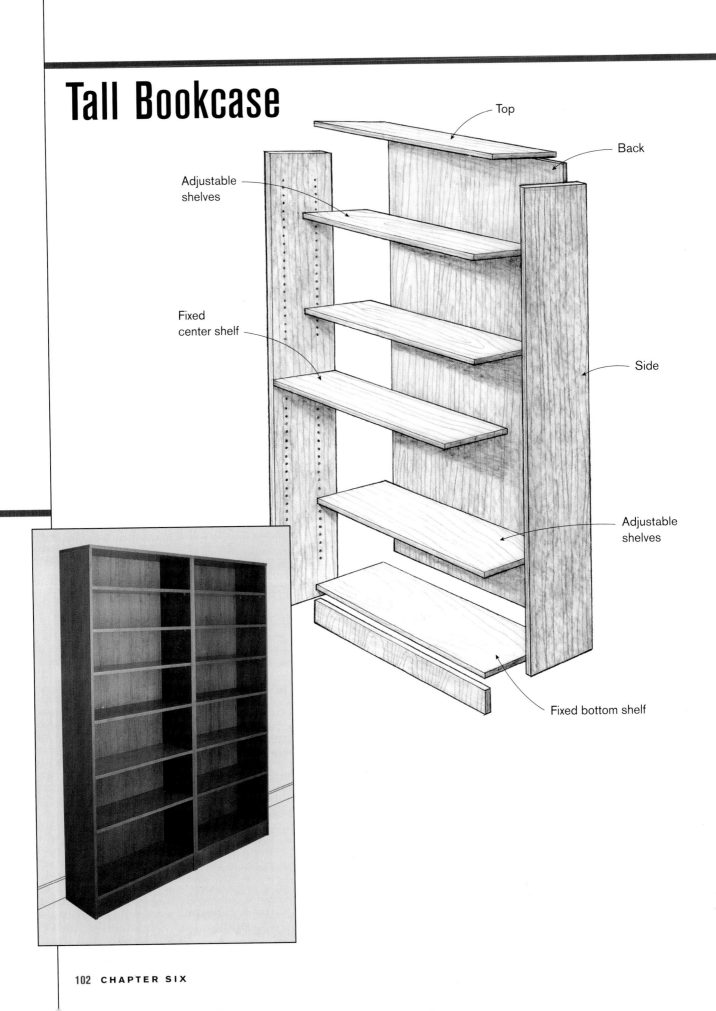

Top

Back

Adjustable shelves

Fixed center shelf

Side

Adjustable shelves

Fixed bottom shelf

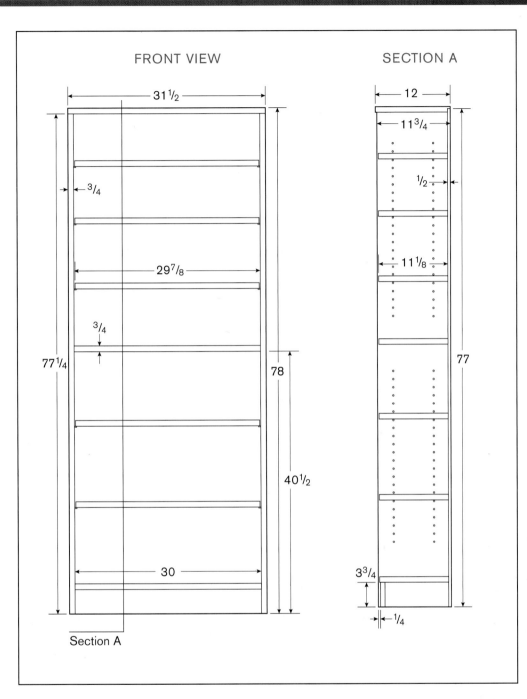

FRONT VIEW

SECTION A

31 1/2

12

3/4

11 3/4

1/2

29 7/8

11 1/8

3/4

77 1/4

78

77

40 1/2

30

3 3/4

1/4

Section A

Construction and Assembly

ALTHOUGH THE CONSTRUCTION of this case is similar to the rest of the cabinets in this book, there are important differences. Most if not all of which involve the relationship between its size and what it is destined to hold: Books, or to put it simply, heavy stuff!

The weight-bearing capacity of shelves depends on the material of which they are constructed. For the ¾-in. plywood being used here, 30 in. is about the maximum length for an unsupported span. Longer spans risk sagging over time if they're loaded with heavy objects—and books are heavy. While softcover books can weigh as little as a few ounces apiece, a row of hardcover novels can easily weigh a pound per inch. Some

CUT LIST FOR TALL BOOKCASE

Case

1	Top	31½ in. x 12 in.	¾-in. cherry plywood
1	Bottom fixed shelf	30 in. x 11⅛ in.	¾-in. cherry plywood
1	Center fixed shelf	30 in. x 11⅛ in.	¾-in. cherry plywood
2	Sides	76½ in. x 11¾ in.	¾-in. cherry plywood
5	Adjustable shelves	29⅞ in. x 11⅛ in.	¾-in. cherry plywood
1	Back	77 in. x 31 in.	½-in. cherry plywood
1	Kick	30 in. x 3¾ in.	¾-in. cherry plywood

Other Materials

Approximately 50 linear ft. edge tape	cherry
24 Shelf pins	
#20 biscuits	
Finish	

PHOTO G: Marking out both sides at the same time ensures that they will be identical.

large art books can weigh four times this amount.

The sides of the bookcase also need support to avoid the risk of the sides bowing. The maximum unsupported height for the materials you'll be using is about 36 in., so the center shelf of this bookcase has to be fixed in place.

This bookshelf is designed around these maximum spans for ¾-in. plywood. The vertical span, or the distance between supports (top of piece, fixed center shelf, and bottom shelf), is 36 in. and the horizontal span (shelf length) is 30 in. The depth is sized to be efficiently cut from sheets of plywood, but you'll find that all but the largest books will fit comfortably in this bookcase. Working from these spans and adding in the thickness of the material, I arrived at a bookcase 31½ in. wide by 78 in. high by 11¾ in. deep.

Layout

You should be able to cut both sides of the bookcase and six shelves from a single sheet of plywood without difficulty. You'll probably find you can cut the top and any additional shelves from the plywood left over from the other projects. If you don't need more than five shelves, you can squeeze the whole bookcase, including the kick, out of one sheet of plywood. Keeping in mind that the top is deeper and wider than the shelves, lay out the pieces carefully, leaving enough room between them for the saw kerf, and pay attention to your cut sequence (see the illustration on the facing page and **photo G**). You will have to cut some of the parts very close to their finished size, so there won't be much waste left for trimming.

Cutting the rabbets

After you have cut all the plywood for the case to size, cut rabbets at the inside back edges of the sides and the top using a router fitted with a ½-in. piloted rabbeting bit. Because the top is positioned over the sides, rather than between them, the rabbet in the top must be a stopped rabbet, as shown in **photo H** on p. 106 (see "Cutting the Rab-

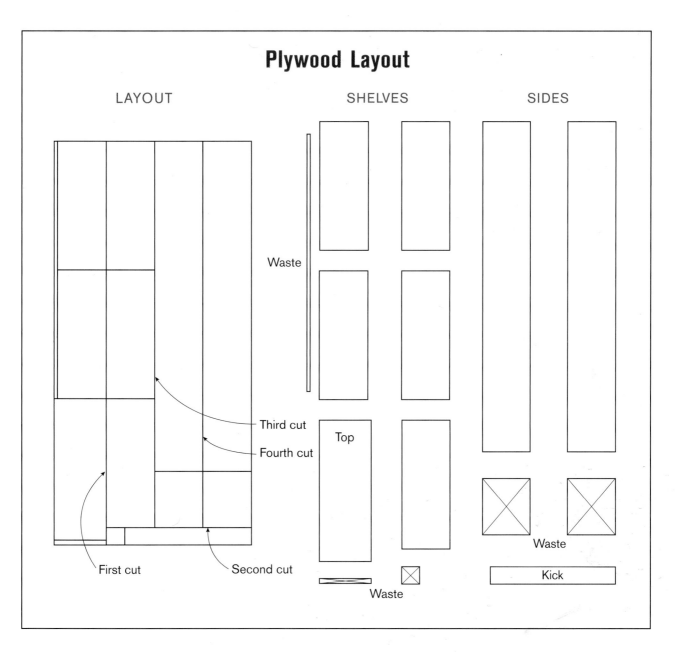

Plywood Layout

LAYOUT

SHELVES

SIDES

Waste

Third cut

Fourth cut

Top

First cut

Second cut

Waste

Waste

Kick

bets" on pp. 85–86 for details). The rabbets in the side pieces can run from end to end.

Cutting the biscuit slots

Lay out and cut the biscuit slots for the case joints, as shown in **photo I** on p. 106. The slots should be cut so that the top of the bookcase lies over the sides and so that the center shelf and bottom shelf are between the sides. When you lay out the slots for the center and bottom shelves, pay attention to how you orient the biscuit joiner for the cuts (see "Biscuit Joinery" on p. 55). This is also the time to cut the slots that you will use to

join the kick to the bottom shelf. You don't need to cut biscuit slots to join the ends of the kick to the case sides. A little glue on these edges when you clamp the case is all that's needed.

Once the slots are cut, dry-fit the piece together to make sure everything is located correctly.

Edgebanding

Edge-band the front edges of the sides and shelves and also the side edges and front edge of the top (see **photo J** on p. 107). Because the top is edge-banded after the biscuit slots are

PHOTO H: Rabbets in the sides can run from end to end, but the rabbet in the top should stop short of the ends so it won't be seen.

cut, the edge tape will be proud of the side of the bookcase. If you position two of these units side by side, they will have a space between them twice the thickness of the edge tape. To attach the units, you would have to add spacers between them at the locations of the fasteners. A washer or two will probably do the job. If you don't like the look of the space, or if you don't want to deal with spacers, factor in the thickness of the edge tape when you cut the top and edge-band the sides of the top before cutting the biscuit slots.

Shelf pin holes

Before continuing with the assembly of the bookcase, drill the shelf pin holes for the adjustable shelves. Two sets of holes are needed on each side, one above and one below the center shelf. It is best to drill the entire row at once, referencing your jig from the same edge for each row. The Festool jig shown in **photo K** has long enough guides to accommodate the whole row, but if your jig

PHOTO I: Cutting biscuit slots at the end of a board is easier if the piece is held in a vise.

PHOTO J: Edge-banding can be easily trimmed by scoring it in back with a sharp knife and breaking it off.

PHOTO K: A long jig is ideal for drilling shelf pin holes in the sides of this bookcase.

is shorter you will have to pay close attention when you move positions. Alternatively, you can make your own jig sized for this operation. I prefer jigs that use a router rather than a hand drill since routers generally cut cleaner holes, but with a little extra care hand drill-based jigs work fine.

All that's really important is being able to drill a row of evenly spaced holes that lines up properly—not only with the other row on the same side of the case but also with the rows on the opposing side. You need to find a way to locate the jig repeatedly at a specific distance from the front and back edges as well as from the top and bottom edges.

Preassembly

To make the final glue-up easier, preassemble the kick and bottom shelf. This reduces the

PHOTO L: Rounded corners left by a router can be quickly squared up using a sharp chisel.

[tip] Gluing and clamping a large piece can be a juggling act, so simplify by creating subassemblies wherever possible.

time for the final glue-up and the number of clamps you will need.

Make sure the ends of the kick are perfectly flush with the shelf during the first glue-up; there is no way to fix it after the fact, since sanding or trimming it to flush it up will change the size of the assembly.

Assembly

Assembling a case this size can be tricky. It pays to prepare the space and gather all of the clamps, glue, and biscuits you will need so you don't have to go looking for something in the middle of a glue-up.

1. Remove the clamps from the bottom shelf/kick assembly and finish-sand the top of the shelf and the face of the kick to 150 grit. Sand the insides of the top, center shelf, and sides to 150 grit.

2. Glue biscuits into the slots in the face of the sides and the top.

3. Lay one long side down on a couple of sawhorses with the inside face up, then glue and position the bottom shelf/kick assembly and the center shelf on their mating biscuits. Glue and place the other long side on top of this assembly.

4. Clamp across the case at the front and back of both shelf locations. Check for square and adjust the clamps if necessary.

5. Glue and position the top on its biscuits and clamp it in place front and back on both sides.

6. When the glue is dry, remove the clamps and finish-sand the outside of the case to 150 grit.

Installing the back

1. With the case lying on its face, use a sharp chisel to square up the corners of the stopped rabbet in the top (see **photo L**).

The routing you did earlier will have left rounded ends.

2. Measure the opening created by the rabbets, and cut your ½-in. plywood back to fit snugly. Fitting the back as tightly as possible gives stability to the case and also helps keep it square.

3. Finish-sand the back to 150 grit and fit it into the rabbets.

4. Mark out and drill pilot holes for small screws around the perimeter of the back and across the backs of the shelves, then insert the screws as shown in **photo M**. (I use 1-in. trim-head screws; see Sources of Supply on p. 152.)

Finishing

I finished these pieces using a spray-on lacquer, but there are several other finishing methods to choose from (see the appendix on p. 151 for details on finishing).

[tip] On a long case, it's best to check for square before the top is clamped in place because clamp pressure along the long sides will often distort or bow them.

PHOTO M: To make the bookcase strong, fasten the back not only around the perimeter but also to the backs of the fixed shelves.

CHAPTER 7

Desktops

AN OFFICE WOULDN'T FUNCTION very well without desktop space, which is as much of a necessity as cabinets and storage units. Not so long ago, you could have gotten away with a medium-sized desk to write out some bills or type a letter. In today's office, desktop space is at a premium. We are being crowded out by computers, printers, fax machines, and scanners. Often there is barely enough room to lay down a pencil. In the matter of desktops, bigger is definitely better.

In this chapter, I will show you how to build the desktop for your office. This may seem straightforward, but the design was actually quite challenging. I started out planning a suite of office furniture whose modular design could be easily adapted to fit most spaces. But it turns out that most of the adapting has to be done in the desktops. More than any other piece of furniture, the desktop is dependent on the size and shape of the individual office space.

The desktops discussed in this chapter are the result of balancing several design requirements. The design had to work in any size and in several different configurations (straight, L-shaped, possibly even U-shaped) and had to span large or small distances with minimal support. It had to fit over the pedestal cabinets, and to complicate matters even more, it had to provide space in the back for the wires that power and link all the office machines as well as the phones and lights.

Desktops

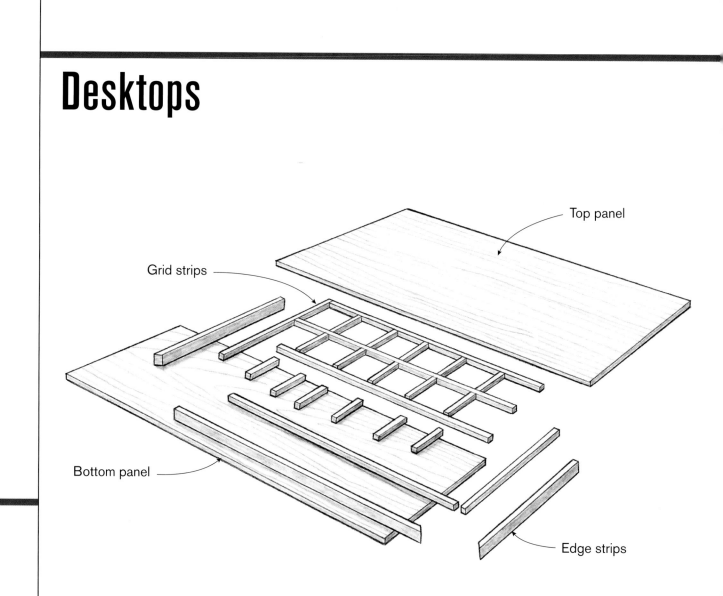

Top panel

Grid strips

Bottom panel

Edge strips

Construction and Assembly

THE THREE DESKTOPS in the example office (8 ft., 5 ft., and 4 ft.) meet the needs I just mentioned elegantly and simply. You can build them in whatever lengths you need. Regardless of length, they are all built using torsion-box construction, a type of hollow-core construction that is very strong and rigid. There are other ways to construct this type of top, but most of them, like the

honeycomb core in **photo A** on p. 116, require special materials and machinery. Even torsion-box construction is easier to do if you have a veneer press, but the method used here doesn't require any special tools or machinery.

The tops shown in this chapter are possibly a bit overbuilt. In retrospect, the smaller tops probably could have been made with more widely spaced grids. Still, it won't hurt the top to be too strong, and the project offers good practice in a valuable technique.

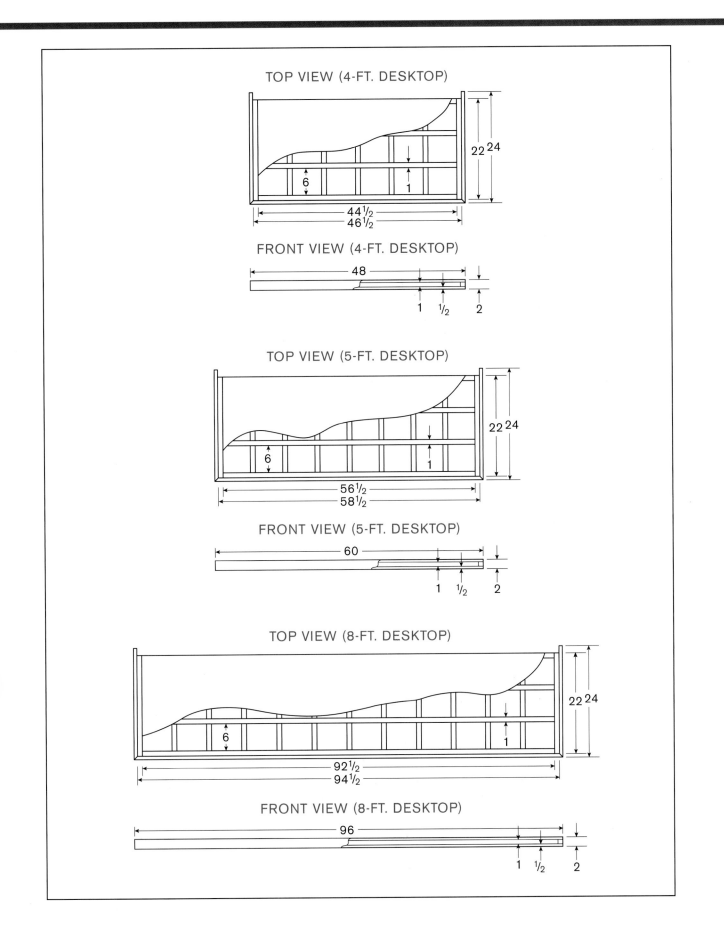

TOP VIEW (4-FT. DESKTOP)

22 24

6

1

44½
46½

FRONT VIEW (4-FT. DESKTOP)

48

1 ½ 2

TOP VIEW (5-FT. DESKTOP)

22 24

6

1

56½
58½

FRONT VIEW (5-FT. DESKTOP)

60

1 ½ 2

TOP VIEW (8-FT. DESKTOP)

22 24

6

1

92½
94½

FRONT VIEW (8-FT. DESKTOP)

96

1 ½ 2

CUT LIST FOR 8-FT. DESKTOP

Top and Bottom Faces

2	Faces	94½ in. x 22 in.	½-in. cherry plywood

Core

4	Grid strips	92½ in. x 1 in. x 1 in.	solid poplar
2	Grid strips	22 in. x 1 in. x 1 in.	solid poplar
33	Grid strips	6 in. x 1 in. x 1 in.	solid poplar

Edging

1	Edge strip	96 in. x 2 in. x ¾ in.	solid cherry
2	Edge strips	22 in. x 2 in. x ¾ in.	solid cherry

Desktop Connectors

2	Blocks	3 in. x 1½ in. x 1½ in.	solid cherry
2	Blocks	3 in. x ¾ in. x 1½ in.	solid cherry

Other Materials

2	Carriage bolts, with nuts and washers	3 in. x ⅜ in.	
Approximately 200 screws		#8 x 1¼ in.	
Finish			

Torsion-Box Construction

A torsion box consists of two skins of plywood glued to a core grid of thin wooden strips. In essence, you are creating many small I-beams within the box. The resulting structure is stronger than either the skin or the core alone and has tremendous resistance to twisting and bending forces. The engineering of the torsion box converts any applied force into shearing stress on the glue lines between the skin and core grid.

To make the core, you could use nearly any clear species of wood, from poplar (which is used here) to maple. Just make sure that the wood is stable and all of the same species—if you used different types of wood, differences in seasonal movement could eventually distort the finished panel. Because you are building 2-in.-thick desktops and using ½-in. plywood as the skins, the thickness of the core strips must be exactly 1 in. The width of the strips is not critical, but

CUT LIST FOR 5-FT. DESKTOP

Top and Bottom Faces

2	Faces	58½ in. x 22 in.	½-in. cherry plywood

Core

4	Grid strips	56½ in. x 1 in. x 1 in.	solid poplar
2	Grid strips	22 in. x 1 in. x 1 in.	solid poplar
21	Grid strips	6 in. x 1 in. x 1 in.	solid poplar

Edging

1	Edge strip	60 in. x 2 in. x ¾ in.	solid cherry
2	Edge strips	22 in. x 2 in. x ¾ in.	solid cherry

Other Materials

Approximately 130 screws		#8 x 1¼ in.	
Finish			

you don't want to make them too thin. Thin strips would be difficult to work with and could compromise the strength of the structure, which comes from the gluelines. For convenience, the strips you will use here are 1 in. square. Whatever dimension you choose, all of the core material must be accurately prepared: It must be flat, uniformly thick, and cut off squarely.

Cutting and laying out the grid

1. Cut to size two pieces of ½-in. plywood for each of the desktops you are building.

2. Rip, joint, and plane as many feet of 1-in. by 1-in. poplar as you need for your desktops, as shown in **photo B** on p. 116. (Refer to the illustration on p. 117 to calculate the length of material you need for the grid.)

CUT LIST FOR 4-FT. DESKTOP

Top and Bottom Faces

2	Faces	46½ in. x 22 in.	½-in. cherry plywood

Core

4	Grid strips	44½ in. x 1 in. x 1 in.	solid poplar
2	Grid strips	22 in. x 1 in. x 1 in.	solid poplar
15	Grid strips	6 in. x 1 in. x 1 in.	solid poplar

Edging

1	Edge strip	48 in. x 2 in. x ¾ in.	solid cherry
2	Edge strips	22 in. x 2 in. x ¾ in.	solid cherry

Other Materials

Approximately 100 screws	#8 x 1¼ in.

Finish

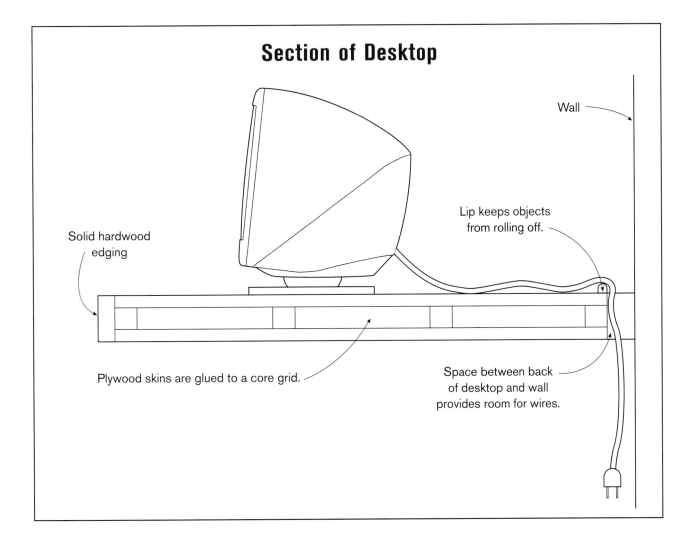

Section of Desktop

Wall

Lip keeps objects from rolling off.

Solid hardwood edging

Plywood skins are glued to a core grid.

Space between back of desktop and wall provides room for wires.

PHOTO A: Torsion boxes can be constructed using various cores. On the left is an example of a shop-built core and on the right, an example of a manufactured core.

PHOTO B: Ripping all the material for the core at the same time will ensure consistency.

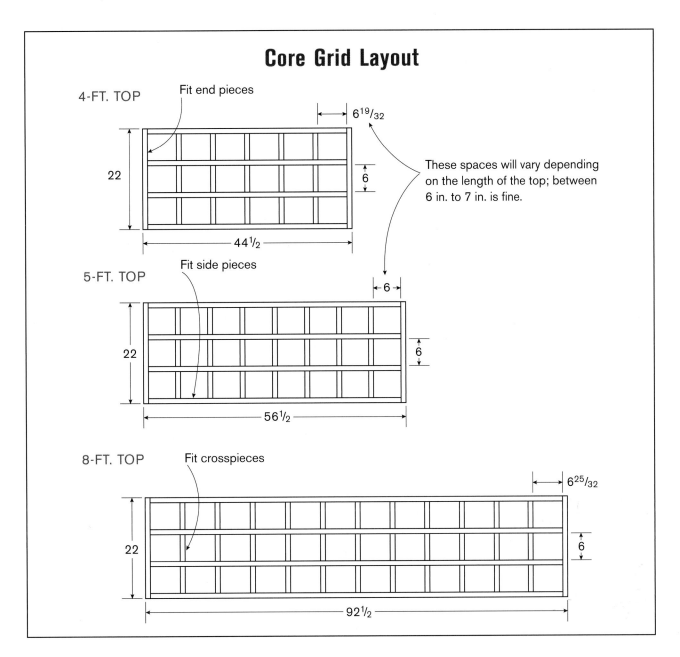

Core Grid Layout

4-FT. TOP

Fit end pieces

22

44½

6¹⁹⁄₃₂

6

These spaces will vary depending on the length of the top; between 6 in. to 7 in. is fine.

5-FT. TOP

Fit side pieces

22

56½

6

6

8-FT. TOP

Fit crosspieces

22

92½

6²⁵⁄₃₂

6

3. Next, lay the top piece of plywood face down on a flat surface. The flatness of the surface is important, since the top will take on the properties of the surface it is assembled on and clamped to. If you assemble the top on a surface that is bowed or twisted, the finished top will also be bowed or twisted.

4. Lay out the two end pieces of the core grid, and clamp them in place temporarily.

5. Cut and fit the four interior pieces that run lengthwise end to end, as shown in **photo C** on p. 118.

6. Temporarily clamp the two outside lengthwise pieces in place.

7. Cut and fit the short crosspieces.

Attaching the core to the top

As I mentioned earlier, a veneer press would certainly make the rest of this process easier—if you have one, by all means use it. If you are using a press, you must first prepare the grid by hot-gluing or stapling the four outside pieces of the grid together so they will contain the inner parts when you assemble the torsion box in the press.

[tip] The interior pieces of the grid should all fit snugly, but you don't have to be fanatical about the fit; the strength of this construction comes from the gluelines and not from how well the core is joined.

PHOTO C: Fit and lay out all the core components before beginning glue-up.

PHOTO D: Bearing down forcefully on the parts when installing the screws will help seat them properly.

If you don't have a veneer press, use the glue and screw method described here. It is very low tech and requires a lot of screws, but it works just fine.

1. When all of the core grid pieces are fitted, remove them, then drill and countersink pilot holes for #8 by 1¼-in. screws in all of the grid parts.

2. Glue and screw the parts in place in the same order you used to fit them, as shown in **photo D**. Be careful not to drive the screws in too deep—you don't want them going through the top.

Attaching the bottom to the core

You can either leave the screws in place (they won't harm anything) or remove them before you attach the bottom. If you choose to remove them, wait until the glue dries before continuing.

1. Place the bottom piece of plywood over the grid and mark the locations of the strips

on it so you will know where to place the screws (see **photo** E). Regardless of whether the first set of screws is still in place, mark the locations of those screws (or of the empty screw holes) so you don't screw into the same places when you attach the bottom. Then mark the new screw locations.

2. Spread glue on the top of the grid and carefully position the bottom piece of plywood over it, making sure its edges are flush with the side pieces. Clamp the bottom in place.

3. Drill and countersink pilot holes at all of your location marks, and screw the bottom to the grid.

4. If you don't like the idea of having these screws visible under your desktop, remove them after the glue is dry and plug the holes.

Attaching the edging

The torsion-box edge, which is now a sandwich of plywood edge and poplar, needs to be finished to match the desktop. The most straightforward solution is to glue a solid

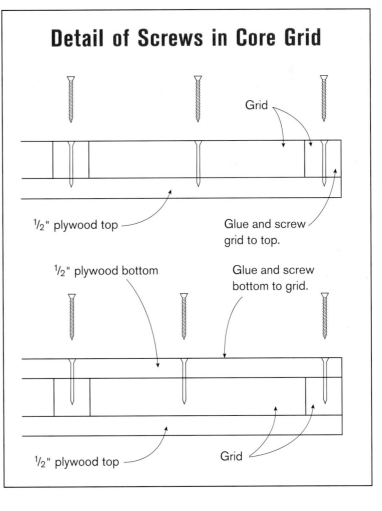

Detail of Screws in Core Grid

Grid

½" plywood top

Glue and screw grid to top.

½" plywood bottom

Glue and screw bottom to grid.

½" plywood top

Grid

cherry edge to the core. The instructions given here are for the 8-ft. desktop.

1. Cut, joint, and plane some solid cherry 2⅛ in. wide by ¾ in. thick, and cut one length to approximately 98 in. and two lengths to approximately 26 in. each. These pieces are slightly oversize; the 2⅛-in. face will be attached later to the edge of the torsion box and planed flush with the faces of the top.

2. Carefully miter one end of each of the three cherry strips at 45 degrees across the ¾-in. face.

3. Line up the mitered end of the long strip at one end of the long edge of the top, using one of the short pieces as a guide to align it.

Clamp in it place temporarily and mark the other end of the piece where it extends past the top (see **photo F**).

4. Miter the other end of the strip at the location you've marked.

5. Next, spread glue on the strip, carefully realign it, and clamp it to the edge of the top, making sure it is about ¹⁄₁₆ in. proud of the top and bottom faces of the top.

6. Spread glue on the short strips and at the miters, align them carefully, and clamp them to the ends of the top.

7. When the glue is dry, scrape off any excess and plane the edging flush with the face of the top using a handplane.

PHOTO F: Solid cherry edging hides the exposed plywood and poplar sandwich.

8. With your table saw fence set to 24 in. from the blade, run the top through the saw with the front edge against the fence. This will trim off the excess edging on the ends of the top, leaving it protruding 2 in. beyond the back edge. The 2-in. space allows you to feed wires down the back of the desktop.

9. Finish-sand the top to 150 grit.

Attaching the lip

The ⅜-in. bullnose lip glued to the back edge of the desktop keeps pencils and other small objects from rolling into the 2-in. gap behind the desktop and ending up on the floor (see **photo G**).

1. To attach the lip, cut, joint, and plane a strip of solid cherry 94½ in. by ⅜ in. by ⅜ in.

2. Sand the top edges of the strip aggressively until they are quite round.

3. Carefully glue and clamp the strip to the back top edge of the desktop.

Supporting the Top

Depending on how you configure your office, the desktop may or may not need some additional support. If you've made a single desktop that rests on cabinets at both ends, you don't need any further support. However, if your desktop ends at a wall, as in the example office, you will need a way to support the top. This is especially important if you have two desktops meeting in a corner with no cabinet underneath to support them.

One approach is to screw ledgers to the wall. On inside corners, such as the corner where the two longest tops come together, ledgers are all but invisible. However, in other places, such as where the 4-ft. desktop hits the wall, they are quite visible and don't look very elegant. More important, ledgers have to be anchored securely, which in practice usually means they must be lagged to the wall into the wall studs. Anchoring them can be a difficult and frustrating process.

A better solution is to build a side panel high enough to support the top and transfer

[tip] When two desktops meet, one of them will have to be supported by the other, so the support underneath them has to be very strong.

Desktop Support Panel

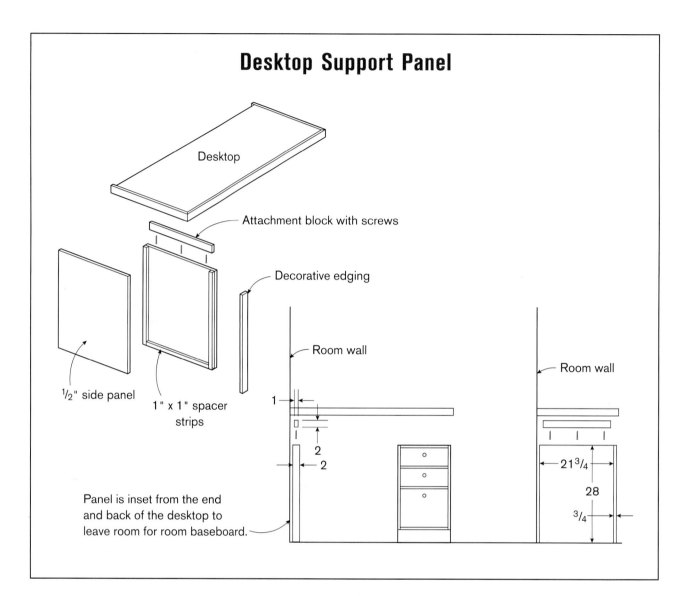

Desktop

Attachment block with screws

Decorative edging

Room wall

Room wall

½" side panel

1" x 1" spacer strips

1

2
2

21³/₄

28

³/₄

Panel is inset from the end and back of the desktop to leave room for room baseboard.

its weight directly to the floor. The panel is constructed similarly to the desktop but without the inside grid core structure. Also, the outside edging goes around only three sides of the panel. The top of the panel is left open to form a pocket into which a strip glued to the desktop will fit.

1. Start by cutting two ½-in. plywood panels each 28 in. by 21¾ in.

2. Cut, joint, and plane solid poplar 1 in. by 1 in. (the same size used in the core grid), and cut one 19¾-in. strip and two 28-in. strips.

3. Glue and clamp the two 28-in. pieces to the front and back of one of the plywood panels, placing each flush with the edge.

4. Glue and clamp the 19¾-in. piece to the bottom of the panel between the other two pieces.

5. When the glue is dry, remove the clamps and glue on the other panel, making sure the edges line up perfectly. Allow the glue to dry again, then clean up any excess and remove the clamps.

6. Cut, joint, and plane a piece of solid cherry 28 in. by 2⅛ in. by ¾ in. This is the same stock used for the desktop edging.

7. Glue and carefully align this piece onto the front edge of the assembly and clamp it in place, making sure it is approximately ¹/₁₆ in. proud of the plywood faces.

STYLE OPTION: END PANELS AND CASTERS

THE SAME DESKTOP SUPPORT PANEL can be used to support the end of a desktop if you choose not to place cabinets there. But even if you position cabinets at the ends of the desktops, you may still want to build side panels. The panels will hide the sides of the cabinets and give the unit a more finished look. They also give you the option of replacing your cabinet bases with casters, so you can pull the cabinets out and move them easily.

The cabinets are constructed with the bottom of the cabinet between the sides. This is not the best arrangement for casters because the weight of the cabinet rests on the cabinet bottom rather than on its sides, where it would be better supported. Rather than attaching the casters directly to the cabinet, add a piece of edge-banded ¾-in.

plywood to the cabinet bottom and attach the casters to it, leaving enough space so that the casters can rotate without extending past the sides of the cabinet. The plywood piece will look less like an afterthought if it is about ¼ in. larger than the cabinet at the front and sides.

ABOVE: Adding a side panel gives the unit a more finished look.

RIGHT: Casters allow the cabinets to be moved about easily.

Casters are available in different wheel diameters and heights, so make sure the casters you choose will work with these cabinets. The casters I used have a 2-in. wheel diameter and an overall height of approximately $2\frac{5}{8}$ in. The casters and the ¾-in. plywood together add approximately $3\frac{3}{8}$ in. to the cabinet. This lowers the overall height of the cabinet by approximately ⅜ in. (compared with the height of the cabinet with a base), allowing it to clear the desktop easily as it is rolled out.

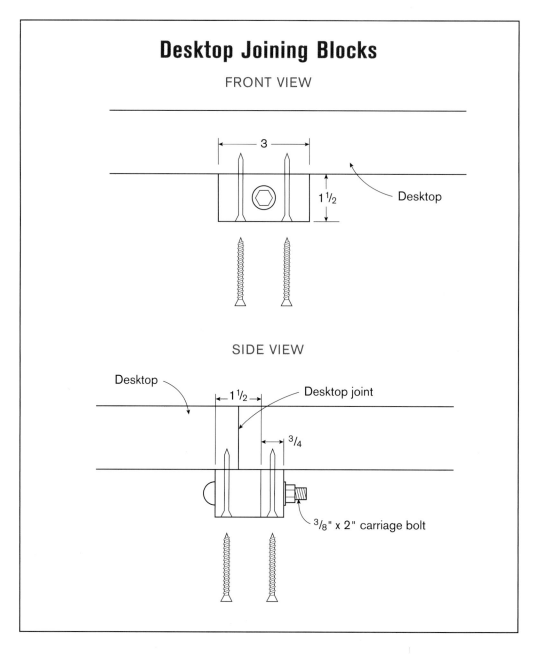

Desktop Joining Blocks

FRONT VIEW

3

1½

Desktop

SIDE VIEW

Desktop

1½

Desktop joint

³/₄

³/₈" x 2" carriage bolt

8. When the glue is dry, scrape off any excess and use a handplane to plane the edging flush with the faces of the panel.

9. Finish-sand the assembly to 150 grit.

10. To attach the side panel to the desktop, cut, joint, and plane a piece of solid poplar 21⅜ in. by 2 in. by 1 in. After chamfering the edges slightly, screw this piece to the underside of the desktop along the side that needs to be supported. It will fit into the pocket created in the top of the support panel assembly. Since you've made it ⅛ in. shorter

than the pocket, which is 21¾ in. long, it can be inserted easily.

Attaching Two Tops

Where two tops come together at right angles, as they do in the example office, they must be connected in some way. This connection must not only join the top surfaces flush but also must firmly support the free edge of the long top. I didn't want to use a connection that required cutting or screwing anything into the edges of the desktops, which might make the edges unsightly if you rearranged the desktops in the future.

Since I couldn't find any hardware that met all of these requirements, I designed the connectors shown in **photo H**. The solution turned out to be very simple.

1. Cut two solid cherry blocks each 3 in. by 1½ in. by 1½ in. and two blocks each 3 in. by 1½ in. by ¾ in. Clamp each larger block to a smaller block. You should now have two block assemblies that are each 3 in. by 2¼ in. by 1½ in.

2. Drill a ⅜-in. hole into the center of one 3-in. by 1½-in. face and all the way through both blocks. Repeat the process for the second pair of blocks.

3. Separate the parts and drill two counter-sunk pilot holes into each block at right angles to the ⅜-in. holes. Locate the pilot holes ¾ in. from the ends of the blocks and ¾ in. from the outside faces.

PHOTO H: This side panel provides elegant support for the top.

PHOTO I: Spacers fitted during the installation of the blocks ensure that the tops will pull tightly together.

PHOTO J: The extending portions of the larger blocks support the second top.

PHOTO K: The tops fit together tightly and flat.

4. Turning the two desktops to be joined upside down, clamp them together in the position they will be when joined.

5. Center the larger blocks on the seam, 4½ in. in from the front and back edges of the larger top with the bolt holes perpendicular to the seam, and mark their locations.

6. Glue and screw the blocks in place, making sure to glue them only to the smaller top. The larger top will rest on the protruding portions of the blocks.

7. Insert ⅜-in. by 3-in. carriage bolts from the sides of the blocks that are not protruding, then spread glue on the bottoms of the smaller blocks and carefully (so as not to smear the glue) slide them onto the bolts. The smaller blocks should be glued to the larger tops as shown in **photo I** on p. 125.

8. Place a ¹⁄₁₆-in. spacer (a small piece of edge tape is perfect) between each set of blocks, install a washer and nut on each bolt, and tighten.

9. Screw the smaller blocks in place. When the glue is dry, remove the clamps, bolts, and spacers, and turn the tops over.

When you're ready to connect the tops, rest the larger top on the protruding portion of the blocks as shown in **photo J**, line up the holes in the blocks, install the bolts (without the spacers), and tighten. The small gap left by the spacers will ensure that the joint between the tops will close up tightly (see **photo K**).

Finishing

I finished these pieces using a spray-on lacquer, but there are several other finishing methods to choose from (see the appendix on p. 151 for details on finishing).

KEYBOARD SLIDE INSTALLATION

YOU COULD PLACE your computer keyboard directly on the desktop, but this arrangement is far from ideal. Unless you're using a very small computer monitor, the monitor and keyboard together will take up most, if not all, of the depth of your desktop. Also, although the height of this desktop is comfortable for most tasks, it's not appropriate for typing. Even in the old days, typewriters were often placed on a separate, lower surface. Computer keyboards are not as high as typewriters, but the desktop is still not the best place for them.

If you're going to spend much time at the keyboard, you should take into consideration the ergonomic research that's been done about long-term keyboard use (see "Computer Ergonomics" on pp. 25–29). Most good keyboard appliances address these ergonomic issues well.

There are two common types of keyboard appliances: keyboard trays, which are basically drawers for the keyboard, and keyboard arms, which hold the keyboard and slide or fold it under the desktop. The keyboard arm, which is the more flexible device, allows you to position the keyboard in a variety of ways. On the other hand, keyboard trays are somewhat more stable. You will have to try them out to decide which is best for you. The installation process depends on the type and model you choose (see the photos on p. 37) but doesn't typically involve more than installing a few screws.

The slide for the keyboard arm is simply screwed to the underside of the top.

The keyboard arm is fitted into the installed slide.

CHAPTER 8

Bridges

THIS LITTLE CORNER of the office, with its small desktop, single pedestal cabinet, and the bridge that is the subject of this chapter, came about because I was getting tired of the modernist, modular approach to office design. It occurred to me that the office had no quiet, personal space for doing simple tasks and getting away from the larger picture (and possibly the computer) for a while. In my quest for the perfectly tailored and flexible space, I had given up intimacy.

The ultimate example of personal space in an office has to be the rolltop desk. Its reputation is well deserved; with its cubbyholes and small drawers, it seems to provide a place for everything. Even if you can't really fit everything you need into one small

space (and this was becoming increasingly difficult even before the introduction of computers), personal space is indispensable in an office. This desktop unit is my answer—a modernist one, I suppose—to this classic piece of furniture. It's a temporary retreat from the larger universe where computers rule and even envelopes are printed on an ink-jet printer.

As with all of the projects in this book, I urge you to view this piece as a starting point. Feel free to customize the compartments for your own needs. However, you should keep some limitations in mind. This piece is designed around the sizes of standard paper, envelopes, and other office supplies, so think carefully about what you want to store if you're going to change the size or layout.

Bridge

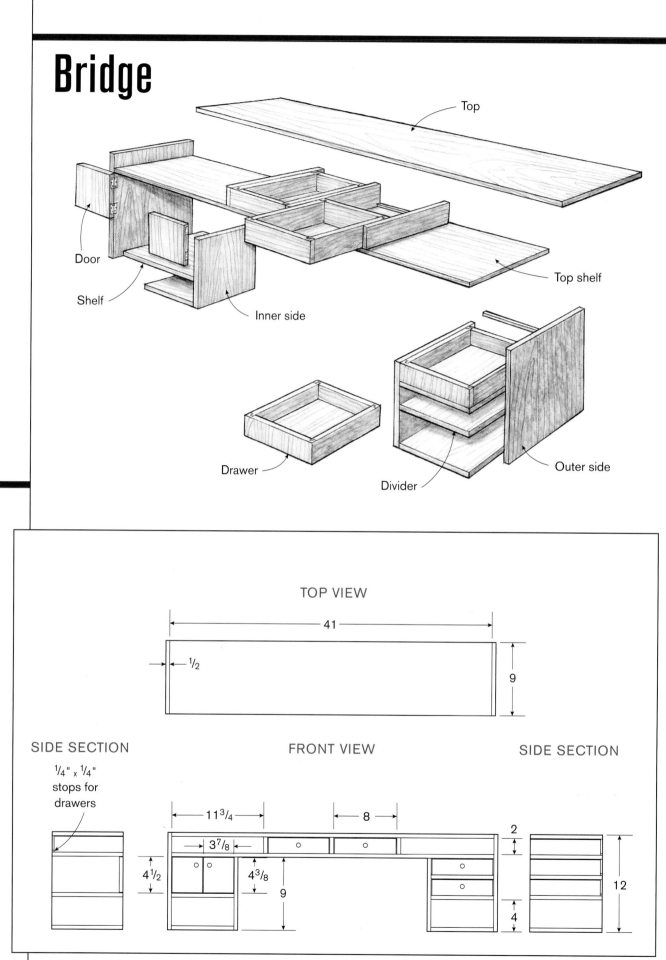

Top

Door

Shelf

Inner side

Top shelf

Drawer

Divider

Outer side

TOP VIEW

41

1/2

9

SIDE SECTION

1/4" x 1/4" stops for drawers

FRONT VIEW

SIDE SECTION

11³/₄

8

2

3⁷/₈

4¹/₂

4³/₈

9

12

4

Construction and Assembly

LIKE THE REST OF THE OFFICE suite, this piece features biscuit joinery and plywood construction. However, it is built with ½-in. plywood rather than the ¾-in. plywood you've used previously. Although the procedure for cutting biscuit slots is the same, there are differences in layout and biscuit joiner settings. Most of the differences depend on your particular biscuit joiner, so I can't be too specific here. I only mention them to alert you that you'll need to figure out your settings in advance and keep them in mind as you work.

Something else to watch out for with ½-in. plywood is thickness variation. In my experience, while all sizes of plywood vary in thickness, ½-in. plywood is the most likely to be thinner than it is supposed to be. The measurements I've given here assume true ½-in. material but, in all probability, some dimen-

PHOTO B: For parts this small, a table saw and miter gauge rather than a radial-arm saw work fine.

PHOTO C: To measure out a length of edgebanding, simply hold it against your workpiece, add a little extra, and break it off the roll.

CUT LIST FOR BRIDGE

Case

1	Top	41 in. x 9 in.	½-in. cherry plywood
2	Sides	12 in. x 9 in.	½-in. cherry plywood
2	Sides	9 in. x 9 in.	½-in. cherry plywood
1	Shelf	41 in. x 9 in.	½-in. cherry plywood
5	Shelves	9 in. x 8 in.	½-in. cherry plywood
3	Dividers	9 in. x 2 in.	½-in. cherry plywood

Drawers

8	Sides	8³⁄₁₆ in. x 1¹⁵⁄₁₆ in. x ½ in.	solid cherry
4	Fronts	7¹⁵⁄₁₆ in. x 1¹⁵⁄₁₆ in. x ½ in.	solid cherry
4	Backs	7¹⁵⁄₁₆ in. x 1¹⁵⁄₁₆ in. x ½ in.	solid cherry
2	Bottoms	8¼ in. x 7⁷⁄₁₆ in. x ⅛ in.	luan plywood
4	Stops	8 in. x ¼ in. x ¼ in.	solid cherry

Doors

2	Doors	4⅜ in. x 3⅞ in. x ½ in.	solid cherry

Other Materials

Approximately 20 linear ft. edge tape		cherry
4	Drawer pulls	
2	Door knobs	
2	Magnetic catches	
4	Hinges	
#10 biscuits		
Finish		

sions of your project will differ from those I've given. You will have to calculate for yourself how to allow for variations in plywood thickness, keeping in mind that the critical dimensions are the inside lengths between the shelves and dividers. Wherever possible, I will give you pointers along the way.

1. Rip and crosscut all of the plywood to size as shown in **photos A** and **B**. In most cases, the dimensions in the cut list will be just right or slightly oversized, depending on the thickness of your plywood.

2. Leave the two outside sides about 1 in. longer than the finished length. You will recut these parts to finished length after their top edges are edge-banded. If you cut them to length now, they will end up too long by the thickness of the edge tape. In this piece you want to make the top edge-banded edges of the sides flush with the top.

Edgebanding

In this project, you will apply the edgebanding before doing the biscuit joinery, so you'll have the finished top edges of the sides to use as reference edges for the biscuit joiner.

Apply the iron-on edgebanding first to the exposed fronts of all of the parts and then to the top edges of the outer sides (see **photo C**). There's a good reason for applying

it in this order: If an object slides forward off the top of the piece, you don't want it to catch on the end of the front-edge tape and damage it. This rule hasn't come up in previous chapters since you haven't edge-banded any other tops that might be used for storage.

Biscuit joinery

As you cut biscuit slots for the joints, pay attention to how each part intersects the other parts and what effect small variations in plywood thickness might have on the layout. One place where plywood thickness might affect the layout is in the spaces for the drawers in the top section.

This piece has four drawers, and to simplify their construction, you'll want them all to be the same size. I've designed the drawer spaces to be 8 in. wide. With a 41-in. top, if you measure in from each end 11¾ in. (the length of the end sections) to locate the slots for joining the dividers, you will have 17½ in. remaining, or just enough for two drawers if your plywood is precisely ½ in. thick (see **photo D**). However, if your plywood is less than ½ in. (and mine was a full ⅛ in. less),

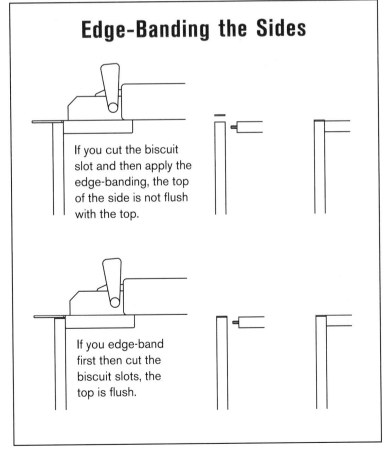

Edge-Banding the Sides

If you cut the biscuit slot and then apply the edge-banding, the top of the side is not flush with the top.

If you edge-band first then cut the biscuit slots, the top is flush.

PHOTO E: Assembly of this piece is easier if it is broken down into subassemblies first.

PHOTO F: Only a few clamps are needed to assemble the finished subassemblies.

then the spaces remaining for the drawers will be larger than 8 in. In my case, they would each have been $\frac{3}{32}$ in. larger, certainly enough to require larger drawers if they were to fit and look right.

1. Start by precisely marking the position of the center divider on both the top and the first shelf, taking into account the actual thickness of the plywood. Carefully cut the biscuit slots in the top and shelf.

2. Dry-fit the center divider in place with its biscuits.

3. Taking the two 8-in.-wide shelves from the right-hand section, place them on either side of the center divider as spacers.

4. Place the other two dividers at the ends of the shelves/spacers and draw them up tight.

5. Mark their locations and cut the biscuit slots for these dividers at these marks.

You've now made the spaces for the center drawers precisely 8 in. wide. The end sections may be a little large, but that's all right—their size is less critical.

You may have a similar problem with the sides because their length is the sum of the four spaces top to bottom plus the thickness of the plywood shelves. If your plywood is significantly thinner than ½ in., you can compensate either by shortening the sides or by lengthening the bottom spaces, where you don't have to worry about fitting doors or drawers.

Assembly

This piece has a lot of parts. It's difficult to glue and clamp them all together at once without messing up the piece. Assemble the case in subsections first, then assemble these sections into a whole.

1. Finish-sand the insides of all of the parts to 150 grit.

2. Glue, biscuit, and clamp the top section (top, long shelf, and dividers), and check for square.

3. Next, glue, biscuit, and clamp the two side sections with their respective dividers, and check for square (see **photo E**).

4. When the glue on the subassemblies is dry, glue, biscuit, and clamp the side sections to the top section and check for square (see **photo F**). This final assembly takes a bit of coaxing, but ½-in. plywood is quite flexible, so you shouldn't have any problem as long as you don't rush the process.

5. After the glue has dried, remove the clamps and finish-sand the outside of the piece to 150 grit.

Building the Drawers

The drawers for this piece are quite small—certainly too small for any but the tiniest of biscuits. However, the scope of the project didn't seem to justify any very complicated joinery. The joinery I chose wouldn't be appropriate for anything larger than these drawer boxes, but it's quick and easy and will

[tip] When you're edge-banding the front and top edges of a piece, always edge-band the front first so it will be protected by the edge tape on the top. (This rule also applies to veneer and laminate.)

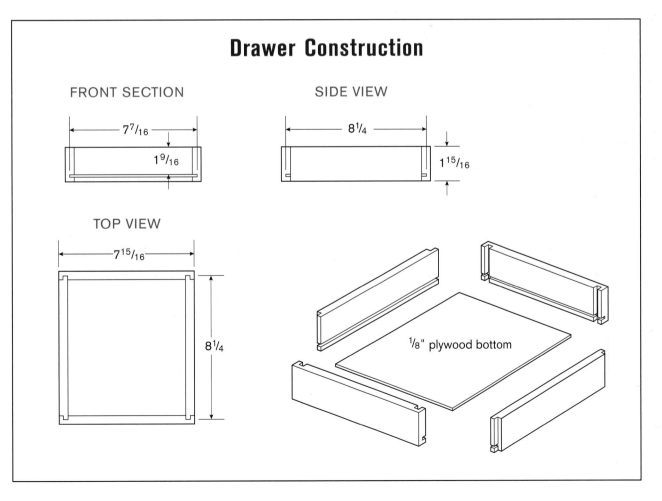

Drawer Construction

FRONT SECTION

7⁷/₁₆

1⁹/₁₆

SIDE VIEW

8¼

1¹⁵/₁₆

TOP VIEW

7¹⁵/₁₆

8¼

⅛" plywood bottom

PHOTO G: A thin-kerf blade should produce a groove just the right size for the ⅛-in. plywood bottoms.

[tip] For a complex assembly like this one, it's helpful to do a trial run without glue, just to make sure everything you need is at hand and you understand the sequence of operations.

PHOTO H: A ¼-in. dado blade quickly cuts the joints for the front and back parts of the drawers.

hold up under the small amount of stress these drawers will be subjected to.

Milling the parts

The drawers are built of solid cherry with ⅛-in. luan plywood bottoms.

1. Cut, joint, and plane enough ½-in. by 2-in. stock for four drawers, and cut the parts to the lengths given in the cut list.

2. Using your table saw blade, cut grooves for the drawer bottom ¼ in. from the bottom inside edge of each piece and ¼ in. deep, as shown in **photo G**. A normal table saw blade is ⅛ in., which might be too wide for some ⅛-in. plywood (there's that plywood thickness issue again). However, a thin-kerf blade, which is about 3⁄32 in., is typically just right. Check the fit to see what works.

Drawer joinery

The joint that connects the corners of the drawer boxes is a version of a lock dado. It's a variation that's simple to set up and that uses the stability of the plywood bottom for part of the strength. Gluing the plywood bottom into its groove significantly increases the integrity of the drawer and allows for a simplified construction. There are only two steps, and the setup of the saw and dado blade is the same for both. The fronts and backs are cut face down on the saw, and the sides are cut on end.

1. Install a ¼-in. dado blade in your table saw and raise it to a height of ¼ in. Position the fence ¼ in. from the blade.

2. Positioning a front or back drawer piece on a miter gauge set at 90 degrees to the blade, with the groove for the drawer bottom facing down and one end of the piece against the fence, run the piece through the saw (see **photo H**).

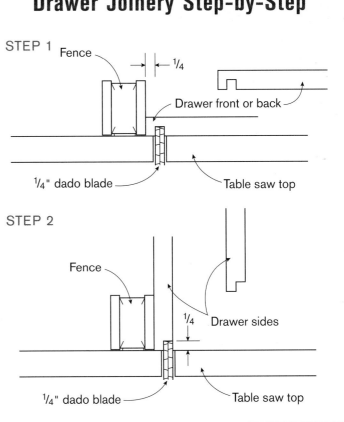

Drawer Joinery Step-by-Step

STEP 1

Fence · ¼ · Drawer front or back · ¼" dado blade · Table saw top

STEP 2

Fence · ¼ · Drawer sides · ¼" dado blade · Table saw top

1. Cut the four drawer bottoms from the ⅛-in. plywood.

2. Test the fit of the joints and adjust them if necessary. The side pieces will probably be a little tight. One or two passes using a sharp handplane, adjusted to remove a tissue-thin shaving, will quickly take care of the fit (see **photo J**). The joints should go together snugly with hand pressure only.

3. Finish-sand the inside of all of the parts to 150 grit. Be careful not to sand the ends of the side pieces that fit into the dadoes on the fronts and backs, since you don't want to alter the fit of the joints.

4. Glue and join two sides to one front, then run a glue bead into the drawer-bottom grooves and slide in a bottom (see **photo K**).

5. Next, glue and join the back to this assembly. Clamp the drawer front to back and check for square.

6. Repeat the process for the rest of the drawers.

7. When the glue is dry, remove the clamps and finish-sand the outside of the drawers to 150 grit.

3. Turn the piece around and cut the dado in the other end, then repeat for all of the front and back pieces.

4. Build a carrier to hold the side pieces upright and against the fence (see **photo I** on p. 137). Positioning one of the sides in the carrier with the groove for the bottom facing the fence, run the piece through the saw.

5. Flip the piece around and cut the other end. Repeat for all of the side pieces.

Assembly and fitting

It is nearly impossible to cut all these small joints and have them fit perfectly right away. Some minor adjustment will probably be necessary. Don't be tempted to force anything; these joints are very fragile until they are assembled and glued.

The drawers should fit the openings side to side, since they were sized 1/16 in. smaller than the width of the opening. However, they probably won't fit top to bottom, since in "Milling the Parts" on p. 136 I instructed you to make the drawers 2 in. high, or 1/16 in. over-sized compared with the finished height shown on the cut list and in the illustration on p. 135. You will have to remove some material from the top edges of the drawers to fit them into the 2-in.-high openings. I've postponed this step until now so you could make the fit more precise.

1. Using a sharp handplane, remove only as much material off the top of the drawers as you need to make them work properly and certainly no more than 1/16 in.

2. Slide the drawers into their openings so they are flush with the front.

3. Measure the distance between the backs of the drawers and the back of the opening (it should be ¼ in.).

4. Cut, joint, and plane four strips of cherry 8 in. by ¼ in. by the distance you measured in the previous step, and glue them to the back edges of the openings as stops for the drawers. Don't worry if the strips end up not being flush with the back. If they are in a little it doesn't matter, and if they stick out a little you can plane them flush.

Making the Doors

These two miniature doors are a lot more difficult and fussy to fit and install correctly than it might seem. Take your time and don't be discouraged if your first set doesn't fit quite right. These doors are easy to cut and use practically no material. Do try to make any mistakes only on the doors however, since any mistakes on the case will be much more difficult to fix.

1. To make the doors, cut two pieces of ½-in.-thick cherry to the sizes in the cut list.

2. Lay out, cut, and chisel mortises for the hinges of your choice (see **photo L** on p. 140).

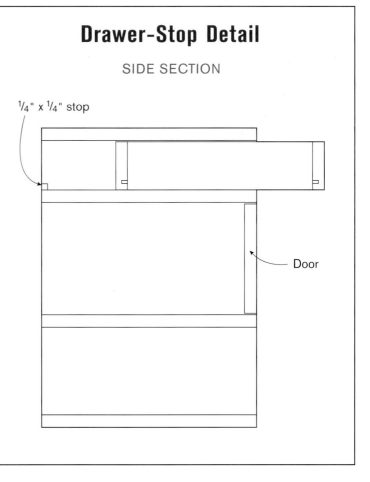

Drawer-Stop Detail

SIDE SECTION

¼" x ¼" stop

Door

PHOTO L: Careful layout and precise cutting of the hinge mortise is critical to the fit of the doors.

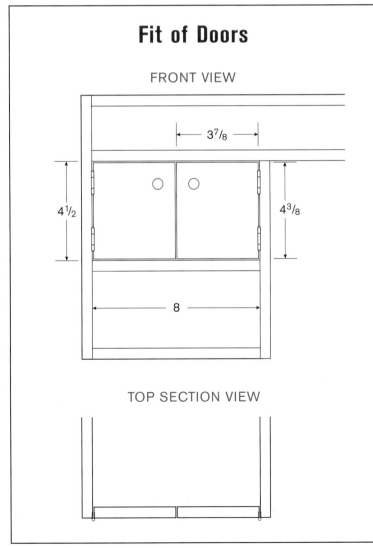

Fit of Doors

FRONT VIEW

$3^7/_8$

$4^1/_2$

$4^3/_8$

8

TOP SECTION VIEW

I used 1-in. by 1-in. satin nickel butt hinges from Whitechapel Hardware #142H94N (see Sources of Supply on p. 152).

3. Install the hinges and check the fit of the doors. Make any necessary adjustments.

The catches I used on these doors require some explanation. I originally planned to use bullet catches to close these doors, but they are so small that even the smallest bullet catch wouldn't work. After searching through hardware catalogs looking for a catch that would work, I decided I would have to make one myself. Whatever catch I used, the doors would have to close against some kind of stop, and everything I tried looked too big. The solution I found works well, but it may be too fussy for some of you, so feel free to use a magnetic catch.

1. Purchase two small, round magnetic-touch latches—I used #98568 touch latches from Rockler Woodworking Supplies (see Sources of Supply on p. 152). Take the latches apart and remove the magnets and the small metal pieces that are stuck to the magnets. You will have to cut the latches to do this.

2. Drill a $\frac{9}{32}$-in. hole exactly in the center (top to bottom and front to back) of the hinge edge of each door. The magnet-and-

Catch Detail

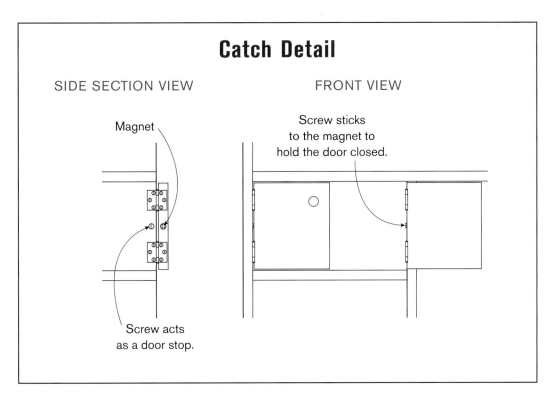

SIDE SECTION VIEW

FRONT VIEW

Magnet

Screw sticks
to the magnet to
hold the door closed.

Screw acts
as a door stop.

metal sandwich will fit snugly in this hole.
Drill the hole deep enough to insert the
sandwich so it will be flush with the edge
of the door (see **photo M**).

3. Mark the location of the center of this
hole on the hinge side of the opening.

4. Drill a pilot hole for a small steel screw.
It is important that this hole be precise and
horizontal and that the screws be steel so
that they will stick to the magnets. The
screws should be less than ½ in. long, and
their heads should be about the same diameter as, or a little smaller than, the hole for
the magnet.

5. Insert the screws and adjust them in or
out until the doors line up with the front of
the opening.

Finishing

I finished these pieces using a spray-on
lacquer, but there are several other finishing
methods to choose from (see the appendix
on p. 151 for details on finishing).

PHOTO M: Custom catches were necessary for these tiny doors.

Style and Layout Options

I DESIGNED THIS SUITE of furniture to be visually suitable for as many situations as possible, and I hope that many of you find it looks right in your home offices. However, I didn't want to lock anyone into building exactly what is shown in this book. Throughout the project chapters, I have suggested how you might alter the look or style of this office furniture by making simple changes. These suggestions were designed to let you consider different approaches to personalizing your office without overwhelming you completely. To reinforce this idea, I'll take a closer look at a few possible style and room layout options and perhaps put a new twist on the idea of modularization that I've talked about throughout this book.

Style Options

The illustration on p. 144 uses some of the style options presented in the project chapters—frame-and-panel doors and drawer fronts, feet, and overhanging tops.

As you can see, it changes the look of the office dramatically.

The differences don't look quite as dramatic in the photos on the facing page and on p. 145, but it's still obvious that these are now different pieces of furniture. If you put your mind to it, I'm sure you can come up with new variations of your own. To point out a few obvious ones, you could easily have used turned feet, block feet, bun feet, or even full legs. Doors, too, can be made in many styles. Raised-panel, arched-top, or glass doors can all be substituted for the basic door without modifying the cabinets themselves (see the illustration on p. 146).

Layout Options

While writing this book, I kept in mind that most, if not all, readers would have offices that were different in size and shape from my virtual office and would have to arrange their furniture differently. I have tried to address this concern throughout, but I would like to

Comparing Style Options

The look of the virtual home office can be significantly altered by making a few changes. Here I've used tapered legs instead of a toe-kick base and added details such as flat-panel doors and an overhanging top, giving it a much different look than the cabinet below.

The low cabinet
unit looks more
formal with frame-
and-panel doors.

present a few additional thoughts on room layout.

It is very easy to line the walls of a room with cabinets and desktops—it's what you might call the kitchen cabinet school of design. However, it's not always the most functional layout, and even kitchen designers are trying new ways of arranging furniture. If you're thinking, "But that's exactly what the virtual office in this book looks like!" you're right. However, I designed it like that for several reasons.

One reason for configuring the office space this way was that I had a whole book's worth of projects to fit into a small room. If you take a look at the office floor plan (shown in the illustration on p. 147), you will see that the virtual room has just about every problem a room can have if you want

to put a lot of furniture in it. To start, it's only about 12 ft. across. When you subtract the space taken up by a 2-ft.-deep desktop on one side and a 1-ft.-deep shelf unit on the other side, you are down to about 9 ft. You need about 3 ft. of space behind a desk to move around comfortably in a task chair, so you really only have about 6 ft. of open floor space. To make matters worse, much of the wall space is taken up by the three doors, three windows, and radiator. The room's only saving grace is its one long, uninterrupted wall, which allows for a reasonably roomy desktop.

However, I still might not have chosen this arrangement of furniture if it hadn't been for two other considerations:

♦ The room has only one entrance and exit, so you don't have to think about traffic

Style Options

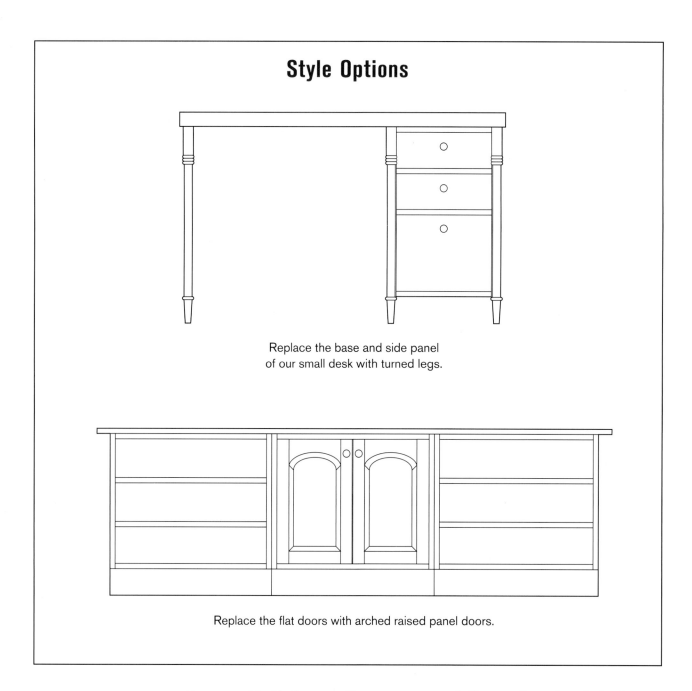

Replace the base and side panel
of our small desk with turned legs.

Replace the flat doors with arched raised panel doors.

patterns except inside the room. No one will be walking through the room, as someone might if it were situated between two other rooms. While you don't want the doorway to be crowded and you don't want the door to slam into the furniture, you also don't need a clear path from that door to another door. If there were another door directly across from the existing door, the bookcases probably shouldn't be where they are, since you would have to sidestep slightly every time you crossed the room (see the top illustration on the facing page). However, I can place the bookcases where they are in the office because the natural traffic pattern takes you more or less diagonally into the center of the room.

◆ The room, although relatively small, is still big enough for accessibility to be an issue. Earlier I discussed the importance of keeping the items you need within easy reach. In this office, you would probably be working at the long desktop, but you would need to retrieve items from other areas of the room. If you were seated at the task chair in front of the long desktop, how

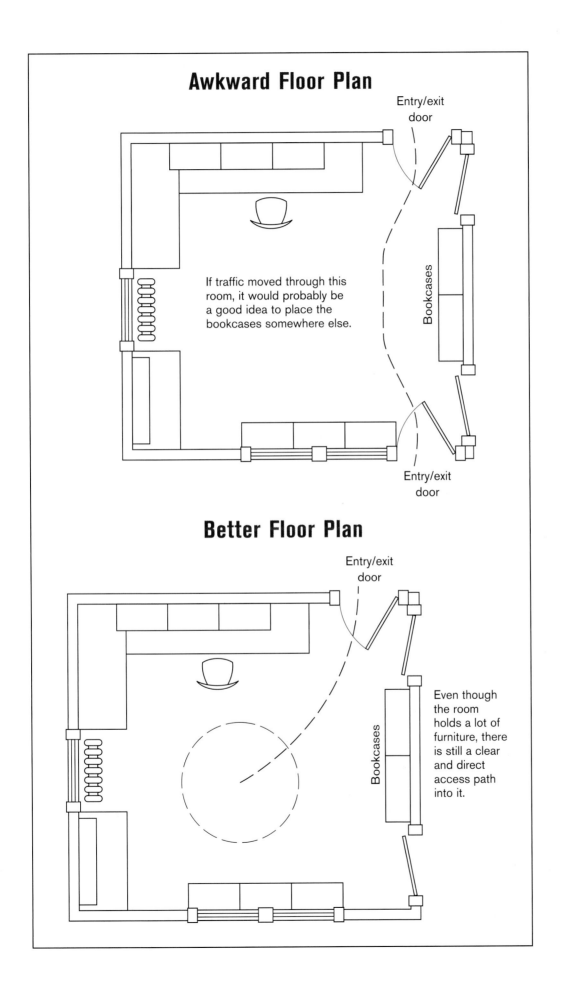

Awkward Floor Plan

Entry/exit door

Bookcases

If traffic moved through this room, it would probably be a good idea to place the bookcases somewhere else.

Entry/exit door

Better Floor Plan

Entry/exit door

Bookcases

Even though the room holds a lot of furniture, there is still a clear and direct access path into it.

Accessible Floor Plan

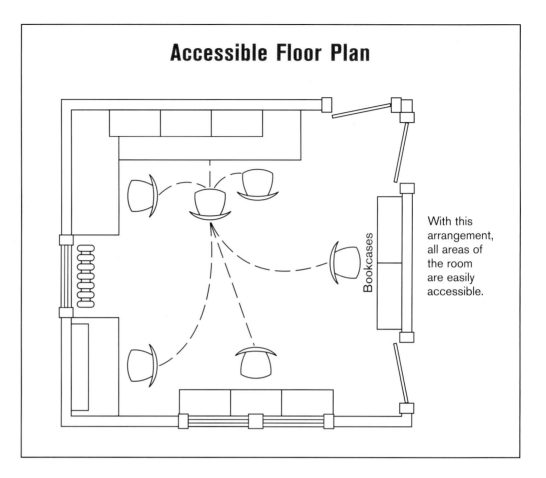

With this arrangement, all areas of the room are easily accessible.

Bookcases

would you get to other areas in the room? Most likely you would push the chair away from the desktop, turn around, stand up, and walk. Alternatively (if you are like me), you might roll the chair across the room and reach for what you want if it is within reach or stand up and get it if it is not. In either case, the one thing you don't want is furniture blocking your path, so the arrangement I've come up with offers a clear path to the other storage spaces and work spaces (see the illustration above).

As you can see, fitting what you need into the room you have available can be quite a challenge. Since you typically can't build a room to fit your furniture, you must give a lot of thought to how to arrange things. Lining the walls with furniture isn't necessarily a bad idea, but before you design the room that way, think about what other options you might have and which arrangement will cause the fewest problems.

Modular Options

You can build as many of each type of cabinet as you need (or can fit in your office space). Generally, I talk about adding two, three, or more cabinets in a row. However, if you think about adding modules, or building blocks, vertically as well as horizontally, you can expand the range of possibilities (see the photo on the facing page). Conceivably, you could fill an entire wall with different combinations of cabinets (see the illustration on the facing page). You would need bases only for the cabinets in the first tier; the upper tiers would just consist of cabinet boxes. This idea occurred to me quite by accident while I was stacking pieces to make room in my shop—but isn't that often how great ideas come about?

One last reminder: There's no rule saying this furniture has to be used for the office. Many of the components would be quite serviceable in other parts of the home.

Modular Options

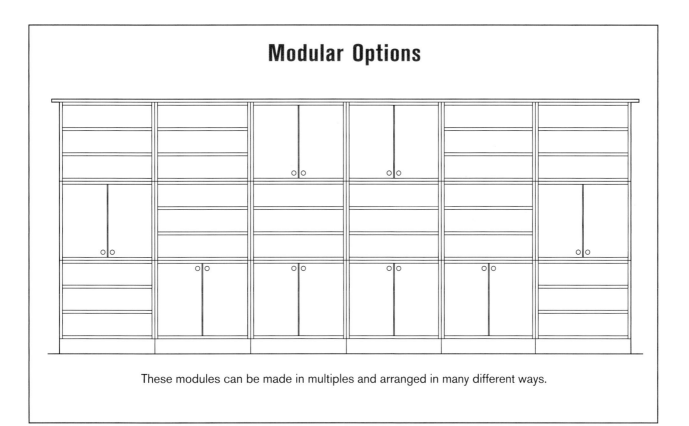

These modules can be made in multiples and arranged in many different ways.

Stacking modular units gives you more storage space. The arrangements are limited only by your imagination.

METRIC CONVERSION CHART

Inches	Centimeters	Millimeters	Inches	Centimeters	Millimeters
1/8	0.3	3	13	33.0	330
1/4	0.6	6	14	35.6	356
3/8	1.0	10	15	38.1	381
1/2	1.3	13	16	40.6	406
5/8	1.6	16	17	43.2	432
3/4	1.9	19	18	45.7	457
7/8	2.2	22	19	48.3	483
1	2.5	25	20	50.8	508
1 1/4	3.2	32	21	53.3	533
1 1/2	3.8	38	22	55.9	559
1 3/4	4.4	44	23	58.4	584
2	5.1	51	24	61.0	610
2 1/2	6.4	64	25	63.5	635
3	7.6	76	26	66.0	660
3 1/2	8.9	89	27	68.6	686
4	10.2	102	28	71.1	711
4 1/2	11.4	114	29	73.7	737
5	12.7	127	30	76.2	762
6	15.2	152	31	78.7	787
7	17.8	178	32	81.3	813
8	20.3	203	33	83.8	838
9	22.9	229	34	86.4	864
10	25.4	254	35	88.9	889
11	27.9	279	36	91.4	914
12	30.5	305			

APPENDIX: Finishing

All of the projects in this book were finished using a spray-on lacquer, a choice I made largely because I had spray equipment and facilities available. If you aren't able to spray, you can choose among many other finishing methods, most of which don't require any specialized equipment. The most important requirements for achieving a good finish are preparation and application. Usually all you have to do, whether you are spraying, wiping, or brushing the finish, is to follow the manufacturer's directions. Applying spray finishes takes some practice, but most other types of finishes are relatively easy to master.

Oil Finishes

Most oil finishes are easy to apply, and in my opinion they bring out the figure in woods such as cherry and curly maple better than any other finish. Since not all oil finishes work the same way, be sure to read the label and follow directions. The downside to oil finishes is that they are not permanent. They dry out and wear and must be reapplied periodically. Initial finishing with oil typically requires a few coats. To apply, wipe on a coat, let it sit for a little while before wiping off the excess, then let the coat dry. You can refresh the finish every few months by repeating these steps.

Many oil finishes are available, but the most popular ones use either tung oil or linseed oil as a base, typically combined with other compounds and driers. Over time I have found that some work better for my purposes than others, but my opinion of one product versus another changes as I try new and different kinds. I usually use products generically known as Danish oil

finishes for light-duty jobs and a high-quality polymerized tung oil for any piece that will get substantial wear. I highly recommend polymerized tung oil. It takes getting used to and applying it correctly is a fair amount of work, but it creates a wonderful, lustrous, long-lasting finish. I have some pieces in my house that still look great after several years of everyday use. Polymerized tung is the closest thing to a lacquer finish you can get from an oil.

Oil finish is also a better choice for projects that have moving or sliding parts, such as step stools, where a film finish would get in the way and become scratched. Also, projects with many small parts are often difficult to finish well with anything except an oil finish.

In recent years, environmentally sound options have become available both for spray finishes (water-based finishes) and, especially, for oil finishes. Distribution of these products is still spotty and sometimes it's difficult to find a reliable source, but with luck this situation will improve. I think it is worth the effort to find these products, some of which claim to be nontoxic and contain no petroleum distillates or derivatives or any heavy metal driers. At least one linseed oil-based product contains citrus solvents, combining a pleasant lemony scent with a nice satin sheen. You can't beat that!

Other Finishes

In my opinion, one underrated finish is a wax finish. Wax looks and feels wonderful, and for certain applications it provides more than adequate protection. Applying wax takes a lot of elbow work, but it's almost impossible to do it wrong. Even if you put on too much wax,

you'll just have to work twice as hard to rub it out to a good shine. Most waxes change the natural color of the wood very little if any. Best of all, wax is self-stripping, which means that applying a new coat dissolves the coat underneath; it doesn't build up and dull the finish you are trying to shine.

Another overlooked possibility is a painted finish. We tend to think of painted finishes as quick and easy cover-ups for some old piece of furniture, but they require more preparation and skill than most people think. A well-executed painted finish can be wonderful and adds a great deal of charm.

One finishing option that some may find odd is not to use finish at all. That may not be appropriate for large office pieces, but smaller accessories may not need any finish. Suppose you have just finished a small box and have handplaned the piece until the wood glows. What is to be gained by applying a finish?

The most common answer is that it will protect the piece. I suppose that is true—finish does protect wood—but by trying to "protect" the piece you are really saying you want it to look the way it does now forever. You want to freeze it in time. Well, that's not possible; the wood will age and the finish will wear. The piece may retain its charm as the years pass, but you won't appreciate this charm if you insist on the piece always looking as it did when you made it. Try to imagine a piece designed from the outset to wear and age gracefully, acquiring a handsome patina. Some woods (butternut is my favorite) age beautifully on their own without any finish.

SOURCES OF SUPPLY

Alienware Corporation
13462 SW 131st St.
Miami, FL 33186
www.alienware.com
(800) 494-3382
Manufacturer of high-end computers for gaming, DV systems, and high-performance workstations

Festool USA
1187 Coast Village Rd., PMB 1215
Santa Barbara, CA 93103
www.festool-usa.com
(888) 463-3786
FESTOOL power tools and accessories, including the FS-LR 32mm hole drilling system and the ATF 55 circular plunge saw and guide

Garrett Wade
161 Ave. of the Americas
New York, NY 10013
www.garrettwade.com
(800) 221-2942
Polymerized tung oil and specialty woodworking tools and supplies

Häfele America Company
3901 Cheyenne Dr.
Archdale, NC 27263
(800) 423-3531
Hardware, hardware, and more hardware

Herman Miller for the Home
855 E. Main Ave.
Zeeland, MI 49464
www.hermanmiller.com
(800) 646-4400
Aeron adjustable work chair and other products and accessories for the home office

Lie-Nielsen Toolworks, Inc.
P. O. Box 9
Warren, ME 04864-0009
www.lie-nielsen.com
(800) 327-2520
Specialty handplanes and tools

McFeely's
1620 Wythe Rd.
Lynchburg, VA 24506-1169
www.mcfeelys.com
(800) 443-7937
Screws, fasteners, threaded inserts, connector bolts, Bessey clamps, tools, and woodworking supplies

One Tech, LLC
23 Acorn St.
Providence, RI 02903
www.onetech.net
(887) 663-8324
Manufacturer of the ECLIPSE computer light

Pendaflex
(800) 211-9605 or (800) 870-6872 (retail locations)
www.pendaflex.com
Information (perhaps more than you need) on filing systems and products

Psion USA
150 Baker Ave. Ext., Ste. 201
Concord, MA 01742-9808
www.psion.com
(800) 997-7466
Mobile computing products, including the Revo palm-top computer

Rockler Woodworking and Hardware
4365 Willow Dr.
Medina, MN 55340
www.rockler.com
(800) 279-4441 (mail order)
(877) 762-5537 (retail locations)
Home-office hardware and accessories, Accuride drawer slides, keyboard slides and trays, wire management products, power stations, grommets, decorative hardware, tools, and woodworking supplies

R & R Clamp, Inc.
2661 Hwy. QQ
Green Bay, WI 54311
www.netnet.net/rrclamp
(920) 863-2987
Stacking clamps

Select Machinery Inc.
64-30 Ellwell Crescent
Rego Park, NY 11374
(800) 789-2323
Lamello Duplex hinges, biscuit joiners, biscuits, Bessey clamps, tools, and woodworking supplies

Whitechapel Ltd.
P. O. Box 11719
Jackson, WY 83002
www.whitechapel-ltd.com
(800) 468-5534
Reproduction period hardware

INDEX

INDEX